Best Practice with Children and Families

D1448629

Best Practice with Children and Families

Critical Social Work Stories

BARRY COOPER, JEAN GORDON
AND
ANDY RIXON

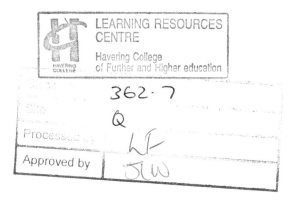

macmillan education palgrave

209362

First published 2015 by
PALGRAVE

Palgrave in the UK is an imprint of Macmillan Publishers Limited, registered
in England, company number 785998, 4 Crinan Street, London N1 9XW.

Palgrave Macmillan in the US is a division of St Martin's Press LLC,
175 Fifth Avenue, New York, NY 10010.

Palgrave is a global imprint of the above companies and is represented
throughout the world..

Palgrave® and Macmillan® are registered trademarks in the United States,
the United Kingdom, Europe and other countries.

ISBN: 978–1–137–00301–0

This book is printed on paper suitable for recycling and made from fully
managed and sustained forest sources. Logging, pulping and manufacturing
processes are expected to conform to the environmental regulations of the
country of origin.

A catalogue record for this book is available from the British Library.

A catalog record for this book is available from the Library of Congress.

Printed in China

Contents

Foreword

Theories *of* and theories *for* practice, in any field, tend to be neat, bounded and refined. In contrast, theories *in* practice are always rougher and more ragged. The complexity and unpredictability of real life generally means that ideas in practice have to bend and adapt, twist and turn if they are going to work. This doesn't mean that theories are irrelevant or redundant. It just means that when a theory is applied in practice, it bumps into reality, and reality being what it is, rarely submits entirely to this or that theory, however smart this or that theory happens to be. This is especially true in the case of social reality. People, and the lives they live, are messy. People have their own ideas about what is going on and what should be done. More than most, social workers, as applied social theorists, know that the cussedness of the real world has to be taken into account as they engage, assess, decide and plan with their clients and service users.

So we have many excellent books on social work theory, skills and interventions which give practitioners a chance to breathe the theoretical airs at their clearest and cleanest. But we have very few books that capture what social work feels like, looks like and smells like on the ground, down and dirty. This is why Barry Cooper, Jean Gordon and Andy Rixon's book, *Best Practice with Children and Families: Critical Social Work Stories*, is so welcome. It *does* tell us what social work looks and feels like in practice. Written in collaboration with front-line practitioners, we are treated to detailed descriptions of 10 cases and the complexities of 'what actually goes on'. Three major themes of social work with children and their families are tackled: the importance of the relationship; handling risk and uncertainty; and the realities of dealing with power, negotiations and problem-solving. Not only do the practitioners describe in their own words who they met, why they met them, what they did, and how children and parents reacted, they also reveal the value of critical reflection, learning from experience, shared endeavour and flexible thinking as they engaged with their families and colleagues.

As the authors explain, best practice is 'the art of the achievable'. Theories and techniques are brought into play, but they shift and re-shape as they accommodate to changing circumstances and evolving situations. This is such a heartening book. It is so good to hear social workers talk about their own cases in ways that ring real and true. The stories, full of warmth and wisdom, give the reader a sense of what it is like to practise 'out there', in people's homes, in the car as you drive a child back to his carers, and in the office as you meet with colleagues. The profession certainly owes a huge debt of gratitude to the practitioners who volunteered to talk and write about their cases with such honesty and engagement. In giving experienced social workers a strong voice, *Best Practice with Children and Families: Critical Social Work Stories* helps us to understand how theory and practice work, indeed are made to work in the real world, and that, without doubt, is wonderfully helpful and vastly reassuring.

David Howe
Emeritus Professor of Social Work
University of East Anglia, Norwich

Acknowledgements

The Editors would like to thank all the practitioners who offered their time and energy in contributing to the stories in this book. We would also like to thank their managers and agencies for permitting our co-authors to be involved and for their stories to be published.

The Practitioner Pathways to Publication project was supported by a research grant from The Open University, Faculty of Health & Social Care, and we are grateful for the help afforded by this.

The names of the children, young people, family members and professional colleagues referred to in this book have all been changed. Other potentially identifying details have also, where necessary, been omitted or altered to preserve anonymity.

1 Introduction

Andy Rixon, Barry Cooper and Jean Gordon

There is a growing interest in bringing social work theory, research and practice closer together, so that writing about social work acknowledges and conveys the complexity and uncertainty of what is involved in doing it. Critical best practice (CBP) is perhaps unique in illustrating how practices and theories are 'enacted' by practitioners through an emphasis on the detail of 'the very "work" that *is* social work, the actions taken, what gets said and done and with what consequences' (Ferguson, 2003, p. 17). It has been argued that while 'service user perspectives' are an established and essential strand within social work writing, the voice of the social worker is largely absent (Beresford and Croft, 2004; Jones et al., 2008). In this book, we have set out to address this imbalance by focusing on practitioners' own narratives and critical reflections upon the complexities and dilemmas of social work with children and families. The accounts and analysis of real case examples offer a new and engaging way of *learning about practice* as the reader is prompted to engage with and respond to the dilemmas and difficulties faced, encouraging them to ask 'What do I think? What would I have done?' The stories in this book offer an opportunity for the reader to accompany practitioners as they explain their struggles to find ways of making a difference in situations where there are few clear cut courses of action. The scope of the book is a wide one, with social workers from statutory, voluntary and private settings, with different levels of experience, describing their day-to-day work with families and children of all ages, from very young babies to adolescents on the verge of adulthood.

Social workers spend a lot of time trying to make sense of situations by negotiating with others and developing agreed and sometimes ambiguous 'narratives' of what may be happening – often bringing together many different and contradictory perspectives. Discussions with service users, consultations with colleagues from different professional backgrounds, writing assessments, supervision or holding strategy and safeguarding meetings, for example, are all about trying to make sense of often fast-moving and complex situations. In these stories we try to highlight how the many different ways in which this happens can have a profound effect on the practices that are carried out and the decisions that are eventually made. The chapters will convey a balance between 'telling the story' from the practitioner's perspective and critical commentary and analysis of the practice presented. This blend between theoretical and practice perspectives will contribute to the development of a shared understanding of the nature of 'best' practices in social work with children and families. Some of the stories mostly speak for themselves through the words of the practitioners while others place a greater emphasis on the analysis of different perspectives, linked to theory and research. No story can ever be complete in itself and there is rarely a clear end to the extent to which analysis will further help to understand situations. This dilemma is explored in the next chapter in which we explain how the stories were gathered and written about, and explore the issues arising from 'narrative' as a theoretical approach.

Why write about practice?

Despite two critically received television series on the BBC[1] and consistent messages of support from Government ministers in the United Kingdom, social work remains a largely misunderstood professional activity. A continuing series of high profile, so-called 'failures' of social work publicised through an often hostile popular media has contributed towards the pervasive air of pessimism which often surrounds social work. The Laming report (2009) quoted from a 'reclaim social work' initiative to the effect that '...social work as a profession has lost it way, lacks confidence, expertise and gravitas, is over-bureaucratised and risk averse...' (p. 48). However, while accepting some of the undeniable problems besetting social work, there continues to be a vast amount of day-to-day *practice* which takes place across all sectors of society that is complex, highly skilled and fascinating. Many social workers continue to act in ways which are autonomous and creative, protecting children and supporting families within, and sometimes in spite of, the systems in which they work. At a time of increasing change and shrinking resources, positive and realistic accounts of the everyday practice of social work with children and families are needed to help ensure that the multiple challenges of practice are understood and represented.

In 2009, the Social Work Task Force in England recommended that in order to create a better understanding of social work, there needs to be 'more effort and expertise in telling the positive stories' (p. 4) and '... a continuously refreshed "bank" of stories and case studies that help to illustrate good social work practice, creating a benchmark for the public of the positive impact social workers can have' (p. 49).

This theme was also evident in Scotland's 21st Century Review of Social Work: Changing Lives. The Review found many examples of good practice that were 'often not acknowledged or celebrated' (Scottish Executive, 2006, p. 13). The review report found that employers of social workers had an important role in promoting and celebrating excellence and learning from good practice as well as from mistakes. In Wales similar concerns have been expressed about a disillusioned profession weighed down by bureaucracy and the need for a systematic sharing of good practice (Association of Directors of Social Services, 2005).

The 'Munro Review' of safeguarding and child protection social work in England argued for fundamental reform, rooted in a set of professionally informed imperatives that have had to find their implementation at a time of severe funding restrictions (Munro, 2011). In a period where both development and retrenchment are being called for, it is all the more important for social workers to be able to assert, with confidence, aspects of their core identities within changing discourses (Wiles, 2013). This book is a contribution to that goal. It draws upon the skills, knowledge, professional values and experience of social workers in practice to help develop a more confident and coherent approach to thinking and talking about social work. It is hoped that this will enable social workers and educators to draw from the accounts a collective strength and belief in what they do. As one of the practitioner authors told us, social work students can often *feel that the gap between the ideal proposed in theory/academia and the reality of doing the job is insurmountable – but it isn't. Something like this project may encourage and give hope and confidence to practitioners.*

A CBP approach therefore has an important contribution to make to the development of professional identity for social workers. Another key purpose of the approach, and, in turn, of this book, is to encourage learning and the development of positive practice (Ferguson, 2003, 2008; Jones and Watson, 2013). Interrogating practice through critical reflection as a source of learning has a long history. In the accounts that follow practitioners highlight the value of opportunities to, for example, reflect on their work during supervision with their manager, debrief with a colleague after a particularly testing home visit, or sit down with colleagues to assess risks to a young child. For social work students and experienced practitioners alike, social work stories create the opportunity to reflect, compare, discuss and critique: What was done well – and why? What might have been done differently? And how can we make sure that new learning is put into practice? To promote this engagement and reflection each narrative starts by posing some questions for the reader to consider. Of course there are many other questions that practitioners may want to explore as they read the chapters; these initial questions are designed to begin to stimulate personal reflection, and to encourage readers to link what they read with their own experiences and dilemmas in their practice with children and families.

The accounts of practice that follow will probably be instantly recognisable to qualified social workers. Practice is constantly on the move as social workers drive to appointments, visit families, play with small children, write court reports, seek resources to support families, engage reluctant adolescents in activities, chair planning meetings and drop planned work at short notice to respond to crises. For readers who are contemplating or engaged in social work training, or perhaps are service users or belong to other professions, the book gives a taste of what it is that social workers actually do. While the roles described are varied, encompassing work in local authorities, voluntary agencies and the independent sector, there are core skills and capabilities that you will read about in each practitioner's chapter. These range from relationship building, assessment and planning to integrating theory and practice, managing colleagues and collaborative team work. The words and language of the practitioners are prioritised enabling the authors to talk directly, through their writing, to other practitioners and people who want to find out more about the world of social work.

The distinctive contributions of a CBP perspective

A CBP perspective has emerged by a number of different routes, informed by a growing interest in bringing together formal theory with knowledge derived from both service user experience and wisdom gained from day-to-day professional practice (Howe, 2009). Ferguson (2003) was first to bring 'critical' and 'best' together in a formal sense to argue for an approach that draws on examples of best practice and uses critical theory as an interpretative framework to promote learning. He argued strongly for a CBP perspective taking a key role in the culture of social work education and practice, seeing this as particularly crucial in the context of rapid change in social work and the wider context of practice. The stories of practice in this book build upon the work of Jones, Cooper and Ferguson (2008) and their arguments to promote a CBP approach in social work through detailed analysis of examples of practice. We wanted to identify further examples of everyday practice that illustrate some of the extraordinary skills, knowledge and values in action that routinely characterise social work with children and families as a complex professional activity. Rather than looking for theoretical principles and models that are abstracted from practice, CBP argues that the values and strengths of social work practice emerge through an examination of the detailed complexities of 'what actually goes on' in interactions between people. It is this warp and weft of the fabric of social work practice that we have set out to reveal in the narratives in this book. First, however, we will take a look at just what we mean by 'best' and 'critical' in the context of a CBP approach.

'Best practice' – the best description?

Ideas of 'excellence' and 'best' practice have become influential in many different fields, including healthcare and business management as well as social work, and have different meanings to different people and institutions at different times. 'Best' is sometimes, for example, used to denote a combination of effectiveness and efficiency that is believed to deliver optimum results for minimum resources. However, a focus on 'best' can be unhelpful if it is beyond what is attainable in the pragmatic world of everyday social work. While there may be a place for models of perfection, in this book we take a more realistic approach, arguing for an acceptance of 'best practice' in social work as being the art of the achievable. The stories in this book contribute towards a greater under-standing of why practice turns out the way it does by foregrounding the practitioner's voice and drawing upon this to help explain what was actually done in practice as opposed to what 'should have' been done or was not done or not achieved. What is 'best' is often what is possible at that particular time in that particular situation with that combination of people, processes and circumstances. Our stories are of social workers *doing their best* in unique situations, and incorporate an understanding of practice as situated in time and place, influenced by past and existing relationships with individuals and institutions.

Another major critique of 'best' or 'good', as descriptors of practice, is that they beg the question: best or good from whose perspective – and according to what criteria? There are of course multiple perspectives in children and families social work, including those of children, parents, different professionals, budget holders, policymakers and the public. While the narratives in this book foreground the social worker's perspective, these knotty questions about 'best for whom?' permeate all their discussions of practice. Rather than assume a single model of good practice one of the purposes of this book is therefore to identify and expose these dilemmas as they happen, and to use them as sources of reflection and learning.

How 'critical' is CBP?

In this book, we take 'critical' to mean an understanding that there are different perspectives and therefore different versions of 'truth'. To this extent we are taking a post-modern view of reality in recognising multiple 'voices'. Social work assessments and interventions through planned courses of action, unless dictated by the exigencies of emergency situations, have to be negotiated with the people involved in order to be successful. Such practices and discourses around practice are constituted by power relations and differential power leads to differential value afforded to different perspectives. This is interesting as it opens up the fundamental point that there is not just the one 'truth' of the situation 'out there' to be discovered through processes of careful information gathering. There are a number of different ways that situations can be assessed and social workers have the potential for privileged access to more powerful judgements that help to define 'the story' of what happened or is happening. In this way the stories and accounts of social work practice can be critiqued. There may be elements of objective conditions in the account but the story or the 'take' on what happened is made up of subjective definitions provided by the practitioner (Parton and O'Byrne, 2000). This important philosophical distinction about the nature of social realities will be explored further in Chapter 2.

Critical practice is arguably an essential, if not defining, aspect of professional social work. There are continuing debates about what it means to practice 'critically' in social work (see Thompson and Thompson, 2008; Fook, 2012 for examples). Being critical in social work requires practitioners to question situations through a constructively sceptical approach. The critical practitioner's starting point is the recognition that things are rarely just as they seem on the surface. There is, therefore, both a surface and a depth to the analysis and understanding of social situations (Howe, 1996). In our everyday lives we intuitively recognise the world to be multi-layered and changing. However, as a professional social worker, this awareness has to be channelled into action. A critical practitioner aims to integrate evidence from research and theoretical literature with an awareness of diversity, power and the rights of children and families. This combination of skilled awareness and in-depth knowledge of situations provides a platform for a critical practitioner to argue for and negotiate about their own judgements and assessments in order to contribute to, and sometimes lead, multi-disciplinary plans and interventions. These are high order expectations and are easier said than done; but this is what critical practice is about. Social work practice as an intervention into private lives is replete with power and authority derived from both legal authority and the 'expert' professional role. However, a professional flexing of state-sanctioned muscles would certainly run the risk of being oppressive if carried out uncritically or unthinkingly. The difficulty for critical social work practice is that appropriate questioning often leads into philosophical thickets where certainties and comfortably mapped life assumptions quickly disappear. The critical practitioner is constantly negotiating these tensions between respect for service users, and a nuanced understanding of the impact of discrimination and oppression, alongside their power, authority and accountability as social workers within their particular practice context (Ferguson, 2008; Gordon and Cooper, 2010). Quite rightly this leads to dilemmas and an argument that practitioners need to question accepted wisdoms and practice in ways that 'challenge domination, exploitation and oppression' (Fook, 2002, p. 18).

Nation perspectives

The key elements of social work practice with children and families in different parts of the United Kingdom are fundamentally the same. However there are also significant differences. An understanding of how practice is situated geographically necessarily requires an understanding of the importance of the political, social and cultural context in which that practice is located. Since the late 1990s, civil decision-making powers have, to varying extents, been increasingly devolved to the four UK nations. This slow but steady shift in public policy and provision, combined with often quite subtle social and cultural differences in each nation, makes it essential for social work practice to be understood in its nation context. For example Scotland, and to some extent Wales, is generally regarded as more committed than England to a universal public sector model of service provision, based to a greater extent upon principles of egalitarianism than those of consumer choice and competition that have tended to dominate in England (Keating, 2010). At the same time it is important not to over-state these differences, with all four nations subject to both global and UK-wide influences, including public sector and welfare reform, that impact in all sorts of important ways on social work practice.

One benefit of divergence has been the creation of opportunities to moderate UK-wide policy and to test out new ideas. This potentially provides opportunities for mutual learning; for example, Wales led the way in installing a Children's Commissioner in 2001, an innovation later adopted by all the other UK nations. By including examples of, and references to, practice from Wales, England and Scotland in this book, we aim, in a much smaller way, to illustrate both the importance of context to social work practice and the opportunities devolution is presenting to learn from practice in different parts of the United Kingdom. There are, of course, other important regional differences in different parts of the United Kingdom which owe more to, for example, rurality, industrialisation and migration, than nationhood, and some of the stories that follow reflect these influences on children and their families.

England

Social work services to children and families in England have arguably been subject to the vicissitudes of opposing party political priorities in social policy and local government funding since the creation of generic social care departments in 1970 (Seebohm Report, 1968). Debates and differences about the roles and tasks of state-funded social work interventions into private lives have been played out through subsequent governmental reviews of social work and social work education (Barclay Report, 1982; Social Work Reform Board, 2010; Croisdale-Appleby, 2014; Narey, 2014). The urgency to 'get things right' and 'learn the lessons' of a series of child death tragedies has led to most than 30 specific inquiries into high media profile child protection 'failures' since the emblematic death of Maria Colwell in 1974. Parton (2011) argues that two of the highest profile and most recent child deaths, those of Victoria Climbié and Baby Peter Connelly (Laming, 2003, 2009), led in turn to very different social policy responses to risk and intervention into the lives of children and families, discussed further in Chapter 7.

The performance management approaches of the New Labour government gave rise to the Every Child Matters agenda for safeguarding and early interventions (Department for Education and Skills, 2004a, 2004b) and the Common Assessment Framework (Children's Workforce Development Council, 2009). Whereas, in apparent contrast, one of the early acts of the Conservative/Liberal coalition government in 2010 was to establish an independent 'Review of Child Protection' that reported the following year in England (Munro, 2011; Department for Education, 2011a). The rhetoric of the coalition government and the subsequent recommendations of the Munro Report (2011) encouraged a familiar theme of 'freeing professionals from bureaucracy'. The 15 recommendations were largely welcomed by the social work profession in England. All had dates for implementation except for recommendation 13 '*Local authorities should review and redesign the ways in which child and family social work is delivered*' which, in line with a broad policy aim of 'localism' was to be enacted 'at a locally determined pace'. At the time of the interviews for this book the extent and pace of implementation of the principles and practices of the Munro recommendations were unclear. This may be understandable in view of the apparent *volte-face* aims of, for example, scrapping target assessments within specific time-frames and deadlines in a professional culture that has developed through two decades of increasing managerialist top-down control (Wastell et al., 2010). More recently, evidence is mounting that the changes envisaged by Munro will be slow and difficult to implement (Community Care, 2013).

Scotland

Scotland has a different legal system from the rest of the United Kingdom, enabling Scotland to develop some distinctive responses to children and families, the most well known of which is probably the children's hearing system based on the Kilbrandon philosophy of 'needs not deeds' (Kilbrandon,1964). This commitment remains evident in more recent Scottish law and policy, most notably the Children's Hearings (Scotland) Act 2011. Scottish social work has been confronting similar crises of confidence about the social work role and capacity of the workforce as other UK nations. Scotland's 21st Century Review of Social Work concluded, 'more of the same won't work: *Increasing demand, greater complexity and rising expectations mean that the current situation is not sustainable*' (Scottish Executive, 2006, p. 8). The Review visualised a revitalised social work profession, less constrained by unnecessary bureaucracy, less risk averse, more autonomous and more able to use their particular knowledge and skills to work creatively and therapeutically with service users and carers. The Review recommended a wide-ranging change programme to build workforce capacity to deliver personalised social services. However, there remain questions about the extent to which the aspirations of Changing Lives have subsequently been achieved in the prevailing economic climate – and to what extent the Scottish Government's vision is one that is recognised and collectively owned by the social work profession in Scotland (Dumbleton and McPhail, 2012).

Debates about child protection in Scotland have parallels with those set out in Munro Review, stressing that 'procedures and guidance in themselves cannot protect children', and that a 'competent, skilled and confident workforce' that can work across agency boundaries is essential (Scottish Government, 2010, p. 5). Social work with children and families is underpinned by a number of policies, including Getting it Right for Every Child and the National Practice Model that place the child at the centre of assessment and planning. A Children's Charter has been in place since 2004, and the Children and Young People (Scotland) Act 2014 aims to strengthen the implementation of the United Nations Convention on the Rights of the Child in Scotland.

Wales

Since devolution the Welsh assembly government has increasingly sought to move children's services towards its own distinctive and progressive agenda. A long-standing emphasis on a rights-based approach to work with children and young people was cemented by the Rights of Children and Young Persons (Wales) Measure 2011 which enshrined the United Nation Convention on the Rights of a Child (UNCRC) in domestic law. Similarly a commitment to address poverty as part of a 'One Wales' (Welsh Assembly Government, 2007) strategy seeks to tackle the needs of disadvantaged families. It seems likely that this process will continue as policies and practices shared with England are reviewed in the Welsh context. Chapter 6 illustrates one way in which policies are able to flow directly into the development of services – integrated family support service teams – a process aided by the more compact structure of government in Wales than that of its larger neighbour. Decision-making is clearer and a smaller gap exists between the service and the ministers responsible.

The social work service itself came into the 21st century with much in common with the rest of the United Kingdom. A profession feeling undervalued, dissatisfied and in need of a 're-launch' (ADSS, 2005, p. 17). Some of the origins of this dissatisfaction are very familiar with joint reviews, inspections and evaluations leading to a target-based culture 'contributing to a shift in the emphasis of the social work role from direct contact with clients' (ADSS, 2005, p. 13). The intention to address these issues of the uncertain role and low esteem of social workers was made clear in a subsequent review of social services. This review advocated improvement in recruitment, retention and quality but acknowledged that it is the 'professional contribution' of practitioners that should be at the heart of services recognising that it is 'the day to day work with citizens that ultimately makes the difference' (Welsh Assembly Government, 2011, p. 24).

The sections and themes of the book

The stories in the three sections of this book are organised within three important and closely inter-related themes in social work practice. The first theme of 'relationships' is one that has been the subject of long-standing debates throughout the history of social work. The second theme of 'risk, uncertainty and judgement' is very much of the present and has become an all pervasive concern in contemporary social work. The third theme of 'power, negotiation and problem-solving' covers inter-related ideas that have been implicit in social work debates but, we argue, are under-explored and should form part of future directions for practice.

Relationships can be demonstrated to have had an explicit influence in social work dating back over at least three centuries but remain a central principle in the present day. The history of social work can be traced back a very long way and some have located it in Biblical times (Seed, 1973). Rather more recently, in 1869, the Charity Organisation Society (COS) was founded to try and organise the wide range of charitable giving on a systematic basis. The COS became a significant influence upon developments in social work and, in so doing, it symbolised some of social work's core tensions. On the one hand it placed great value upon locally based, person-centred approaches and an individualised understanding of relationships and family difficulties. At the same time, however, it was also striving to increase its efficiency through 'scientific' administration and became an early example of how the humanistic values of social work can be challenged and compromised through the imperatives of 'efficiency'. Nonetheless, as Cooper (1983) proposes,

11

The COS casework method of social assessment and of family and individual support based on relationships established between the worker and the recipient of the service was a major contribution to the development of professional social work. (p. 17)

It can be argued that this core tension, between helping relationships and the development of efficient systems to deliver such help on a large scale, is indicative of the increasing role of the State in private lives. Consequently, the developments from historical, piecemeal charitable activities to the universal state-delivered services of late modernity are among the factors that drive the recent emphasis upon 'risk' and the assessment of risk. There are few people in social work today in the United Kingdom that would not identify the assessment and management of risk as a major, if not the major, factor influencing practice and policy decisions. However, the present-day preoccupation with risk in social work can only be addressed and receive a service level response in practice through person-to-person level relationships. It is at these points in social work practice, where relationships and risk meet that the far less explicit influence of power exists. As Smith (2010) argues:

in the contemporary era, risk and its representations are central to the practice of social work [and are, as such] a powerful exemplar of the dynamics and consequences of power relationships in social work. (8.1)

If relationships and risk can be located as both past and present preoccupations, it could be argued that power and negotiation should be part of the present and future concerns for social work today. Power is both essential and ubiquitous in social work practice and yet at the same time it is, as commentators such as Foucault have famously noted, frustratingly disguised and under-recognised. It is a slippery term that is difficult to grasp conceptually although most practitioners will intuitively have some understanding of how it operates. In 'Section 3' power is coupled with the practice skills of negotiation towards solutions to problems. These links, between power- and solution-focused practices, are drawn out through risks and relationships and look to future directions for social work. The following paragraphs offer a taster of what is contained in each section.

Section 1: Relationships

Inside every social work story there is a story of relationship. The relationship may be substantial and long-lasting; it may be short and conflictual. Even where a social worker feels they were completely unsuccessful in forming any relationship with a service user there is still a story to be told and explored. The fundamental importance of relationship in social work has long been recognised (Perlman, 1979; Ruch et al., 2010) although it has struggled at times to have a high profile in policy, training, supervision, or even practice. Arguments for the reorientation of social work practice across the United Kingdom discussed earlier also brought a re-emphasis, at least within the rhetoric, on the vital importance of relationships and even 'therapeutic' relationships (Scottish Executive, 2006; Munro, 2011).

Answering the 'why' question about relationships is an easier one than the 'how' question but detailed explorations of practice can provide valuable insights to enable that discussion to take place. Consequently although all the chapters in this book will inevitably contribute to the discussion about social work relationships in practice, in three instances practitioners were asked to talk directly and in depth about how they went about planning, forming and maintaining relationships in specific situations. In Chapter 6, this discussion goes beyond practice with service users to consider the role of relationships in creating the context for advancing CBP in organisations.

Section 2: Risk, uncertainty and decision-making

Social workers, like the rest of society, practice in a context that is 'saturated with and preoccupied by risk' (Webb, 2006, p. 23). Risk – its identification, assessment and management – has become a major preoccupation for the social work profession. This changing emphasis is evident in the assessment frameworks for qualifying social work education in all four UK nations, reflecting the resolve of policy-makers to ensure that risk is central to health and care social policy (Whittington, 2007). The importance of effective risk assessment and management, supported by training, has been stressed in successive inquiries into child abuse. Although there is recognition that it is impossible to eliminate risk – and indeed, that risk-taking can have positive as well as negative outcomes – governments and employers have tended to respond to potential risk defensively. The skilled practitioner must identify and respond to risk of harm to children, while negotiating their understanding of risk and its impact with families, employers and multi-disciplinary colleagues. At the same time they must balance their assessment of risk and need with people's rights – the developing child's right to increasing independence and autonomy, and the rights of parents to make decisions about their children's welfare. These tensions are encapsulated in the Codes of Practice in the UK nations, through, for example, the requirement to 'promote the independence of service users while protecting them as far as possible from danger or harm' (e.g., SSSC, 2009). The four examples in this section of the book illustrate a range of practice situations in which risk – its assessment and determining a proportionate and safe response to the potential for harm – is the dominant issue for the practitioners concerned.

Section 3: Power, negotiation and problem-solving

This section of the book argues that the purposeful uses of power and negotiation are under-recognised within social work but, arguably, constitute the *sine qua non* of the professional practitioner. However, power and negotiation are not ends in themselves but are essential means through which social work addresses the very reasons for its involvement: identifying problems and finding solutions to those problems. Despite power being both a relevant and complex socio-logical concept as well as an everyday word, it is not always clear to what extent practitioners are aware of their power – in practice. An acknowledgement of power by practitioners often appears to conflict with the deeply held values of anti-oppressive practice and service user empowerment. But in order for the professional aspirations of empowerment to be realised there first needs to be an understanding of how power accrues personally and as a professional worker with authority within welfare networks. A major way in which power in social work operates is arguably through purposeful talk and negotiation.

However, whereas power can be argued to be a ubiquitous aspect of social work, the same cannot be clearly asserted of negotiation. It's not always apparent how practitioners negotiate with people in open and transparent processes to bring about change. A negotiative approach to the social work process recognises power differentials and proceeds with as much transparency as possible during interventions into the lives of parents, children and families. Social work problems need to be defined but ways forward have to be created through detailed and often-contested negotiation, in collaboration with multi-disciplinary colleagues, and with children, young people and their families as a central part of the process. The three stories of practice in 'Section 3' illustrate how the workings of power and negotiation are complex, interlinked – and sometimes absent!

Note

1. Someone To Watch Over Me, 2004, and Protecting Our Children, 2012, BBC & Open University.

2 Telling Stories: A Journey into Narratives of Practice

Barry Cooper, Jean Gordon and Andy Rixon

Introduction

This chapter is about the significance of stories to social work practice. Roscoe and Jones (2009) propose that 'In social work ... we speak ourselves into existence within the stories available to us' (p. 10). This is a profound thought. However, stories or narratives in social work are not unproblematic. By explaining some of the struggles and dilemmas that arose from writing with practitioners we aim to draw out some key arguments and theoretical insights into the relationship between story-telling and social work practice. Two key questions help to frame these discussions: 'what story?' and 'whose words?' Some of this discussion may seem complex. But this is only because social work practice *is* intrinsically complicated. So we would urge readers interested in these explanations to stick with it. However, the stories in the three sections that follow are self-contained and readers can choose to return to this and the more theoretical section introductory chapters at any time.

Our journey into narratives of practice has been an interesting one. We started out facilitating a discussion with practitioners about an example of their 'best practice'. Recording these discussions seemed relatively uncomplicated and we will describe how we did it. However, turning a recorded discussion into a written story of practice is far from straightforward. Some of the details of our experience of 'writing up' a conversation about social work practice and trying to subsequently 'write down' various narrative versions of 'the story' have, we believe, important implications for both practice and research into practice. As Marie, one our participants, commented in reflection upon the processes of writing a chapter: *'I think it captures for me the importance of the "little things" in social work that can often make a big difference and people don't always have the opportunity to really reflect on decisions they make*. So, we are going to tell you a story about our journey into narratives of practice that will help you to explore the stories of social work in the rest of this book with open eyes.

Talking to practitioners

The interviews and resulting stories in this book arose through a research project funded by the Open University, Faculty of Health and Social Care, that we called 'Practitioner Pathways into Publishing'. The OU social work programme is offered in four nations across the United Kingdom, in England, Scotland and Wales as well as, on a smaller scale, in Northern Ireland. We were able to use our contacts in England, Wales and Scotland to make a general enquiry along these lines:

> Are you interested in contributing to a book that will showcase examples of best prac-
> tice in Child Care Social Work? Or do you know someone who might be?
>
> If you are a social worker or senior practitioner, and enjoy opportunities to reflect,
> talk and possibly write about your work, you may be interested in becoming involved
> in a project that aims to explore the challenges, dilemmas and complexities of social
> work practice with children and families from a practitioner's viewpoint. We plan to
> interview up to 12 children and family social work practitioners in different settings in
> England, Scotland and Wales about their work.

The 'sample' of participants was inevitably opportunistic as it depended upon people volunteering to be interviewed. Social work is a complex and diverse set of services and it was unrealistic to aim for a small-scale project to cover all possibilities. Nevertheless over time, from the resulting response, we were able to choose a number of social workers whose practice reflected aspects of the range of different services and settings in children and families social work across these three nations. They included practitioners from the statutory and independent sectors, working with children of different ages and a range of needs as well as parents and foster carers. The participant group includes a mix of gender, range of ages and practitioners with widely varying lengths of experience working in both urban and rural areas, although we were less successful at including practitioners from minority ethnic backgrounds.

We asked our volunteer practitioners to select an example that they thought was illustrative of the kinds of work that they do and which could, within the parameters of 'best practice' defined in Chapter 1, be used as the basis for an exploratory discussion. We also asked them to tell us which of the three themes of the book – relationships, risk or negotiation and problem-solving – that this example of practice particularly illustrated. Often practitioners identified more than one theme. We asked both the practitioner and a representative from their employer, usually a line manager, to sign a consent form that confirmed that they had read an information sheet about the project, and agreed that the social worker was able to take part. The agency information included an explanation of 'critical best practice' and our policy in relation to issues of consent, anonymity and confidentiality. These issues were resolved in different ways in each case, sometimes through seeking consent of a service user or Guardian ad Litem, sometimes by changing details of the case and, in one case by use of a pseudonym by the social worker. In every case the names of parents, children and other professionals, as well as any identifying details have been changed.

As editors, we also discussed the possibility of involving service users, either in interviews, or inviting their commentary on the practitioners' stories. After much debate, we concluded that this was going to be too complex to do well – and all too easy to do badly if service users were involved in ways that could appear tokenistic. Additionally, many of the individuals described in the narratives were or are involuntary service users, and in some cases the relationship between parents, children and/ or social workers was fraught, and sometimes hostile. Perhaps inevitably, it was these very difficult cases, involving skilful, highly reflective and personally challenging practice that social workers wanted to talk to us about.

Writing with practitioners

The project was titled 'Practitioner Pathways into Publishing' because we were keen to involve participants as active joint-authors of the developing stories and viewed it as crucial that the social worker had a central role in turning their verbal accounts of lived experience into text. This kind of collaborative endeavour between academics and practitioners is known to be one way of helping to overcome the barriers that many practitioners experience when trying to combine day-to-day practice with dissemination of knowledge through publication (Staudt et al., 2003).

Most contributors were willing, in principle, to be involved in commenting upon and verifying the draft chapters although there were differences in practitioners' time and availability to engage in the time-consuming tasks of writing and editing texts. In nearly every case the writing process was a gradual one, which started with practitioners and editors annotating the typed interview transcript and ended with the production of the final chapter. Typically there were numerous drafts, and sometimes long gaps in communication with practitioners, most of whom were working at full tilt in busy social work teams and other settings. Nevertheless, it is notable that, with the exception of one practitioner who was unable to continue with the project owing to ill health, the social workers have stayed with the writing process over the three years the project lasted. Its iterative nature seems to have allowed a steady flow of ideas, and, to varying extents, the development of a sense of 'co-producing' the chapters with the three editors. Many of the practitioners who took part have given us positive feedback about their experience of being involved in writing about practice, and told us of their plans to find ways of continuing to write about practice. For example, Jock Mickshik (see Chapter 9) explained how his involvement with this project *directly influenced me in thinking how I could help other practitioners*. The experience has led to his co-authoring of a local guide to help professionals manage and treat sexually harmful behaviour and sexual victimization among young people with learning difficulties. At the same time, like many of the practitioner authors, he reports *an inevitable struggle* to make time to write when there are so many other demands on his time in his workplace.

The many phases of the process described earlier, from verbatim transcripts of spoken discussions in the initial interview through numerous versions of text-based stories to the final published version, raised some important questions for the authors about the use of narrative. Two central dilemmas became clear from the process of writing down the stories which turned on the questions of 'what story?' was finally selected and 'whose words?' were used to write it. We will explore these two questions as a way in to some of the theoretical issues arising from the use of narratives and stories of social work practice.

What's the story?

The 'story' is a particularly loaded word in the English language. From earliest childhood memories most people will recall being warned by adult authority figures about 'telling stories' with the clear message that this is tantamount to 'telling fibs'. In written media contexts the story has also become synonymous with newspapers spinning accounts that are designed to sensationalise and maintain circulation figures regardless of the impact upon people's lives. For social work this popular association of stories with untruths and an abuse of power would seem to be particularly dangerous territory. Perhaps because of this, there have been few published attempts to convey the powerful stories of social work or to use them as a valid source of knowledge for assessment, planning and interventions. One attempt, by LeCroy (2002), set out to let practitioners in a USA context speak about themselves and what they do in practice and to tell their stories in their own words with little visible editorial commentary or academic critique. This approach has many advantages but has also been criticised (Butler, 2003) for smoothing over the complications of narrative work in the social sciences and for rendering as largely invisible the inevitable selection processes of editing stories from interviews.

Squire et al. (2008) argue that narratives are used in a variety of different ways in research. These include the use of stories as ways of expressing or building professional identity. Phillips et al. (2012) go so far as to claim that 'Research is the ultimate telling of a story' (p. 785). In the context of our project interviews, social workers were telling their stories not only as a version of events but perhaps also as a version of themselves as social workers. To step outside of conventional views on social work might be seen as a risk and so their explanations of events need to be plausible and defensible. What appears to be a straightforward interview can, from this perspective, be seen as a self-censoring performance by the interviewee that, in turn, is influenced by the interviewer, and, ultimately, the readership, as 'audience' (Salmon, in Riessman and Quinney, 2005, pp. 398–9).

In this sense a complex process has already begun even before the more active co-production of the final text had commenced. When social workers reviewed their transcripts after the interview, they occasionally wanted to edit some of the content on the grounds that this might appear, for example, too indecisive, unprofessional or even controversial. For example, one practitioner author was concerned that he came across as too blunt with service users and this might be seen as poor professional practice even though the circumstances justified a 'direct' style. So, in producing these accounts, any changes made to transcripts were negotiated in each case by the editors and practitioners, though ultimately the practitioner had the final word on which direct quotes were included and how their practice was represented on the page.

Reflecting the complexity of social work practice was a challenge at all stages of the project. Most of our interviewees would have been happy to speak for much longer about their practice, but as editors we were only looking for an arbitrary two hours of their time. The twists, turns and dilemmas of direct practice that may have taken place over weeks, months and sometimes years are impossible to capture in their entirety, and certainly not in less than 5,000 words. Some interviews also went into some fascinating places that just didn't 'fit' the book's three themes. Quite often interviews 'circled' around the topic – the circling often seemed important not only because it helped establish the context for the practice but also because it was often part of the practitioner's reflective processes: 'Now I'm thinking about this again, I am beginning to wonder if.' However, much of this discussion does not appear in the chapters. Some of the content of interviews that was lost was taken out because it could be 'neatly' removed without detracting from the particular story that the chapter tells. So, some of the selection decisions were guided by the need to tell a comprehensible and readable story with due regard to maintaining anonymity. It was a long and sometimes quite painful process to remove some of the interesting ideas and discussions that disappeared into the recycle bin. And, in a book about complexity, it makes the stories look simpler, tidier and more uni-directional than they ever were in practice. At the same time, in making these practice stories accessible, we have tried hard not to smooth over the challenges of 21st-century social work, and just how the practitioners we interviewed met these.

In making a case for the importance of stories of social work there is undoubtedly a need for what Paley and Eva (2005, p. 83) describe as 'narrative vigilance' in differentiating between stories of practice as narratives with some degree of objective accuracy and stories that are designed to deliver emotional persuasiveness. However while the word 'story' may be an emotive one, as Paley and Eva point out, the word 'narrative' is also problematic. 'Narrative research' can be found across many disciplines but with little consistency in its definition or theoretical underpinning. Narrative is also used in popular culture and political dialogue and so is 'strikingly diverse in the way it is understood' (Squire et al., 2008, p. 3). Nevertheless, it is generally agreed that 'narrative stories refer to discourses with a sequential order i.e. they are chronological, meaningful and social' (Eliott, 2005, in Larsson and Sjoblom, 2010, p. 274). It is this broad understanding of narrative (or story) that we draw on in this book, rather than its more restricted uses, for example, in sociolinguistics.

Paley and Eva maintain that for a story to be called a narrative it should be 'an account which, at least implicitly, makes claims (which may be either true or false) about the causal links between some of the events described' (2005, p. 86) and seeks to offer an explanation.

However, 'causal links' and their role in creating stories that offer 'explanations' of events are persuasive and powerful concepts that require examination. Social work remains a professional activity that continues to value the importance of feelings and skilled practitioners seek to purposefully negotiate the stories that bring private lives into the realms of professional duties and obligations. The mechanisms and processes in deciding what story achieves priority in social work practice are similar, we would argue, to those that help decide literary publication. Both processes inevitably involve power and selection and, in fundamental ways, challenge implicit assumptions of 'causal links' and 'explanations' of events. The next section sets out some important theoretical perspectives.

Constructing a story: theoretical thoughts

A full theoretical argument to explain why psychological and perceptual processes of selection are intrinsic to human interaction and use of power is beyond the scope of this chapter. However, we cannot explore the status of stories without, to some extent, questioning the nature of knowledge in social work. As part of a much wider consideration of the importance of constructivism for social work, Fisher (1991) sets out the differences between traditional objectivist epistemologies and the more radical constructivist ways of knowing. On the one hand, an objectivist approach to social science and the process of knowing reality would hold that knowledge consists of verifiable facts about the world and other people and that we can gain access to this reality through a process of discovery. The assumption is that social scientistic methods require fine-tuning in order that variables can be identified and isolated and linear chains of causality understood. This approach is exemplified by 'evidence-based' arguments for social work (Sheldon and Chilvers, 2000) although there are also arguments that seek to broaden out the conceptions of what legitimately constitutes evidence and knowledge for practice (Gray et al., 2009). On the other hand, in comparison, a constructivist approach accepts that, although there is a reality 'out there' made up of objective conditions, we only have access to our constructions of subjectively perceived realities through our definitions, experienced relationships and interactions. This personal knowledge, as a product of our assumptions and anticipations of our world, is pragmatic knowledge that is continually tested by us in our daily lives and interactions. Polkinghorne (1992) suggests that, 'the test for pragmatic knowledge is whether it functions successfully in guiding human action to fulfil intended purposes' (p. 151). Arguments for the 'humanisation' of human science research are reflected within aspects of social work literature that explore and emphasise the value of purposeful communication and engagement between people. As Howe (1993) clearly puts it,

> [T]here are no objective fundamental truths in human relationships, only working truths. These decentred contingent truths help people make sense of and control the meaning of their own experience. (p. 193)

The interplay between our social worlds, of relationships and culture, and our internal world of thoughts and feelings is an enduring philosophical conundrum. But it is what gives rise to our stories as ways of making sense of what we do and what we experience. Commentators upon the two theoretical perspectives of social constructionism and psychological constructivism recognise that the differences between 'the social' and 'the personal' are ones of emphasis as both interact with and derive from the other. In other words, a greater awareness of the social actually deepens an understanding of the personal; and vice versa. Paris and Epting (2004) argue that it is through our stories that we create understandings of what we do within socially constituted situations. The essentially relational aspects of people as beings-in-the-world can only be understood through a complementary awareness of how stories influence our social and personal meanings and constructions. They very succinctly convey the crux of the matter like this:

> How we experience what we call reality is isomorphic with how we go about making sense of our lives and ourselves and with what sense we make of the world. The terms we use to describe ourselves and others (and that others use to describe us) come loaded with definitions, implications, and connotations, around which we spin stories that we live by. In this way, these descriptive terms are standing invitations to construe others and ourselves in ways that are consistent with them. (p. 17)

This quote could hardly be more germane to social workers in their practice stories and assessments of people and social situations. A constructivist theoretical perspective is based upon the fundamental assumption that individuals have an ability to construct themselves through their stories. On this perspective, social workers, like everybody else, will attempt to exert some power and control over how they present themselves and their practice through systems of selection that decide which aspects of their available knowledge will help to construct particular stories and versions of events. One of the biggest challenges in social work is to recognise and accept the power potential to privilege some versions and interpretations of events over others.

So, the theoretical ground upon which we were operating, to write about social work stories with the practitioners concerned, is particularly complex. The stories are the practitioners' versions and there is value in these stories being told. In trying to answer the question of 'what's the story?' we had at the same time to grapple with the question of 'whose story to use?' This next section will draw out some of these issues and also reflect upon the parallel implications for practice.

Whose story?

It is tempting to view the initial phases of getting stories as being one of relatively straightforward data collection; we talked to people and we recorded it and this was transcribed. So far, so simple, it seems. Whereas, by comparison, the subsequent processes of creative writing that produce the stories are far more complicated. However, Atkinson (1990) argues that data collection is not at all straightforward and has captured the way that ethnographers collect and write down stories as data and then afterwards begin to write those stories up. Although he differentiates between 'writing down' and 'writing up' he makes the point that, '*both* phases of the work involve the creation of textual materials; both are equally matters of textual construction' (p. 61). For example, our discussions with practitioners were audio-recorded and later transcribed verbatim or written down. However, although this was done by a professional transcriber, even before this process began the stories had begun to be constructed in particular ways. They were framed through the kinds of questions that were pre-provided by the editors; thought about and reflected upon by our interviewees; and then shaped through the dynamics of the minute-to-minute decisions taken by both interviewer and participant as their conversation unfolded.

As explained earlier, in drawing upon a broadly constructivist framework, these processes of selection are central to interactions and communications in personal and social activities. The issues that arise in professional writing reflect similar issues in professional practice. That is, we as academics and educators struggle with decisions about whose words and whose voice should be used with practitioner colleagues in writing about practice. The issues for practitioners in working with service users are, or should be, similarly accentuated. For example, in setting out to write with practitioners and trying to 'co-produce' the chapters there followed a long process of selecting, editing, commenting and analysing which felt like an incremental process. Riessman (1993) suggests that this method is better understood as a series of 'transformations' from spoken word to published text. As such, there were constant issues of power and who decides what goes in and why. The decisions involved questions of whose words should be used and to what extent was it legitimate for us, as editors, to amend and add commentaries that subtly but powerfully broadened, deepened and thereby changed 'the story'?

While we were able to shape the stories on the basis of our interviews, we were dependent upon the practitioners' decisions about what to include and what to exclude in their accounts of practice. It is a dynamic that most practitioners will commonly recognise in compiling assessments. The service user, social worker and other practitioners in multi-professional contexts are all engaged in helping to create, reinforce or contradict their own ideas about 'the story' of the situation. In an important sense, social work principles about empowerment should ensure that service users are involved in making 'executive decisions' about what goes into the story and the processes of sharing, checking and validating the 'final' version. This is a crucial counterbalance to the power of the social worker 'through statute, language and perspective to define the experiences of others' (Butler et al., 2007, p. 1124). In writing the chapters for this book we remained acutely aware of the 'privileging' effects of the written word in creating a permanent record which defines the experience of others at that particular moment. Social work practice takes place in changing and dynamic social situations and so trying to capture 'the story' from an interview at one moment in time, sometimes seemed akin to trying to capture a whole movie with a single click of the camera. As in practice, the interviews, and the nature of the information that was recorded to use as the basis for the chapters, was influenced by a range of different factors in each case. The relationships between us as individual editors and our varied participant practitioners inevitably impacted upon what was talked about. Questions, selections and analysis were all also influenced (consciously or unconsciously) by our own views on what constitutes 'good' practice, informed by our own social work histories and theoretical perspectives. So, just as in social work practice, we cannot be construed as 'naive listeners'; as interviewers and editors we were busy story-making too (Larsson and Sjoblom, 2010, p. 279).

Learning from stories

We are all interested in stories: we tell them, listen to them, read them and watch them on television, computers and the stage as well as in 'real life'. 'Narratives are everywhere' (Silverman, 1998, quoted by Sikes and Gale, 2006, p. 47) and much of human life is conducted through narrative accounts of events and experiences (Roscoe, 2009). However, our interest in stories in this book is a quite specific one: to use relatively structured narratives of practice as a stimulus for reflection, learning and development. This is congruent with one of the central aims of a critical best practice approach, to analyse what social work 'routinely does well by developing knowledge of best practice on which to base learning and positive growth' (Ferguson, 2008, p. 16).

Social work practice, like the narrative approach, takes place within the context of human interaction, spoken, written and non-verbal. Both share an interest in people's stories, and 'giving voice to marginalised groups' by listening to and responding to those stories (Larsson and Sjoblom, 2010, p. 273). We highlighted earlier the way in which social workers develop their own stories through practice, and how these stories interact, and sometimes compete, with the perspectives of others, including service users, carers, other professionals and their employers. Narrative approaches are also used in more systematic and explicit ways in social work. For example, life story work with adopted children, and therapeutic use of reminiscence, or 'de-briefing' after a traumatic event, are long-established forms of intervention which rely on the power of story-telling and the importance of personal biographies. Story-telling is closely entwined with identity, a key concept in social work practice, and narrative approaches have been shown to provide opportunities for positive re-framing of personal identity and the development of alternative stories through processes of 're-authoring' (Altenberger and Mackay, 2006; Roscoe, 2009).

Narrative as a form of pedagogy – to promote critical reflexivity and learning – also has a substantial history. Reflective writing, as a means of developing self-awareness and improving practice, is a well-established element in social work qualifying and post-qualifying education and relies heavily on narrative processes. Social work supervision may involve the sharing of 'stories' about social workers' interactions with service users – as well as a complex co-construction of meaning from this interaction by the social worker and their supervisor. (Interestingly, however, our discussions with the practitioner authors suggested that this act of 'telling the story' is an increasingly rare oral experience for practitioners at a time when traditional processes of supervision and consultation are changing under pressure.) The stories of practice in this book follow a similar tradition by using stories to promote learning. However, in contrast with the story making that goes on in a social work senior's office or on the pages of a student's reflective journal, our aim is to make these practice narratives visible. Our detailed explorations of practice provide a means of communicating with social workers, other professionals and service users about the doing of social work. Like reflective practice, much of the real work of social work, the time spent with children and families, takes place in private spaces, in the home or a review meeting. For the uninitiated, this gives social work a certain mystique, as well as a lack of visible accountability, which may hide both good and poor practice. The participants in the 'Practitioner Pathways into Publishing' project have bravely agreed to open up their practice, including their reflections on doubts, mistakes and wrong turnings, to the reader's scrutiny. Importantly, these stories have a wider purpose: to trigger reflection and critical thinking about the relationship between what is read and the reader's particular experience of social work. The questions at the beginning of each chapter are designed to encourage individual readers to make links between what they read and their own experiences – of childhood, of being a service user and/or a social worker or other professional. This final transformation, through the many transformations involved in bringing this book to fruition, is about the use you make of these examples of practice to clarify your understanding of what best practice means to you and the people you work with.

Part 1

Relationships

3 Relationships

Andy Rixon

That social workers require the ability to form relationships with the people with whom they work has always been accepted even, perhaps mistakenly, taken for granted. However the emphasis on the centrality of relationships to the social work role and what we really mean by this has fluctuated over time as the thorny debate about what it is social workers should actually be doing and how, has continued. This section explores, through descriptions of practice, some of the reality of how social workers view the idea of relationships and what they actually do and don't do in their direct work to create, foster and then end them. No ideal will be proposed; so varied are social work encounters and the contexts in which they take place that this would be impossible. But this is not to say that learning cannot emerge from following the struggles of practitioners to form meaningful relationships as they search for the best practice they can achieve in complex situations.

Looking back/looking forward

Recognition of the importance of interpersonal relationships in social work stretches back to its earliest organised forms in the Settlement movement and the Charity Organisation Society of the late 19th century. The highpoint of practice that could be described as 'relationship based' is often seen as being found in the 'casework' of the 1950s and 1960s; an approach strongly influenced by psychodynamic theory. Here 'the casework relationship is a form of treatment' (Beistek, 1961 cited in Prynn, 2008, p. 104) whether within the family or with children outside of it:

> It is the relationship – found in the foster home or Children's Home – provided by the case worker which is the healing factor in the child's life. (Heywood, 1959 cited in Prynn, 2008, p. 104)

In the subsequent decades of the 20th century this emphasis declined as new debates emerged within the profession and new social and political contexts outside it. Flaws in the underpinning assumptions of casework were identified by the radical social work movement of the 1970s as the primary purpose of the casework relationship emphasised 'helping the client achieve a better adjustment between himself and his environment' (Beistek cited in Trevithick, 2003, p. 165) rather than challenging that environment and the disadvantages experienced by clients within it. In turn the emphasis on both the relational aspects of social work and on radical social work were subsequently eclipsed by the rise of a culture dominated by audit, managerialism and bureaucracy (Ruch 2010).

One key influence in the development of this managerialist culture was the rise of neoliberalism and its emphasis on individualisation and the primacy of markets. As service users were positioned as consumers so social workers became service providers open to scrutiny for efficiency and value for money. Arguably, policy and practice towards children and families became driven less by the possibilities of what could be achieved within the social work relationship than by 'managing and monitoring a range of abstract factors' (Parton, 1998). Targets and timescales can play an important role in the development of practice and can be introduced in response to feedback from parent and carers or research identifying where social work practice could be improved (see, e.g., the education and placement stability of looked-after children (Jackson, 1998; Stein, 2009)). However, the fact that a visit had been done and the assessment completed in time sometimes seemed to assume more significance than what actually happened during the visit. In the case of risk, in relation to children in particular, this may have stemmed from a concern to 'manage out' the messy reality of practice.

> such developments are in danger of overlooking a central characteristic of child welfare policy and practice in terms of the pervasiveness of uncertainty and ambiguity. (Parton, 1998, p. 6)

Entering the 21st-century social work seemed to many to be dominated by this bureaucracy and the computer systems and forms they required (Garrett, 2005). At the same time the profession was repeatedly found to be uncertain and unconfident in its own skills and expertise in relation to children and families (Scottish Executive, 2006; Laming, 2009).

Although the argument for the role of relationship-based practice has continued to be made (Ruch, 2005; Trevithick, 2003, etc.) the early

21st century saw it regain prominence in at least the rhetoric of policy. The impact of time spent filling in forms, recording, data inputting and co-ordinating resurfaced for discussion and debate along with a re-examination of what it is that social workers should be doing.

In Scotland 'Changing Lives' emphasised the importance of developing 'therapeutic relationships':

> [Yet] social workers consistently told us that it is this very aspect of their work which has been eroded and devalued in recent years under the pressures of workloads, increased bureaucracy and a more mechanistic and technical approach to delivering services. We must now legitimise and restore the centrality of working for change through therapeutic relationships as the basis of strengthening the profession for the 21st Century. (Scottish Executive, 2006, p. 28)

This was echoed in England in the Munro review of child protection which was equally critical of the balance between the emotional elements of social work and bureaucratic tasks such as keeping records.

> The centrality of forming relationships with children and families to understand and help them has become obscured. (Munro, 2011, p. 8)

The debate about what social workers do has sometimes crystallised around the label of social worker as 'care manager' something questioned directly by a review of social services in Wales along with a suggestion of a much more radical shift in the basis of practitioner–service user relationships:

> We believe that the concept of 'care management' is outmoded – conveying a sense of control by the service, not by the citizen. We know that social workers are not simply the deliverers of pre-determined care, but co-creators of the support that people need. (Welsh Assembly Government, 2011, p. 24)

The extent to which the debate will really change the nature of social work practice and set the tone for its future remains an open question (see Parton, 2012). It seems highly unlikely that the existence of targets and performance assessment frameworks will disappear nor many of the pressures on resources. However perhaps the importance of relationships and the skills associated with it will be restored as a priority in the profession. As the Welsh quote above indicates, it is also increasingly likely that the question will be answered differently in the different nations of the United Kingdom as devolved governments shape services according to their own priorities and values. Devolved governments have also looked beyond the United Kingdom for models of practice; the centrality of relationships in work with children in a range of settings is not questioned in social pedagogic traditions across much of Europe (Petrie, 2011).

Professional identities

The changing emphasis on relationships in social work has often followed reviews of the roles and tasks of social work which have been drawn and redrawn at regular intervals. Social work has had a fragile professional identity which has often been under pressure from within and without (Rixon, 2010). It is particularly exposed to changing political and economic ideologies and, child care social work in particular, buffeted by the reactions to various enquiries. What constitutes its knowledge base and the evidence for its efficacy is also subject to continuing debate.

The increasingly inter-professional working environment (and a good example of this features in Chapters 4 and 6), brings social work roles and skills and what is distinctive about them into sharp focus. Qualitative studies with social workers seem to reinforce the idea that (for example) not only is direct work with children not always done but is not always seen as a core professional task. Rather this type of work is something that can be done by other professionals and social work assessments can therefore be dependent on the quality of a child's relationships with others (Winter, 2009).

As a consequence while the profession might broadly welcome the idea of a return to an emphasis on relationships, as signalled in some policy documents, recapturing 'relationships' for the profession might not be a straightforward matter. Lack of recognition of the emotional dimensions of professional practice in favour of the technical and bureaucratic has arguably encouraged practice prone to defensiveness. Ruch (2010) argues that as a result some social workers may lack the skills in communication and relationship building and the confidence and support to develop them. Consequently for relationship-based practice to succeed it may require not just a reconceptualisation of practice but of practitioners themselves (Ruch, 2010).

All three chapters that follow in this section show workers who are clear that the skills of communicating, engaging and relationship building are a central part of their social work identity. It is less clear how their training prepared them to think about relationships in social work practice or specifically aimed to equip them with relevant skills. In addition two of the social workers stress just how much the ability of social workers to really engage in relationship building and deal with the stresses and strains it creates, is influenced by the team, managerial and organisational environment within which they work. The third chapter directly addresses this environment and how understanding relationships – with policymakers, organisations and team members – are equally important. This chapter also addresses social work identity and how it can be maintained and even enhanced in this integrated team.

A good relationship?

Lack of communication between practitioner and child has recurred frequently as a key finding in inquiry reports. This is often phrased in terms of the ability to ascertain the wishes and feelings of children but is inextricably linked to the need to form a relationship; for example in the inquiry in to the death of Victoria Climbie:

> ...a point that was returned to time and time again was the need for a relationship of trust between practitioner and child. (Laming, 2003, p. 353)

There is a substantial amount of research confirming the importance of relationships and the types of characteristics that children and young people value in their social workers; being reliable and accessible, trustworthy, supportive and non-judgemental, being prepared to listen and take their views into consideration (Bell, 2002; Morgan, 2005; McCleod, 2007; Buckley et al., 2011). For some disabled children (Turner, 2003) and children looked after (e.g. Department for Education and Skills, 2007), the desire for a greater degree of continuity in relationships features particularly strongly.

This is not just an issue of the quality of relationships but arguably it is through a quality relationship that children are more effectively protected and have their rights secured. Several studies have shown that the experience of getting their views heard in the child protection process is a frustrating one and the extent to which children feel involved in the process is dependent on a good relationship with their social worker. Jobe and Gorin's (2013) interviews with children and young people in England on help-seeking behaviour adds to the growing body of research that finds that children and young people are unlikely to disclose abuse to a professional in the first place without that professional being able to establish a relationship.

> *Young people need consistent, trusting relationships to disclose maltreatment and to enable them to successfully engage with the social care system. Without these crucial relationships young people are likely remain at risk. (Jobe and Gorin, p. 8)*

An earlier study of children's views in relation to child protection investigations emphasises the way in which relationships can be used to help ensure children's rights – to participation, choice and representation (Bell, 2002). For children in care and accommodation a lack of relationship with a social worker undermines their power to influence decision-making about them (Department for Education and Skills, 2007, cited in Winter, 2009).

Power is a dimension of any relationship, particularly a professional one and it is important that workers recognise this because children and their families do and are conscious of how it is exercised (De Boer and Coady, 2007). While there is little overt discussion of power and rights in the social workers' own descriptions of their work in the following chapters, more implicitly it is clear that they see establishing a relationship as crucial to enabling children's choices and their ability to express their views. It is equally clear that the social workers are explaining choices and showing genuine interest in children's views to help establish those relationships. They also recognise that to ensure children's rights and protection, social workers need to form relationships that are distinct from those with parents and other family members.

Of course children and young people do not always see relationships in ways that fit with professional preconceptions. Giving 'practical help', being 'like a friend' and 'an equal' have all featured significantly in interviews with young people in care (McLeod, 2010). Each of these is challenging to professional boundaries (even if after more detailed exploration it is clear that young people are not naive about the power differences and limits of friendships) and also to the limits of the role social workers can play.

The idea of professional boundaries in relationships (often discussed in social work training) can raise other issues rarely addressed in social work (Doel et al., 2009). The subject of touch, for example, is highly problematic and would seem to be outside of any discussion of social work relationships even with adults let alone children. Yet Ferguson insists that 'professional touch' should be seen as 'a routine part of day-to-day practice that keeps children safe' (Ferguson, 2011, p. 95). On an equally sensitive topic Turney (2010) argues that love, liking and positive feelings in professional relationships are inevitable (as indeed might be dislike and negative feelings) and need to be recognised and processed. Turney cites Hem and Heggen (2003) in highlighting our high expectations that professionals should be both 'intimate and distanced' – 'human and professional'. It may be that it is the very act of stretching professional boundaries that children and their families appreciate most and enables the strongest working relationships (De Boer and Coady, 2007). These different perspectives certainly under-line the complexity behind what we mean by a relationship in the social work context. And of course there is no single social work context but many contexts surrounding each ultimately unique encounter.

Doing relationships

The characteristics of a good relationship highlighted above blur personal attributes, skills, values, knowledge and basic practicalities. Even if the importance of a relationship is acknowledged – what do we know about how they are created? What are their constituent parts? Why and in what way are they effective? The broad message is clear with policy drawing on literature citing the importance of the 'thera-peutic bond' and 'therapist credibility' (Munro, 2011, p. 88) and the Scottish Executive promoting the concept of the 'therapeutic alliance' (Scottish Executive, 2006). These are all terms which need further unpicking (when does a relationship become a therapeutic one? what makes a social worker a therapist?) Further, there is some recogni-tion that work with families in a relationships-based approach is partly intuitive:

> [W]hen an experienced social worker meets a family, he or she can quickly pick up an intuitive awareness of the state of the dynamics in the family – the warmth of the relationship between family members, or the level of fear felt by a child. (Munro, 2011, p. 90)

There has been no shortage of guidance in social work text books about 'the first problem to be solved in being of help to another person: how to connect, how to come into some alliance in a vital way with the person who wants or needs help' (Perlman, 1979). The importance of respect, empathy, warmth, genuineness, and spontaneity (e.g. Egan,

2002) is repeatedly stressed. The difficulty of pinning down all the elements of the skill of forming relationships is illustrated with reference to Trevithick's in-depth consideration of social work skills (Trevithick, 2005). She accepts that the relationship is central to the social work task and process 'a vital part of the repertoire of skills' (Trevithick, 2005, pp. 148–9). Establishing and ending relationships are broken down into basic components – establishing rapport, informal conversation, empathy and sympathy, styles of questioning, self-disclosure, use of humour and of physical touch, etc. – while at the same time acknowledging that 'we know very little about the specific characteristics' of social work relationships because relationships contain so many 'unique' and 'intangible factors' (Trevithick, 2005, p. 149). Ultimately we lack the knowledge of which factors within the overall idea of a relationship or alliance are most effective (Ruch, 2010). It is possible that relationships may just be too central to our very being and self to be amenable to analysis beyond a certain point.

The interviews that follow tend to reflect this mix of elements. The social workers, – all experienced, – stress the importance of skills and attributes such as planning, being respectful, being curious, projecting a genuine interest in their service users point of view but also argue that other factors – such as 'feeling at ease with children' – is fundamental. These elements are harder to teach or learn and less apparent in the literature but take us back to the vital importance of self-awareness and the value of critical reflection in trying to understand the role of the self in any interaction.

Without drawing a discrete definition of 'relationships based practice' Ruch et al. (2010) argue for 'sound and coherent theory' for relationship-based practice to succeed. They then draw on psycho-social (e.g. Hollis, 1964), psychodynamic and attachment perspectives; that past experiences affect our current behaviour, the importance of subconscious processes and the inseparability of internal and external worlds.

In the accounts that follow practitioners did not view working with relationships in a tightly defined way. The extent to which the social workers drew explicitly on psychodynamic ideas or indeed other theory bases such as child development varied as did the extent to which they felt the therapeutic 'label' explicitly attached to their work. Through their reflections we explore to what extent this matters – how does it influence the work they do and the outcomes they are trying to achieve?

Central to a critical best practice approach is the understanding that there are various perspectives on any given social interaction. At the very least each social work encounter will have two understandings based on the unique world views of the individuals drawing on the difference and diversity of a whole range of experiences and beliefs. Understanding the world view of the service user is the key first step to creating solutions. This is essentially a constructivist approach which does not only emphasise the importance of service users being able to tell their own story in their own terms and having it heard respectfully but also focuses on the importance of the medium through which it occurs or is constructed – talk, language, narrative (Parton and O'Byrne, 2000).

In other words the process of making relationships, sharing perspectives and working towards agreements about different ways of understanding situations, are all ways in which outlooks are shaped and social realities constructed (Cooper, 2008, p. 92).

Frequently there are multiple relationships to be managed. Further layers of understanding and skill are needed to communicate with children of different ages and abilities and negotiating those relationships with children separately from those with their parents and carers.

Accounts of practice

All the accounts of practice explored in this book will inevitably touch on elements of relationships; this is one of the key components of practice whether the focus is on risk or negotiation. In the accounts in this section however practitioners were asked to include a greater degree of reflection on, and be more explicit about, how they saw themselves forming and sustaining their relationship with the service users. How much is this a planned strategy? How much is it an intuitive process, responses created on the spot? What knowledge or theory did they draw on?

None of the social workers questioned the fundamental importance of relationships and there are many similar features to their approaches and beliefs. However, while the accounts of the social workers reinforce some long-standing basics of the social work literature firmly rooted in personal and professional values, each describe relationships in different ways. The workers are performing different roles in different agencies with many different constraints on their work. Above all what we see illustrated is that the work is complex and rarely unproblematic even for the most experienced.

Niall works in an integrated team specialising in work with families where there are parental drug and alcohol problems and, consequently, risks to children. A key feature of this team is the highly intensive but short-term nature of their work. The account related by Niall gives an insight into the role of social work relationships in the context of this compressed time period in a project that also has a clearly defined approach in terms of the underpinning theory, research base and tools that practitioners use. It also illustrates the complexity of forming working relationships with both adults and child in the same family.

The story of practice related by Michelle is one in an overtly thera-peutic setting where families are coming for longer term work following experiences of abuse. Here the role of relationships is more explicitly acknowledged but just because a relationship is more 'voluntary' in nature does not mean that engaging and maintaining it is any less complex. Questions about the meaning of therapeutic relationships are explored again in both the world of the adult and the world of the child.

The chapter by Mike revisits the Integrated Family Support Team that is the setting for the first of these three chapters but views relationships from the perspective of the manager. It explores the multiple role of relationships in establishing and developing an integrated team and in turn how such a team can support work which maintains the impor-tance of relationships at its heart.

4 Relationships in Intensive Short-Term Work

Niall Casserly and Andy Rixon

Niall has worked in the field for longer than he cares to remember, qualifying in 1991. He has been a probation officer, a substance misuse project manager, and a training and development manager. He is currently a consultant social worker working for an Integrated Family Support Team in Wales.

Questions to ask yourself as you read:

- What are the implications for practice in social work relationships of prescribed timescales for interventions?

- How do you form effective working relationships with children and young people separately from their families?

- Do specific models, tools and evidence-based practice help or hinder relationships-based practice?

The project

The context of this work is an Integrated Family Support Team in Wales. These interdisciplinary teams (social workers, community psychiatric nurses and health visitors) were introduced by the Welsh Government, supported by the Children and Families (Wales) Measure 2010, to work intensively with families where there are risks to children through parental substance misuse. The origins and development of this particular 'pioneer' team (and the role of relationships in its development) are explored in more detail in Chapter 6.

The nature of the intervention provided by this team provides an opportunity to explore one perspective on how the social work relationship is shaped by the parameters within which the practitioner has to act. There are two particularly significant features. First, the team works in a short term and intensive way with the period of involvement being fixed at 4–6 weeks so compressing the time to form, work within and end a relationship. The team are involved in subsequent reviews over the following year with the possibility of 'booster sessions' but the primary work is done in this intensive phase. Low-case loads and highly flexible working arrangements allow a level of contact very different from families' previous experiences of professionals. The family under consideration, for example, would have had input of, on average, three hours per day. This phase might be viewed as a 'luxury' in social work terms where other casework responsibilities place limitations on the amount of work one may enter into with the family; the corollary of this intensity is that it can be demanding of family and worker, and expectations are high. Secondly the service draws explicitly on learning from the evaluation of a ten-year long project (Option 2) working with parents with substance misuse (Forrester et al., 2008, 2012). This evidence-based approach means that the structure of the work is 'semi-formalised' in terms of theoretical models, for example, the cycle of change (Prochaska and DiClementi, 1984), motivational interviewing (Miller and Rollnick, 2002), whole family approach and the selection of tools, such as 'values and strengths' exercises and goal attainment scoring used with families.

The referral

This family consisted of Sharon the mother in early forties, father Steve late forties and son – Dominic age 12. There was also an older son who had now left home. The family are white UK. Steve had history of alcohol misuse and a local reputation as a loud, public 'drunk' which son and mother found to be both humiliating and frightening. Both parents had been in care and Sharon had recently been suffering from depression/anxiety that was being aggravated by her husband's alcohol use and their son's response to it.

The key criteria for the involvement of the team are:

• Parental drug and alcohol use
• Risk to children
• Willingness to engage
• Timeliness (that a crisis point had been reached in their lives).

This family fitted the criteria not only because the father had long-term drug and particularly alcohol related problems but also had indicated a preparedness to address it . Although originally a Child in Need case (s.17 Children Act 1989)[1] the referring social worker was getting increasingly concerned about the level of volatility between father, mother and son. Dominic, a boy previously thought of as educationally very able, had deteriorating behaviour at school, at home and with peers. Behaviourally this played out as being confrontational, through substance misuse and alternating between co-operating with and rejecting of authority.

The initial aims therefore related to establishing some of the building blocks the family needed before addressing the issues around parenting – in this case reducing the levels of volatility at home, supporting Steve'sattempt to detox and reducing the risks to Dominic. Out of the myriad of elements that there are in any such case, we have picked out four aspects that seem particularly pertinent to exploring-some of the realities of relationships in social work. Across the trajectory of the work we start with the initial difficult interview through to the ending of the work using therapeutic letters: in between we look at the difference between trying to construct a connection with the young person separate from their family and the issue of dealing with changing agendas as interventions do not always progress in the way everyone hopes.

A whole lot of yelling

It is often argued that first contacts are very significant in terms of relationship forming; yet in complex and conflictual cases these can be far from straightforward encounters. As Ferguson points out the home visit 'crossing the threshold' (Ferguson, 2011) into the heart of someone else's space is a taken-for-granted and under-explored area of practice despite its potential tensions and pressures. Even for Niall – a worker of considerable experience who felt confident in his relationship-building skills – the initial visit with this family proved extremely challenging. The first interview with Sharon and Steve (Dominic was at school) was less of an interview and more just 'witnessing a whole lot of yelling' with a powerfully de-skilling effect. All the more frustrating when there is a specific 'model' of intervention to try and apply.

> ... so I went in and there was forty minutes of high volume yelling at each other from the two parents, and after about twenty minutes I thought,

how do I intervene and then another twenty minutes went by and I thought well this is not a good use of time, but actually, I can't just get up and walk out... because it's not very kind of strength based [in line with the values of the project]. I felt a bit intimidated... I didn't feel that anybody was going to hit me, but I was amazed at the speed at which they went into a proper full on yelling, top of their voices, you did this, you did that, you know, if I'd asked them to role play it, they couldn't have done it better and I felt hugely de-skilled, I came out feeling, where do I go from here...?

Niall reports a 'fight or flight' adrenaline fuelled wish to 'have my say' – this tone of course would have simply added another strident voice which (together with both the television showing a fighting couple on Jeremy Kyle in the background and the dog barking) would have added to the mayhem. At the same time he was feeling a strong sense of wanting to leave to remove the discomfort he felt at this level of confrontation (while searching for the professional tools to deal with it).

Out of all the confusion of the first encounter, Niall did feel that he was able to begin to field some of the emotion in the room and make at least one positive contribution before leaving:

'The one thing I can say that I find really heartening about this is that nobody could ever say, "you don't care". Nobody could ever say that you don't care about your child, because this is full of passion, it was full of you know, desperation, it's full of all sorts of stuff which comes from a good place essentially, but next time we meet I think we are going to have to meet separately'.

I don't know whether they heard that or not but for me it was great, to be blunt I was really pleased that I'd managed... cos it did strike me as being absolutely true, what I'd said, it was honest and I was just pleased that I'd been able to pull something positive out of the bag then and there which allowed us to make a start.

As well as feeling that something had been salvaged from the situation, that it was 'true' or authentic seemed vital in this exchange. For Niall the atmosphere in the room was not the sort of place for subtlety, nuance or even politeness; congruence lay in 'genuineness' or 'straight-talking'.

The way in which the project is organised enables workers in this team processing such experiences to immediately debrief with colleagues back at the office, and get support and help to reflect and reframe.

There is a buddy system and even where one's buddy is not immediately available it creates an expectation within the team that their professional role encompasses a responsibility to proactively address the needs of colleagues. The purpose of this is to build the capacity for emotional resilience within the team recognising the emotional labour (Hochschild, 1979) involved in social work. The team use the same framework for professional reflection as is employed with the families, drawing on the OARS framework (Open-ended questions, Affirming, Reflecting, Summarising (Miller and Rollnick, 2002). Such debriefing was available to Niall and subsequently he moved from seeing the initial interview as having been unsuccessful, unhelpful and possibly even counterproductive in terms of the initial plan, to an understanding that it was an extremely valuable first-hand insight into the much reported volatility of the family.

> sometimes it's just gold dust to be right in the middle of something like that because otherwise you're just guessing. There's no way these people were bluffing, you know, it was just – here, warts and all.

Although it seemed important to have said the same thing to both parents there had been a strong sense that home was the mother's domain. Niall was interested to see how Steve functioned on neutral territory. The conversation continued the following day in terms of tone (straight-talking) and content (observation on the nature of their conflict).

> I took Steve out and said to him, that was pretty hairy yesterday, and he said, "Oh yeah, yeah, we're always like that, people always say we bicker" and I said by way of a summary of the previous day, "Well, what struck me ... was that some of the stuff you were arguing about has already happened and can't be changed, some of the stuff sounded genuinely hurtful and some of the stuff was pretty unimportant and more just you being angry and shouting.

The gender issue seemed pertinent not just in terms of territory but also, taking the lead from Steve, deciding that trying to create a therapeutic relationship required using a directness in language that he would expect from another man.

Strictly speaking Niall's overall approach early on was directive; with the time period short he 'cut to the chase'. Clarifying some of the important features in the conflict was a first point in developing a strategy to address it and make working relationships possible.

> Quite quickly I could actually have them in the same room and I also got to know them a bit better so ... I never quite said 'oh shut up' if they started arguing, but I could be a bit more assertive you know ...

Words such as 'true' and 'genuine' frequently crop up in the literature in discussions of relationship forming (see, e.g., Egan, 2002; Trevithick, 2005; Ruch et al., 2010). They also feature in much of the feedback that this project gets from service user evaluation. Genuineness is used here both in terms of the congruence that Niall insists is fundamental to relationship-building and therapeutic interventions and also communicating a genuine interest in the families' perspective:

> So people understand that you are genuinely looking to listen to their take on their lives and the specific skills used are evidence to the client that they have at least been very closely listened to. We are looking to get to peoples ambivalence about change and that can be very threatening for everyone as it involves articulating their resistance to change. To enable that conversation it needs to be clear that the worker will take on board the inconsistencies and the contradictions that the client is having to live with.

> Part of the genuineness equation involves clarity about the overarching concern i.e. that we wouldn't be involved if there wasn't some sort of child protection, child in need issue, you know, so there are some things which are just there, I mean, they have to be explicit.

> If people never trust you enough to be realistic then you might as well not start – which is why the engagement is so important.

To achieve this perception of real interest and concern having a specific range of techniques and tools at your disposal is of great help, they do not have to be a shield to hide behind. The use of tools is flexible but as Niall explains if workers in the project are not utilising them they need to have a good rationale. Specific tools are valuable at specific points in the process. So for example the miracle question (a commonly used technique in solution focused therapies to help people envisage a positive future) feeds into the notion of genuine interest as it is an entire exercise designed to allow the client to be heard – and the more it allows the worker to examine aspirations the more the service users views around preferred futures can be articulated. This may not be easy in terms of relationship-building as in the short term people often like to be rescued by being told what to do but the legacy of this style of work is a respectfulness for the clients' ability to develop their own solutions. Prescribed tools or techniques can therefore be a valuable asset rather than a constraint within the context of a relationship-based approach.

The same but different

Forming working relationships with children and young people raises both similar and distinct issues to those with adults. Issues of genuineness and curiosity in order to engage were equally true for the later first meeting with Dominic. Niall had thought carefully about the approach.

> I did want something of my own in terms of, not mine, but particular to me, about the relationship in that I wanted to be clear with him that I was prepared to take his view on himself. We are both particular individuals and if I acknowledge that then he may accept that I see him as someone with his own particular story to tell which will make sense in his own particular way. So, for example, everybody had told me that he was fantastic at sports at school and it became clear fairly quickly that one of the paradoxes in his life was that he was getting an extra, or he perceived that he was getting an extra, bit of a hard time because of his missed potential, everybody had said, you could do so well, so his talents were used as a stick to beat him with in that sense. So I promised him for example all the way through that I would never mention sport again!

Initial work with children and young people also requires delicate positioning to put the basis of forming a relationship on firm ground within the complex dynamics of families.

> I would always see him outside the house, I would do my best not to kind of 'big up' his father too much by saying how well he'd done in stopping drinking. You know, just a question of him not seeing me as an ally of his father.

Again the issue of territory – the choice of location for work with young people can be crucial. There may be reasons why home is not ideal yet school, while it may represent a secure base for some, can be problematic and inhibiting for others (Jones, 2003). In this instance an informal space seemed to be the best environment to generate the basis for a relationship.

> [W]e'd talk on the way down to KFC in the car we'd talk as we had the KFC and we'd talk on the way back and some of it was about anything,

just to lighten up the conversation. But I did think that we'd developed enough of a relationship for him to be honest with me about, for example, stuff about making unfounded accusations in order to get at and hurt his father.

Ferguson (2011) argues that the car is an under-researched site of practice 'where vitally important opportunities for meaningful communication and therapeutic work with children arises...' (p. 111). He acknowledges that many social workers have long understood, intuitively, the value of the car in day-to-day practice. For Niall the physical setting shoulder-to-shoulder (rather than face-to-face) and one which safely excludes others is important and the incidental-ness of the conversations ('about anything') allows for important matters emerge unforced and be discussed. This can enable a less pressured approach to developing relationships particularly with young people while needing to be appropriate to age and gender. In this case contact was over an hour in each instance which might compare favourably with a session sitting face-to-face in a more formal environment.

Niall tried to explore how Dominic saw himself in a range of roles – son, pupil, friend, etc. – with a view to trying to establish his pro-social strengths in each. Again the technique of the miracle question was used in some detail to establish his aspirations and provided the foundations for a discussion about cognitive dissonance – what he valued in one situation he would see critically in others. Many of the tools used with adults can be equally appropriate to use with young people – goal sheets, strengths and values cards and solution-focused ways of talking.

So many elements intertwine in whether working relationships can be established. On reflection Niall believes that in the past he would not have found this relationship as easy to develop. But at this point, with the experience of children of his own of this age and contact with their adolescent friends he felt more obviously 'at ease' in talking with Dominic. This might be achieved by different workers through different experiences but a sense of ease (or unease) has the potential to subtly enable (or betray) our most professional attempts to form relationships.

Understanding the implications of change

One of the dimensions of trying to affect change in social work is that over time as issues are addressed with one person so new ones emerge as other family members in the same system respond to those changes. So as Steve began to undergo abstinence, while a positive change, there were other seemingly less positive consequences. The perspective used by this project is taken from Harbin (2006) who in adapting Prochaska and Di Clemente describes this process as one in which while the person undergoing detox or abstinence is moving around the 'cycle of change' other family members might be moving the opposite way in reaction. The need to understand the implications of change and shifting agendas for everyone was emphatically made in this case.

> So how that played out for the son was that as his father progressed so his behaviour started becoming worse. He became more confrontational with his father, so I would get phone calls from Steve and Sharon with him smashing mirrors and that in the background.
>
> Dominic had gone from being the victim in the situation, to the 'baddy', because his dad had suddenly decided, you know, after... messing them around, humiliating him publicly, being a laughing stock, etc., etc., all of a sudden, he turned into the hero, everybody is saying well done Dad, well done Dad and suddenly he is expected to change, well why should he? Why should he care? Why should he believe the changes? Now he was more angry than ever.

So as a result of Steve's successful new abstinence his son's behaviour deteriorated and therefore the demands on the father's parenting skills increased markedly at the same time as the father realised that he had developed very few. He would take Dominic upstairs physically or put him outside the front door physically to get him to go to school. Dominic would make allegation that he had been hit by his father.

> [W]e'd talk about the sorts of things that he said, and he admitted to me, he said, "I do them because I know that they're the way that I can get at my father" – annoying, that would be a complete understatement, hurting, he wanted to hurt him for all the hurt that he'd inflicted on him and as he saw it, on his mother as well.

The precondition (addressing the alcohol) to achieving progress meant that some aspects of the situation became more marked. There was also a clear need from the start of the process that all agencies, in particular the school were prepared for this, perhaps counter-intuitive, eventuality and that their response was consistent with the common experience of the children of substance users.

Therapeutic letters

Niall had assessed that in terms of risk, Sharon was a protective factor, and ultimately it seemed that it was the relationship between father and son that needed to change to achieve the reduction in the volatility and risk that had triggered the original referral.

As the intensive phase was moving towards its conclusion one option Niall considered was the use of 'therapeutic letters' a strategy regularly used by the team. They can act as a way of making permanent 'affirmations' made during a session as part of the OARS approach.

> One of the things that we do is that we write therapeutic letters so that when you have a session with somebody you try and write it down, you put it in a letter and you send it to them, or you give it to them and they have a family file that they keep all these things in. Which a lot of people find very useful because it kind of puts a stamp of approval, it's like the difference between thinking something and saying something, you know, something becomes slightly truer when you say it, and if you write it down as well it becomes slightly truer as well. The expression of it changes your relationships to it, it can add emphasis and permanency.

In this instance the therapeutic letter was to be used slightly differently between the parties as a powerful tool for enabling their communication. It illustrates Niall working within the relationships he had built with both Steve and Dominic to bring them to the point where a shift in the relationships between father and son was possible. This required careful preparation, as there was only a limited amount of what they had to say to each other that could be useful at this point.

> The last couple of weeks of the intensive intervention, I ended up, I didn't think that this was kind of in the model that we work to as such but I ended up getting the father to write a letter to the son, and the son to write a letter to the father. People had mentioned this here, kind of in general terms, but this felt like high stakes stuff.

And in the event the meeting Niall arranged for the exchange of letters was extremely difficult but also powerful.

> ...and what we ended up with was a letter from the father saying that he loved his son and this is why he's doing all this, and he knows that he doesn't always do it very well but he'll always be there for him. And the other one was from the son effectively saying, "I know you're trying but I still hate your guts,"

50

...so the father had actually in that moment, possibly for one of the first times in his life, realised that he had taken on a proper parenting role because if you like, his love had trumped his son's anger...no that's the wrong phrase, but it had managed and held his son's anger, because his letter had said, no matter what etc.

And funnily enough, because we do reviews at one, three, six and twelve months and at the one month review Steve told me that he'd written Dominic another letter...

This specific exercise had only been possible because of the relationships that had been created between social worker and family members within these few short but intense weeks. Both father and son felt that the worker could be trusted at several levels – first that their individual position was understood, secondly that it was adequately represented and thirdly that the exercise itself held out the prospect of things improving at home. Improvements were indeed forthcoming over the next six months as measured against the original goals in particular in relation to the level of conflict. The case was later closed by the referring social services department as concerns about Dominic significantly reduced.

On reflection

Niall felt that this case represented an example of the reality of building relationships in the context of not only short-term intensive work but also of a robust framework for intervention. Exploring it in more detail also revealed to him how theory, research, experience and use of self (both conscious and unconscious) all played a role. Some risks had also been taken but Niall felt they were calculated and managed. Within the context of the referral it seemed an effective intervention. A year later some new issues emerged for the family requiring further social work involvement which has led to further reflection on his work. However in terms of relationship-building, while there are always new things to learn promoted by the reflective stance of the team, Niall sees this as a positive piece of work at the time in the circumstances of the case. How we measure a 'successful' outcome is a complex issue for social work; perhaps we could only judge in the much longer term.

Note

1. The equivalent legislation in Scotland is s.22 Children (Scotland) Act 1995.

5 Relationships in a Therapeutic Context

Michelle Hyams-Ssekasi and Andy Rixon

Michelle is a social worker of over 30 years experience as a manager, supervisor and practitioner working with children, young people and adults whose lives have been affected by abuse and trauma. She is a practitioner in the NSPCC, a large voluntary organisation offering post-abuse therapeutic support primarily to children and young people but also, when required, sessions for their parents or carers. The team is in a large urban area of England.

Questions to ask yourself as you read:

- How would you describe your 'knowledge base' for developing and sustaining relationships?

- What kind of opportunities would help you to develop your knowledge or communication skills?

- What are the key elements of 'stepping in to the child's world'?

- What factors could improve your ability to build relationships with children?

The importance of relationships in an overtly therapeutic context is widely accepted. However this does not necessarily mean we can assume that developing appropriate relationships is an easier task than in any other social work context. Neither can we take for granted the skills that are involved in engaging families in therapeutic work. This chapter focuses on the knowledge, skills and values that are central in the building and sustaining of relationships with both adults and children to support a family affected by sexual abuse. It concentrates on three key aspects of this case – the initial visit, direct work with the child, and subsequent work with the mother in the family.

The family

This family was referred to the agency via the police and a Sexual Assault Centre following an investigation of sexual abuse. The remit of Michelle's team is to support families where sexual abuse is a feature; pre-trial, post-trial or where a criminal prosecution has been considered but not progressed at the time the work is being undertaken. The role in relation to this family was one of offering therapeutic support. The children in this white UK family, Emma aged ten years and Ben seven years, had alleged that an adult outside of the family had sexually assaulted them. Their mother Sandra was struggling to cope with the aftermath and emotional impact of this allegation of abuse. Sandra, had childhood experiences of intra-familial abuse and, as a result had been in care for many years.

The children were clearly traumatised by their experience. They had been interviewed by the police under the 'Achieving Best Evidence' guidelines[1] and had undergone medical examinations. At the same time, a social work assessment was being undertaken by Children's services. The communication between the local authority and the voluntary organisation was therefore important in trying to achieve a seamless service for the family. Michelle's involvement continued for nine months via a combination of individual and joint sessions with family members.

Making a connection

> If you don't make that initial connection with the service user for whatever reason within that first 10 or 15 minutes, I think, you're on a hiding to nothing, because they are checking you out as much as you're checking them out.

Many parents are sceptical of social workers and are fearful of being accused of not being a 'good enough parent'. So there are nearly always challenges facing the worker, in whatever capacity, in achieving some kind of engagement. When visiting a family faced with the impact of sexual abuse they may be severely traumatised by their experiences and as a result may not be receptive to social work intervention even if the service being offered is assumed to be beneficial and on a voluntary basis.

Michelle argues therefore that preparation for visits is essential. Phoning and writing to a parent before a home visit and responding to any initial queries is in fact the first contact and therefore the first vital impression. In this context, home as well as office visits are essential and enable parents like Sandra to make informed choices as to whether they want to access the service. Equally there is a need for clarity from the outset about the boundaries and limitations of the worker's role including time and length of involvement.

> I can be with you today for up to an hour and a half. If we need to meet again, then we can do that. So I place a clear time boundary for the visit. I'll tell them what I know, and offer reassurance – I'm here to listen to what you want to say and what you see as the situation. The relationship is the key to everything.

Reassurance was important with Sandra because of difficult relationships with agencies in the past stemming from her care history and the lack of protection she experienced in her childhood. During these recent events she felt that the police had not believed her and that people were dismissing what she was saying because of the way that she presented. Suspicion and resistance were now built in to any equation with any new professional.

For Michelle the priority in building a relationship with adults is to be able to see them as unique individuals as well as parents and/or carers. Parents need opportunities to tell and share their own narrative or story of life events. Some have a consistent story, others have a narrative with many gaps and omissions and others may be unable, or unwilling, to remember or recall any significant life events. The challenge was to try and attune to Sandra and offer encouragement for her to share her ambivalence, anger and fear in relation to her experiences.

> Many parents ... you know, they've got like this third antenna, this hyper vigilance about them, that they kind of instinctively know whether somebody is interested in them or not. Sandra would frequently say, 'Well, you're just doing your job aren't you, because you're paid to do this job aren't you?'. The psychological unspoken message was 'Do you care about me and my children?' 'Are you really interested in me?'

The overt message was 'Well as long as the kids get some help, I'll be all right' – but clearly, I could see that she was struggling.

Michelle has been working with families in distress for many years, is used to dealing with issues related to sexual abuse and so can convey that she has 'heard lots of things', and nothing will shock or surprise her. Relaying that kind of reassurance is an important and concrete communication skill that helped to settle Sandra's anxieties. Engagement skills and techniques are vital to put in place the building blocks for a relationship within which to work – but ultimately social workers must also convince families that they have something to offer.

> A real relationship begins to form and develop when the parent believes that I have the ability, knowledge and skill to support and work with them and their children.

Michelle first made a home visit. As well as trying to engage with Sandra in the first ten minutes this first home visit was also the initial meeting with Emma and Ben. For Michelle, when meeting children for the first time it is important to meet them in the same room as the parents and equally important to make a connection with them.

> I would offer an active commentary, not talk about everything we were doing, I often play act a bit to help the child feel at ease, 'You're mum's told me your name, but I can't remember what letter of the alphabet it begins with?' kind of just playing with them really. Not being as direct with the children. I would say like, 'Do you know why I'm here, did Mum tell you?' 'Well, we knew you were coming but we don't know why you're here'. I say, 'Well, I need to come and talk to your mum about some of the tough stuff', you know, something that they could relate to, and then I'd ask them about what toys or whatever they had, making some comment about what they were wearing… then invariably they then sat next to you drawing pictures, it's crucial to engage the child on their level really, and not talk to them like they're miniature adults, because they're not, they're children.

> I think it would be unfair to say to a child do you want to come and see me for six times or something, [rather than] how about if you come with mum, come and have a look round and we can have another chat and you can decide whether you want to come and see me again and then we can decide together how many times we're going to meet. It's on that basic level really, so when they come to the office, it is building on what

> you've already done, you're still a stranger to them, but you've taken an interest in them and then they come in the office here and they see me in a different environment, it kind of works, not kind of, it 'does' work. It helps to build confidence in the child when they are offered choices.

This recounting of the initial visit touches on several important points. First just as with adults the aim is to achieve some level of engagement and trust with children 'on their level'. The ability to do this is often taken for granted in child care social work while numerous reports and inquiries over many years show that in fact it is often not achieved or even made a priority (see, e.g., Blom-Cooper, 1985; Laming, 2003; Munro, 2011). The introduction to this section argued that a relationship is not only essential to children's safety (Jobe and Gorin, 2012) but also to supporting their rights (Bell, 2002) – it is important that some choices are retained for the children to make. Secondly Michelle notes how quickly children will pick up on a practitioner's unease or anxiety with children; this raises the question of how personal experience and attributes – 'use of self' – can be combined with skills that can perhaps be more easily 'taught'. Finally, within this initial relationship building, difficult topics still need to be raised to achieve some level of clarity about why a social worker is there and what is likely to happen next.

Although this analysis is focusing on trying to tease out how relationships can be created, such is the nature of social work that inevitably this is intertwined with other roles such as the need to be assessing the family situation. Michelle was conscious of her observations of the children's use of language, behaviour, social interaction and play; whether they are engaging, fearful or clingy.

One outcome of the initial assessment was the decision that Michelle would undertake individual work with the eldest child, Emma.

Stepping in to the child's world

> Kind of what you are doing is stepping into their world through the play to look at the impact of the abuse. ... that's what we do when you're working with children, I think, as a social worker and as a therapist. In order to understand what's going on from there, you have to try and look at the world through their eyes, what's happening for them, so whether it's through techniques or tools that you'll use it's all about encouraging them to share what's going on for them.

The work with Emma was complicated initially by a potential criminal prosecution pending; in this situation children cannot be asked directly about their experiences and specific practice guidance must be followed (Crown Prosecution Service, 2001).

The techniques to encourage children to share their perspective are drawn from a variety of sources. It may be through a picture they've drawn or through play, or tools from a more explicitly psychotherapeutic source such as exploring a child's script – their unconscious psychological formation – through a questionnaire which asks children a series of questions. Partly it is also a search for a medium of communication a child uses naturally. Emma would pick out some craft equipment to use and then as the sessions progressed she was interested in looking after the baby dolls, dressing up, and using the telephones to communicate 'indirectly' with Michelle.

> ... what I've tended to find over the years, that if children have experienced trauma in their lives they're usually developmentally stuck at the age of when the ... if it's an abusive experience, started. So their choices of play materials are linked to child development.

Therefore, Michelle argues, social workers need to be familiar with a range of child development theory to inform their practice and approaches to the engagement of a child or young person. This raises the question of how much weight should be placed on knowledge about child development and attachment for social workers. Michelle's emphasis would certainly accord with the official descriptions of key/professional capabilities (Scottish Social Services Council, 2008; Social Work Reform Board, 2010b; Care Council for Wales, 2013) required by social workers, and the findings of serious case reviews (Brandon et al., 2011).

Quite quickly an issue emerged that needed gently challenging or 'naming'. Emma as a child whose parent had also abused alcohol could be a 'pseudo adult' herself expecting to have to look after other unreliable adults.

> ...she initially said what she thought I wanted to hear. So, I let that go for one session, but in the next session, I said, 'I've been thinking about when we last met and some of the things ... and I kind of wondered whether you were just saying what you thought I wanted to hear, or what you wanted to say really, because you know, these sessions are not about me, they're about you and you know, even if it's yucky stuff, that's absolute fine with me'. I can't remember exactly what she said, but I remember there was

an acknowledgement and relief on her face that said, 'oh, so I don't have to do that'.

...with a lot of the children they want to look after you...it is not a challenge to work with this therapeutically but it's a challenge to them because you are encouraging them to be different, not be different but to kind of step into themselves rather than caring for the adult, you know, which is different. So I think that takes me down a road of, how social workers in assessing what children need or what's happening for a child, have to be very cautious about not focussing too much just on what's said.

The last comment highlights the tension between listening carefully to what a child actually says and what they might want to convey – the surface and depth of communication. Another important aspect of the work is always being conscious of boundaries and safety (especially in the context of sexual abuse) and clarity of roles between worker, child and parent.

... the safety's important because it is about protection, whether its for the adult or child, and you're also modelling, you say... you are important, I am here to keep you safe when you're with me.

These boundaries and relationships are underpinned by a clear written agreement with all parties.

The huge difference about relationship building with children and adults is that any of my work with children and young people will have an agreement with the adults, you know, with the parents, because ultimately, a child isn't an island on its own, they are part of a family structure and there is a point in the work where you start involving the family more or the carers more because they're the ones ultimately who are going to move forward with the children.

Moving forward in this case required some work with other family members.

Caring confrontation?

... we had a three way meeting between Sandra, me and the social worker and Sandra actually said at that meeting, 'So, does that mean then if I don't have these sessions that there's going to be an issue about whether I'm a good enough parent?'

In Michelle's assessment it was apparent that, as well as the work on the abuse with Emma, what was really needed was work with her mother, Sandra, who seemed to be having difficulties in holding things together emotionally. Sandra maintained her challenging style from the initial meeting:

> She was a very challenging person to work with because she would test you out... she'd test me in a way where she'd check out whether I had been listening to what she'd been saying and different things and I'd kind of, what's the term I'm thinking of, I would use caring confrontation, I would bring it back, I would say, it seems to me that you need to check out with me that, whether I was listening, and at first like, there'd be lots of denial and all this business, but then it got to you know, why she was doing this, because she basically didn't trust people.

Even in a therapeutic context developing relationships might still require some upfront clarification and even confrontation, and the ability to accept some confrontation from the other side.

> *Michelle*: She wasn't used to endings because she was into flight or avoidance mode most of the time, that's what she'd learnt as a child and her adolescence, because she hadn't had any healthy relationships around her really. So she struggled with the ending and I think that is why she was sacking me ever so often... It was kind of when... we had gone to an area that she found difficult to talk about. Or where she had shared quite a lot about herself, it was like, she needed to try to withdraw.
>
> *Andy*: What would she say?
>
> *Michelle*: 'Oh, I don't think any of this is doing me any good' and 'I don't need this, I don't know why we're opening up all of this and in fact, I don't think I want to see you again Michelle...'
>
> *Andy*: Right... and you'd respond...?
>
> *Michelle*: 'Oh, if that's what you want then – I'll be here next week...' yeah, my colleagues used to laugh about it in support, you know, has she sacked you again! It was kind of that push me, pull you, that tension, that working with the relationship.

This exchange repeats the theme noted earlier – listening carefully to what people say – but then also trying to understand the difference between what they say and what they mean and reflecting your understandings back to them. Probing beyond surface meaning, demonstrating 'compassionate scepticism' without probing too much is a skilled professional judgement (Jones and Watson, 2013). It may be that in more time and resource-pressured environments Sandra's 'sacking' would be accepted more easily, yet such moments, and how they are responded to, may be crucial in building trust and achieving real change:

> She told me some weird and wonderful things from her life and I think it surprised her that I didn't kind of recoil … or reject her, it was kind of, I was still there, so she had to push me away and then you know, we'd get back together again, and she learnt from that and she did say to me when we'd finished the work, 'definitely it's helped me'.

This may of course create problems for the real ending when it comes. Michelle's interpretation of Sandra's actions above already included the impact of poor endings and the idea of a flight response framed in terms of attachment and loss.

> I mean, age old concepts, attachment, separation, loss, grief … in talking about the relationship that's what we are looking at doing aren't we? And at whatever level, we are looking at forming an attachment. Now, for people that we're working with in social work they could have had healthy, unhealthy, problematic, multi separations, loss through abuse, through multiple moves, through death of a parent, you know, so all that, all of these issues and a lot of times the social worker …. you're trying to model a healthy relationship. …

Social workers cannot promise open-ended relationships (they may of course find ending difficult themselves) and even in a longer term therapeutic situation like this there are still defined time and resource constraints which should be clear from the outset. Social workers need to aim to model a professional boundaried relationship even if there is no one definition of what this actually is. For Michelle specifically planning the ending is always introduced about three quarters the way through the work.

> But a lot of times the kids don't want to finish and the adults don't want to finish … they will be reluctant to give it up. They may want to cling on to you even more. A social work skill in itself is knowing how much is enough.

> [I'd say] "I've been thinking about when we finish working together, what would you like to do, the last time we meet, how do you want to remember the time we had together?

So much time can be invested into forming a relationship as the basis for achieving change; caring can be demonstrated by being there for someone but equally by being clear that this is not indefinite but is going to end.

You're a social worker; you know how to do relationships

I was thinking about the first visit where you are meeting with the family and stuff, you are dealing with current relationships, you are dealing with past relationships … you're planning for future relationships and social workers aren't valued or are not seen for that level of skill that they are using in managing all those different relationships.

… but it's kind of taken for granted isn't it? ; you're a social worker, you know how to do relationships.

Exploring examples of day-to-day social work practice, as here with Michelle, the complexity of forming and maintaining relationships and the skills required to do it are clear. Do social workers learn these skills? And what sort of specialised knowledge do they believe is required if any? Articulating the answers is, not surprisingly, difficult. In response to these questions, at different points in the interview, Michelle made slightly different comments:

you can learn relationship skills, how to relationship build: you use the term empathy, but whether that connects with somebody else and you show that you are empathetic and genuine, is another matter. Because it's not a mechanical process, you learn the skill, you practice it. …

you can learn to not make those faux pas and stuff like that, but ultimately … creating, building and maintaining relationships are about the person, the actual social worker and what they bring to that relationship. I don't know whether that answers what you're asking. Because a lot can depend for me, on what the worker's experience is of relationships.

going back to what we said earlier which is that, that's where I think mentoring has a role. You know, people who've walked that journey and have done it and have come across a lot of the pit falls …

Even when specifically exploring and reflecting on relationships 'how it's done' is complex to unpick. As noted in the introduction to this section, relationship skills can be identified and practiced but it seems likely that much more needs to be done to provide qualifying training that focuses more clearly on working with emotions and self-reflection

(Ward, 2010). In this account 'personal attributes' also features as does the importance of learning from the experience of others.

This is not to say that 'knowledge' is not also a key component. Michelle holds strongly that theoretical knowledge can be learnt and that this depth of knowledge can enhance social work practice.

> Relationship is about creating a connection with another, so if it's going to be therapeutic what you are looking at is a deeper connection ... the core principles are the same.

One key influence for Michelle has been the work of Erskine and Trautmann (1999) who developed the concept of eight relational needs which span a human life (security, valuing, acceptance, mutuality, self-definition, making an impact, having the other initiate, to express love) and which Michelle argues must be taken into account to engage in any constructive and meaningful intervention with both children and adults.

> I think there is probably too much practice where because there's been a superficial connection with say parents from social workers that there's an assumption that the relationship is going to develop and work, you know, progress is going to be made. ... There can sadly be an over reliance on parents turning up for appointments saying what they think you want to hear and sadly there is no positive change ... I know that being a therapist and a social worker has helped me to differentiate between the clients psychological needs and my own and to be mindful and aware of the intra-psychic processes that can and will be triggered by being in 'relationship' with another.

Knowledge and self-knowledge are obviously inextricably linked here and Michelle's personal view is that all social workers would actually benefit from personal therapy. This perspective on emotional and professional development is underpinned by her use of regular clinical supervision but most importantly the work needs to be supported by quality agency supervision particularly given that the focus is frequently on sexual abuse. In her view workers do not always get what they need from supervision beyond the management of cases. Attention needs to be paid to the process of relationship building, maintaining and ending them but also the impact of working in the area of sexual abuse on the supervisor and supervisee. Team support, structured and unstructured, practical and emotional, also plays an important role in working with family situations such as the one described here.

On reflection

Evaluating the longer term impact of therapeutic interventions such as this is challenging. Michelle values the feedback from child and adult service users and her own assessment of reported changes in children's lives. This sits alongside the use of the trauma symptom checklist in the agency, a recognised standardised measure of change in symptoms of trauma such as the experience of bad dreams, levels of anger or self-harm (Briere 1996 – http://www4.parinc.com/Products/Product. aspx?Productid=TSCC). In fact the agency now places a much greater emphasis on evaluation and a case such as this would now be undertaken within a more structured evidence-based programme of work.

This piece of work illustrates the typically multi-textured nature of relationship work in this context with a range of relationships to juggle while trying to ensure that the needs of the child remain central. Michelle suggests social workers need 'a map, satellite navigation and compass' to find a way to build and maintain these relationships in a meaningful way.

Note

1. Guidance for interviewing children in England and Wales http://www.justice.gov.uk/downloads/victims-and-witnesses/vulnerable-witnesses/achieving-best-evidence-criminal-proceedings.pdf

6 Managing Relationships

Michael Waite and Andy Rixon

Mike has been a qualified social worker for 15 years working in youth offending and residential social work. Mike has managed the Families First project which is a multi-agency team set up to work with families where parental substance and alcohol misuse has been identified as having a negative effect on the children and young people in the family. Mike was then seconded to project manage the setting up of an Integrated Family Support Team which he has managed since the pioneer areas were launched.

Questions to ask yourself as you read:

- How can managers try to support 'critical best practice'?

- What are the challenges of creating an inter-disciplinary team?

- What is the role of relationships in work across and within organisations?

While most of the chapters in this book will focus on analysing individual examples of face-to-face social work practice, this chapter is set in the broader context in which this practice takes place. The 'stories' of practitioners will inevitably make reference to the role played by management, supervision, organisations, the possibilities of team support, relations across professional boundaries, issues of resourcing and politics with a small p or occasionally a large P. This raises questions about how their attempts to achieve best practice can be supported? How can the right conditions be created and maintained within organisations to help it develop? These issues and questions are frequently acknowledged but often insufficiently addressed. This chapter explores the pivotal role of the manager in trying to answer some of these questions.

The context of practice from the political to the organisational to the individual team will be illustrated through the development of one project – a pioneer Integrated Family Support Team (IFST) in Wales. This setting also enables an exploration of social work practice situated in the contemporary and increasingly inter-professional environment with all its attendant tensions surrounding the professional social work identity.

However, this chapter is also a personal 'story' of the creation of a team and the role played by Mike, the manager, in its development. It is another perspective on critical best practice which explores the skills needed to shape a service and an environment that can in turn foster a best practice approach to work with children and families. As the story was unfolded and examined so it seemed apparent that at every level the importance of relationships was a key feature mirroring its fundamental importance in social work practice. This chapter can be read in conjunction with Chapter 4 which explores the experience of one social worker working within this IFST.

The political and the inter-agency context

The aim of the IFST is to provide a skilled, multi-disciplinary team to intervene with families, referred by Local Authority Children's Services, who present a high level of need and risk due to parental/carer substance misuse. Their role is to reduce the level of risk and try to ensure positive outcomes for the most vulnerable children, delivering a service based on robust evidence of effectiveness and best practice. The issue of evidence is significant, the IFSTs were backed by politicians because they believed that they has been trialled and worked – they saw their introduction as 'evidence based policy'. Popularised, particularly by the 'modernising government' agenda of new labour governments, policy, it is argued, should be shaped less by ideology and more by evidence of 'what works' (Cabinet Office, 1999). Despite reservations about the extent to which this really has led to policy being more evidence-based (Bilson, 2005), the rhetoric remains a powerful driver:

> *The Welsh Government is committed to using good quality research to support its decision making. Research helps us identify and respond to emerging issues, evaluate the impact of our initiatives and find better ways of doing things.*
>
> (Welsh Assembly Government, 2012)

65

Support for this principle being applied within social work is strong in Wales as it is across the United Kingdom. A government-commissioned review of the profession advocated 'more use of research and evaluation to support continuing professional development and to inform frontline practice' (Welsh Assembly Government, 2010). The evidence-based nature of the project is also significant in providing a structure, theoretical underpinning and tools for practitioners to use with families.

Another key focus of the IFST is to provide consultation and advice to the wider workforce utilising the knowledge, skills and experience of the team's staff to provide 'an engine for system change' in Wales in work with the most vulnerable children and families.

The creation of this team can be seen to have its roots in the national Hidden Harm reports (Advisory Council on the Misuse of Drugs, 2003) on the needs of children who have parents with problem drug use, the Vulnerable Children's Strategy, and the 'One Wales' commitment by the Welsh Government to address child poverty by providing integrated services to children and families (Welsh Assembly Government, 2007). Significantly the service is not just the product of a policy measure but the Welsh Government has written it into the legislative framework (Children and Families (Wales) Measure, 2010) and underpinned it by regulation.

The scale and shape of the initiative can also be seen in part as a product of devolution. Government is smaller, more focused with clearer decision-making. It was only in 2006 that the Welsh Assembly gained primary law-making powers but as a government its legislation was immediately distinctive, in children's services, for example, through its high-profile adoption of the United Nations Charter on the Rights of the Child (UNCRC) as a benchmark for other law and policy to be measured by. Indeed policy documents such as that of the task force reviewing social work makes reference to 'Welsh political values' (Welsh Assembly Government, 2010). In terms of social work, the ethos of policy is geared towards 'rediscovering the heart' of the profession, an ethos that is positioned in direct contrast to the marketisation of social care in England.

Devolution has also meant a smaller gap between the service and the ministers responsible with levels of contact between them, and the potential for the development of personal relationships, which would be highly unusual for an individual project particularly in England where there might be multiple tiers of management in-between.

[T]he family support function under the legislation is really important and again, something different that's happened as a result of IFSS (Integrated Family Support Service). In order to strengthen that, the Lead Policy Advisor and a lawyer from Welsh Government are coming to speak to the IFSS Board next week so I think that evidences a really close link. I do feel that if I had an issue I could speak directly to the Policy Lead at Welsh Government about it and I've never been in that situation before.

Mike feels that this is equally true within of the next 'layer' of contact across agencies – health, the voluntary sector and other departments of the local authority – and their senior management. At least having these direct lines of communication creates the possibility of developing real working relationships. Through these relationships it was possible to ascertain to what extent the service was getting, or perhaps more importantly not getting, support and why.

I have never been in a situation where you're emailing Directors, Senior Managers or Heads of Service on a regular basis, it's having those key people and getting that 'buy in' from them, knowing that they're embracing it.

There is of course another side to this coin as all of these closer links between policymakers and the service means greater visibility and more opportunity for close scrutiny from senior management and politicians; they want to see a successful service – and value for money.

But obviously, they want to see results and it's about cost effectiveness; I am totally conscious of the political landscape that we exist in. They are going to want to see results but you get used to being in a goldfish bowl after a while. There is a lot at stake and you are bound to get closely scrutinised at every level due to that, it goes with the territory I guess.

The importance of leadership in creating new services that require networking and boundary crossing is increasingly recognised (Anning et al., 2010). Some of the skills and characteristics that Mike suggests are required here to develop and sustain networks might seem mundane, yet they have proved crucial to the project's success.

I think that probably the most important skill that I've acquired over the last nine months in terms of trying to build those bridges between the different services and the different areas is patience, to understand that the people, you know, I am dealing with people on the board who are the group directors and the director of Nursing and these are huge

> organisations and you need to understand that it can often be very difficult for people to respond to you in terms of their availability or information that you require from them, when you want that information so sometimes its about understanding that they have lots of different priorities and sometimes they are not always able to prioritise what you want them to do. ...

Referrals to the project come from the children services teams and so again networking skills are vitally important for the manager. However the newly established IFST service is seen as being well resourced and so it is not just a case of establishing good working relationships but establishing them with tact and diplomacy.

> So we've had to be very, very sensitive in the way that we've got 'buy in' from the wider workforce, because they are absolutely fundamental in order for the success of this project. So we've had to be very mindful that we are not seen as this elitist 'Rolls Royce' service, it's about selling it in the way of how we can be a resource for those social workers on the ground with regard to families who are probably most time and resource intensive on their caseload. We learned very early on that an easy way of annoying social workers is to offer them an IFST Mousemat, Mug or Lucky Gonk when they feel they haven't got enough staff and resources to even fulfil their statutory obligations.

Collaborating and influencing skills along with those of creating partnerships have been increasingly recognised across the United Kingdom as crucial facets of leadership in social care[1]. For Mike they are underpinned by basic social work skills and the building blocks of forming relationships.

> [B]eing able to communicate on a number of levels, obviously is very important if it's with group directors one day to, you know, talking to a panel of service users the next day, and the skills of engaging them, communicating with people have been quite important in that.
> ...and being a social worker by trade if you like, I think lots of those are transferable skills, the core competencies you know, communicate and engage... These are just as relevant in a multi-agency setting.

A broader argument could be made for the importance of leadership and networking skills for all social workers transferring their skills in relationships with service users in to this important area of professional practice.

The team context

Beyond the constraints of the politics and the larger organisation it is perhaps the manager who is most able to influence some of the structures around the individual team and whether or not they support the possibilities for practice development. As highlighted in the introduction this is also a story of the creation of an integrated team and one which has also had to develop a different way of working, drawing strongly on a theoretical framework. In exploring both these aspects of the project the relevance of relationships in the team context is apparent.

The shift towards social work practice being performed in an inter-professional environment has been inexorable. The drive for one-stop shops, co-location and greater information sharing has been experienced across all jurisdictions of the United Kingdom. From the outset a central feature of the IFSS was that the teams would be inter-professional in nature. The role of professional identity in inter-professional working is much discussed in the literature. Issues of professional knowledge, skills, values, status and accountability, are frequently recurring themes (Easen et al., 2000; Frost et al., 2005; Anning et al., 2010) and finding a structure and way of working that would address these issues was a challenge for this team too.

The team comprises of a Team Performance and Development Manager and administrator, two Consultant Social Workers and six Intervention Specialists. The Intervention Specialists are from a variety of professional disciplines including child and adult services, mental health, substance misuse, Community Psychiatric Nurse and Health Visitor backgrounds. Cases can be allocated to any worker, each using the same model as a basis for their intervention. The team is characterised by a relatively flat structure with each team member being recognised both by their Grade (and consequent level of remuneration) and the level of expertise they bring. This has served to provide an environment where each member appreciates and respects the importance and difference of every role and how each cannot work effectively without the others. In this way, Mike argues, a kind of synergy has been created where, although the Team is placed within local authority Children's Services, the expertise provided by staff with backgrounds in the other disciplines and agencies are all viewed as equally beneficial thereby transcending agency limitations.

The inter-professional nature of the project has proved an interesting mix for all the workers of being both 'expert' and 'novice'.

> They were all an expert in their field and now they come to something that's brand new, so everybody is starting from a clean sheet and they feel something of a novice.

Mike argues that this is a great 'leveller' creating an important starting point for the team to develop despite their different professional experiences. At the same time clinical supervision and recognition that each worker is bringing extra expertise to the team tries to ensure the experience is stimulating and not deskilling. The team structure has therefore been carefully put in place to maximise the impact of the variety of skills and minimising the potential conflict which could distract from the work with families. Mike has had to be instrumental in this process as 'effective leadership is crucial in providing an environment that values people and celebrates the diversity of different professionals (Anning et al., 2010, p. 105). The need to make staff from the health sector feel equal partners in a relationship which had been created to sit within the social care framework was a major factor. Attempting to create an environment where lively discussion could take place and where all workers could see that their views are valued by management seemed key.

> It was not unusual for the 'Any Other Business' part of Team Meetings to run into double figures with staff from Health and social care backgrounds offering very different perspectives on everything from the value placed by professionals on 'drug testing' to the need for a rota to ensure the IFST always had clean tea towels. Although challenging in terms of managing this, it did provide clear evidence of the genuine commitment, belief and determination of staff to make the IFST as effective and efficient as it could be.

While the boundaries issues with other professional can have challenges for the social workers involved, the experience of working in this team does not seem to have a negative effect on social work identity. If anything, as far as social work is concerned, the nature of the project could be seen as 're-skilling' and restoring belief in the opportunity to make 'real' interventions based on therapeutic relationships:

> We do get the sense that what we're delivering here is actual direct therapeutic interventions with families, – this, to a greater or lesser degree, has been diminished within social work because the role has just been so process driven in terms of key performance indicators and time limits on core assessments and initial assessments and all those sort of things Social workers have become care coordinators rather than actually delivering those interventions by working directly with families.

Another important element of the nature of the project is its particularly intensive model of working:

> If you think, in four to six weeks, we probably spend the amount of time with a family that a field social worker might do in twelve months on weekly visits. We are really compacting that. So the effect on workers be it emotional or psychological, can be and often is absolutely huge.

There is therefore a clear recognition of the need to set up structures and practices that will support workers and their practice development. Mike has established the use of reflective groups where issues with individual cases can be shared with the team and the worker benefit from the critical but supportive questioning of their colleagues. In addition practitioners get a greater level of supervision. Of course a greater quantity of supervision is not necessarily significant (although some social workers would no doubt welcome it); what is important, as Mike recognises, is that it is supervision that supports the discussion of emotions as well as the audit of cases.

As Ruch (2012) argues,

> *Front line managers are in the unenviable position of having to find a way of responding to the ostensibly rational demands of the performance-driven agenda determined by senior managers within their organisation, while being directly exposed to the emotionally charged experiences that practitioners present to them from the front line of practice. (pp. 1317–18)*

For Ruch it is clear that reflective practice and relationship-based social work can only really be promoted within reflective and relationship-based management practices.

Realising the potential for personal or professional challenge wherever possible, for example in the reflective groups, can be difficult when there is a sense that you are 'laying yourself bare' in front of your colleagues even if this does take place within a structured framework where everybody is valued for their opinions and feels safe to express them. The project tries to start from the same point as they would in engaging families, for example, openness and honesty. Anning et al. (2010) outline how many of these features are essential to help enable both integrated working in general and the development of an effective community of practice (Wenger, 1998) in particular that can allow but contain conflict. Mike is also aware that the fact that reflective groups exist does not mean that genuine reflection always takes place and even the dangers of over-reflection, substituting for action, need to be guarded against.

The efforts to create a positive culture of reflection illustrates another important principle – that of attempting to make a connection between the way in which supportive relationships are fostered 'out there' with families and 'in here' between manager and practitioners and practitioners with each other.

> Similarly, the importance placed on the robust system for staff to debrief and reflect on their interventions with colleagues provides a safe and mutually supportive environment where people feel they have the support of the whole team. This 'systems' approach also reflects and validates the whole family systems approach of IFST.

The systems approach noted here is part of the overall approach of the project which is, as noted earlier, firmly rooted in research, theory and specific tools for practitioners to use.

> It was drawing on research generally, but specifically from what was known as the Option 2 Project which had been running for ten years in Cardiff and the evaluation carried out showed that families who had been through this intensive whole family intervention, if their children did result in becoming looked after, then those episodes of looked after were for shorter periods than for families who hadn't received the intensive intervention. So the main thrust of this is trying to keep children safe, that is the most important thing, but looking at what's different about it, it's looking at the whole family, so a systems approach which takes place within an intensive brief period.
>
> ... it is an intensive intervention where we work with a family intensively for four to six weeks and the methodology, or the methods of working if you like, are based around solution focussed brief therapy, motivational interviewing, cognitive behavioural techniques and a systems approach where you are looking at the whole family.

The practitioners work within a prescribed methodology. However rather than being a constraint Mike argues that the prescription is valuable so long as there is still some space for creativity. It is a fine line that can create some tension, and his description of how the model works reveals the complexity of what really shapes the context in which practice is enacted – the 'highly prescribed model' meets the messy reality of 'complex families'. Both elements of this – its value and its constraints – are explored in Chapter 4 through the work of a social worker in this team.

Chapter 4 also reveals the connection between the model and the fundamental role of forming and sustaining working relationships with families. From a management perspective one important way of supporting this connection is for the day-to-day operation of the team to attempt to mirror the values of the project. If staff experience management using the same approach in their role to that which practitioners use with families, this can only, in Mike's view, endorse and reinforce the values of the organisation. This results in staff feeling credible in their role and that they been given a mandate to practice in this manner as modelled by management.

> By creating an environment of openness and honesty where staff are encouraged to discuss issues as soon as they arise in a 'solution focussed' context in team meetings and supervision sessions, we were striving for social work best practice where openness, transparency and the desire to build on strengths are critical factors. Also the way of working, the range of methods of intervention, for example utilising OARS [Open Ended Questions, Affirming, Reflecting and Summarising]. We try and ensure that this strand goes right through the organisation as well.…a team dynamic of openness, honesty and support that mirrors the therapeutic relationships with the families with whom we work.

Another possibility of 'affirming', 'reflecting' and 'summarising' where staff feel they are at in terms of their intervention with a family is the creation of a common language within the organisation which then contributes to a sense of identity and belonging that has positively affected staff morale and performance as well as recruitment and retention.

Already the exploration of the team context above shows how the style of supervision, support of reflective groups and overall culture of the team is recognised as important by the manager in trying to enable a particular approach to practice. Undoubtedly some strategic decisions were important – a seconded project manager as a single point of contact to set up the project was cited as one example – but perhaps the least-well-analysed factor in how such a service can be effectively established, but one we emphasise here, is about what kind of person needs to be leading it. What are the knowledge and skills? Are there personal qualities that are essential? There may, of course, be more than one way of achieving an outcome but reflecting on this with Mike gives an opportunity to gain some insight into achieving the best outcome in a complex set of developments.

In the other chapters in this section the social workers consider the boundaries of formal learning, personal characteristics and experience. Mike was drawing on previous knowledge of managing a team working with the same service user group for three years. This was also a multi-agency team including social workers and Health Visitors. While this experience was clearly valuable it also needed to be combined with the ability to transfer this into the uncertainly of a new project – one where some facets were highly prescribed and others are not prescribed at all. This can be quite daunting for managers who have been used to working within concrete parameters in the statutory sector. Personal qualities seemed key to the whole process:

> ... equally as important I would say, is approaching a new challenging project like this with a positive, 'can do' attitude and recognising that the model of work and the whole ethos behind the IFST is something that could, I think, shape wider practice in the future. What I've needed to have is that belief that this really can provide positive outcomes for families and children within those families who are some of the most vulnerable in our communities and keeping that at the forefront of your mind.

> That said, I believe that people make organisations effective. You can have the best, evidence based model of intervention, policies and procedures in place, but without the building and sustenance of key relationships at every level, between the IFST worker and the family, the social worker, management and the wider workforce, any potential for best practice is made much more difficult.

Note

1. See, for example, in Wales: http://www.ssiacymru.org.uk/home.php?page_id=3777 and Scotland: http://www.stepintoleadership.info/managers.html).

Part 2

Risk, Uncertainty and Judgement

7 Working with Risk: Fine Judgements and Difficult Decisions

Jean Gordon

Introduction

Social work with children and young people, has always required an understanding of risk. Youth and adolescence, for example, a time of life that is 'synonymous with transition' (Cebula, 2009, p. 9) involve negotiating the often rocky path between childhood and adolescence and, almost inevitably, taking risks. Decision-making about risk – what constitutes a risk, whether the risk is harmful, whether it is right to intervene to reduce risk – is a core and enduring aspect of social work practice. Making these kinds of 'judgement calls', which intersect with individual, organisational and societal attitudes towards risk taking, has always been one of the most pressing and testing tasks faced by welfare professionals (Titterton and Hunter, 2011). This chapter provides a brief synopsis of some of the debates, dilemmas and difficult decisions that surround our understanding of risk. It can only give a taste of the extensive and growing literature on the subject of risk; the references at the end of this book will enable readers to go on to explore these interesting and important debates in greater detail. This introduction will set the context for a discussion of the place of risk in day-to-day social work practice, and for four practitioners' stories about their experiences of working with risk in different practice contexts.

Understanding risk

Concern about risk has come to dominate the practice of social work. This shift has not happened in isolation, but, it has been argued, come as a consequence of living in a society characterised by constant change and dislocation, and a pre-occupation with safety (Giddens, 1990; Beck,

1992). Whether or not the world is becoming a more dangerous place to live in is a matter for debate, but, in a modernist western society, it is argued, our life decisions are no longer regarded as being 'in the lap of the gods' but subject to reasoned decision-making and a belief that we have control over the outcomes of our actions (Power, 2004, p. 4). This increasing pre-occupation with minimising risk and uncertainty is alive and well in social work practice, fuelled by intense media attention on the actions of social workers, and public, and sometimes political, condemnation of decisions that social workers and other child care workers have made that have failed to protect children from harm. Paradoxically, at a time when improvements in child protection practice have contributed to making child abuse deaths rare events, rather than celebrating and learning from success, the 'defining approach' has become one of minimising the risk of failure of child protection systems (Ferguson, 2011, p. 33). Governmental response to the fear of risk to children, as well as the risk of unwanted media attention, has been to produce increasing quantities of regulatory guidance, checklists and procedures that seek to reduce the possibility of uncertainty in decision-making through administrative change. This approach seems to be founded on a premise that, *if only* social workers could apply procedures properly, then child abuse, and in particular, child deaths from abuse, will not happen. Munro, in her review of child protection in England suggested that this increasingly prescriptive approach to social work practice arises from 'the false hope' that risk of harm can somehow be eliminated (Munro, 2011, p. 134). The outcome of this approach, she suggests, is that professionals are responding to uncertainty with increasingly defensive practices, aimed at protecting their reputations and those of the organisations they work for. These approaches can be as much about satisfying organisational demands as meeting the welfare needs of children.

Pre-occupation with risk of harm also has the potential to create new risks which themselves may be damaging. Littlechild (2008) has argued that fear of risk itself can lead to 'the risk of fear' by creating a level of anxiety and defensiveness in social workers that is inimical to the confident use of social work practice skills and knowledge. He has also suggested that risk assessment tools and processes may be constructed in ways that under-estimate some areas of risk to children as well as risk to workers themselves, for example of harassment or aggression directed at social workers by parents. A focus on risk assessment and management may create other dangers, for example that, by spending large amounts of time satisfying complex bureaucratic demands to assess 'high risk' cases, other work with children at risk, or to prevent risk of harm, may receive less priority (Beckett, 2008). Study of the use of the plethora of computer-based recording systems introduced to manage and monitor social workers' performance, with the aim of reducing unpredictability and ambiguity in child protection practice, suggests that these may sometimes have the unintended consequence of obscuring risk to children (Pithouse et al., 2012).

There is then an increasingly active debate about the meaning and significance of risk in social work practice in the United Kingdom. Bringing together the many threads in this complex discussion, the Munro Review has identified in unequivocal terms that the child protection system in England requires substantial reform to enable it to move 'from a system that has become over-bureaucratised and focused on compliance to one that values and develops professional expertise and is focused on the safety and welfare of children and young people' (Munro, 2011, p. 7). Eileen Munro identified a central challenge for social workers, and everyone else involved in child protection, to move from a focus that remains predominantly 'risk averse' to one of being 'risk sensible' (2011, p. 135). A similar discussion about the 'right' balance between prescription and autonomy is playing out in a range of different social work contexts in different parts of the United Kingdom. For example, The Scottish Executive's 21st Century Review of Social Work, 'Changing Lives', saw the social worker's role with children (and adults) subject to increasing constraint, over-regulated by procedure and management oversight. The Review argued that social workers need to be accountable – to the public, to their employers, and, above all, to service users and carers – but need scope to exercise their professional judgement in identifying, assessing and managing risk (Scottish Executive, 2006).

Up to this point this chapter has focused on risk of harm. However, although risk tends to be associated with adverse consequences in social work practice, it also has more positive connotations. So a particular risk can be seen in one context as dangerous, reckless and damaging, and, in another as life-affirming, adventurous and creative.

The understanding that risk can be positive as well as negative is implicit in the growth of interest in the significance of resilience and protective factors to children and families. Both children and adults need to negotiate a degree of risk and adversity to develop coping strategies to respond to future circumstances. Over-protection of children, such as adolescents eager to test out their growing autonomy, can create its own risks to children's well-being, including reducing their capacity to manage future life challenges. Assessment frameworks, such as

Scotland's Getting it Right for Every Child National Practice Model (Scottish Government, 2012), implicitly embed this understanding of the importance of resilience in professional practice with children and families. The notion of positive risk-taking is also a key element of emerging developments in adult health and social care, such as personalisation, self-directed support and self-management of long-term health conditions (Titterton, 2011). These changes are bringing about some important changes in the language of risk. For example, the term 'risk enablement' is increasingly used to refer to ways in which individuals, including adults and children with disabilities, may be supported to take positive risks as part of a personalised approach to self-directed assessment and support (SCIE, 2010). It would seem then that there are the seeds of change in our attitudes towards risk, as well as changes in our language. This shift in meaning is congruent, Stalker (2003) finds, with some of the fundamental tenets of social work, including principles of self-determination, choice and empowerment.

Judgement and decision-making

Titterton and Hunter (2011) suggest that it is hard to imagine a more interesting – or challenging – time for social work students and practitioners to be studying risk. On the one hand social workers are being urged to use professional discretion to take a creative and nuanced approach to risk, and on the other to respond with certainty to avoid or minimise risk, working within complex systems of audit and performance management where 'safety first' is the main maxim. The fear of fallibility – of making 'the wrong decision' – in child protection practice will be familiar to every social worker working with children and their families. One of the social workers interviewed for this book recalled the impact of the reporting of the death of 'Baby P' in London in 2007 on practitioners in her local authority:

> I think when you are working in a climate that social workers have been working in, you are very fearful, aren't you? And you know, and I think probably at the time of Baby P, I know that in places where other local authority employees worked, social workers were being talked about in very derogatory terms.

This worker illustrates what Lord Laming confirmed in his report on Baby Peter's death: that hostile media and public attention had had 'serious implications for the effectiveness, status and morale of the children's workforce as a whole' (Laming, 2009, p. 44). Significantly, this atmosphere of 'fear of risk' also, for some time, changed the way in which social workers and other professionals perceived and responded to concerns about children's welfare. There were unprecedented increases in applications for child protection proceedings in England almost as soon as Baby P's death was reported, with consequent increases in the number of children in foster or residential care. These changes in practice have been attributed to a more cautious approach to decision-making by individual practitioners and managers, as well as increased risk aversion at an institutional level (Douglas, 2008, cited by Elsley, 2010). The impact of an event like the death of Baby P on social workers' decisions, and therefore on the lives of children and their families, is a reminder that our conception of risk is not fixed, but socially constructed. It is influenced by the perceptions of individuals, groups and communities about what 'risk of harm' means.

We all experience risk – it is 'an essential part of the subjective experience of being human' (Titterton, 2011, p. 32). Baker and Wilkinson suggest that one of the difficulties in moving towards a different conception of, and response to, risk is a tendency for 'over-simplified and caricatured responses' to risk (2011, p. 14). These responses are partly influenced by our own perceptions and experiences of danger and the ways in which we have, successfully or unsuccessfully, managed to negotiate both positive and negative risks in our lives. Social workers therefore have to be sensitive to their own, and others', experience of risk, and of strategies for managing the unpredictability of everyday life. Crucially this includes the experiences and understanding of children and their families of what risk means to them. It is important for social workers to gain an understanding of how parents and other caregivers have developed strategies for protecting their children from harm – and enabling them to take risks to grow and develop. It is not the case that children just passively respond to parental behaviours and attitudes. Instead they play an active role in negotiating risk-related decisions with significant others, and develop their own ways of measuring and responding to risk (Kelley et al., 1998, cited in Stalker, 2003, p. 226). Working in partnership with children and families to negotiate understandings and plan responses to risk of harm is therefore essential to effective social work practice. An international literature review of effective approaches to risk assessment confirmed the centrality of the relationship between the practitioner and service users to good practice in risk assessment and management (Barry, 2007). However, Barry's review also found evidence that this relationship was being eroded by the language and politics of risk. Barriers to relationship-building identified included a pre-occupation with thresholds and short-term crisis intervention resulting in 'minimal scope for learning from mistakes and a lack of user involvement in decision making' (Barry, 2007, p. 1).

The following chapters in this section explore how four practitioners responded to situations in which there was risk of harm. Each practitioner 'story' involves weighing up different kinds of risks, positive and negative, and making judgements about whether and how to respond to complex situations. Sometimes these were major decisions to act to reduce risk of harm, such as the decision that Myra should move out of her family home into local authority accommodation (see Chapter 10). In other cases the decisions were smaller, day-to-day ones, such as those to enable Amy to take increasing responsibility for caring for her young daughter, Grace (see Chapter 8). Each chapter tells a very different story about decision-making but there are some common elements. First, the social workers were engaged in a continuous process of balancing people's rights to privacy and self-determination with the social worker's duty to respond to protect children from harm. Secondly, they were not making decisions in isolation, but in the context of their particular team and organisational setting. This positioning often required them to negotiate different and competing understandings of risk expressed by the children and young people involved, their parents, foster carers and other professionals. Finally, all four social workers brought a good deal of knowledge to the decision-making process, and used evidence from a range of different sources to inform the judgements made. We now go on to examine these three particular elements of decision-making about risk – balancing rights and responsibilities, the context for practice and evidence-based practice – through the lens of critical social work practice.

A critical approach to risk

A key element of critical best practice in social work is that it is 'critical', involving processes of skilful reflection, balancing respect for service users, and awareness of oppression and vulnerability, with social work authority and accountability, and an understanding of the current working context for social workers (Ferguson, 2008). Glaister (2008) sees forging relationships as a key foundation for critical practice. As the previous section of the book emphasises, this requires a willingness and ability to build relationships with children and families, and the time and support for doing so. Working with risk of harm to children also requires a constant balancing and re-balancing of what is often referred to as 'care and control' in the exercise of what Ferguson calls 'good authority' (2011, p. 37). That authority is conveyed in a range of ways not least through social workers' mandate to practice in accordance with legal principles and duties under, for example, in Scotland the Children (Scotland) Act 1995 and, in England and Wales, the Children Act 1989. These statutes also, crucially, convey rights – to children and to parents. The balance between children's rights and those of their parents and of representatives of the state is one that has undergone considerable change over the last century. There is increasing recognition that children have rights – to provision of services, to protection and to participation in decisions about their lives (United Nations Convention on the Rights of the Child, UNICEF, 1989). With rights come responsibilities, not only for social workers but for everyone who comes into contact with children: in the words of a Scottish policy review, it has become 'everybody's job' to make sure that children are 'alright' (Scottish Executive, 2002). At the same time it is often the role of the social worker to take the lead in 'calling time' when anxieties are mounting about a child's safety; in this section both Jock and Clive illustrate the tensions inherent in making and following through judgement calls about when and how to intervene when there is perceived danger to a young person (Chapters 9 and 10).

Social workers derive their authority to act through their organisational role and professional standing as well as the law. However, as Ferguson points out, social workers also wield personal authority, without which they are unable to make effective day-to-day decisions about when and how to intervene to protect children from harm. Authoritative practice of this kind requires a range of knowledge and skills, underpinned with compassion and a commitment to ethical principles, including partnership working and empowerment. The nature of this power to act, and how to ensure that 'good authority' is just that, is a central theme in all four accounts of practice that follow.

The need for a critical understanding of the *context* of practice is also evident. First, all the social workers interviewed reflected in their interviews on the size of workloads, and the challenges of effective engagement with children and families in often complex and anxiety-provoking circumstances. Excessive caseloads have repeatedly been identified as a contributing factor to failures to protect children and young people from harm (All Party Parliamentary Group on Social Work, 2013). Understanding the context for child and family, and the impact of their particular circumstances and community is also necessarily a central feature of critical social work practice. For example, we know that children's life opportunities may be affected adversely by structural factors, such living in poverty and dangerous communities (Scottish

Government, 2008). The importance of locating risk to children and young people within an understanding of the 'child's world' – their individual needs, their relationships with people who are important to them, and their environment – is stressed in Getting it Right for Every Child (Scottish Government, 2012) and other systemic and ecological approaches to assessment that focus on 'the big picture' (Howe, 2009, p. 109). In this section the outcomes of structural disadvantage on parents and children are perhaps most evident in Chapters 8 and 9, in relation to risk of harm to David and to Grace, and the impact on them of their parents' significant difficulties in providing consistent parenting in environments that failed to support healthy child development. On the whole, however, while all the social workers interviewed demonstrated their awareness of inequality and deprivation on the families they were working with, it tended to be their relationships with children and parents that practitioners spoke about most in the interviews.

Another highly significant aspect of context for practice was its multidisciplinary nature. The important role of teachers, lawyers, housing officers, doctors and other professionals was apparent in each case example. These multi-disciplinary relationships introduced richness, complexity – and sometimes frustration or miscommunication – as different practitioners and their agencies introduced different understandings of risk and the actions thought necessary (or unnecessary) to reduce perceived risks. The literature on risk and social work suggests that social workers tend to defer to decisions of the judiciary and of the medical profession when decisions are made about risk in child protection (Barry, 2007). There are, therefore, issues of power which play an important role in mediating decision-making processes between professionals and their organisations. These mirror the imbalance of power between social workers and the children and families that they work with; this is explored in greater detail in the next section of the book. Barry's review of the international literature highlighted the need to find ways of fostering trust, reciprocity and openness between all parties, including service users, carers, managers and practitioners from different backgrounds when assessing and managing risk (Barry, 2007). The critical element of practice was especially visible in this book's interviews when social workers were working with complexity and uncertainty, making fine judgements alongside colleagues from other disciplines about appropriate thresholds for intervention. This was thrown into particular relief when the young person and/or their family was resistant to or, as in Clive Rosenthal's case example, very negative, about the involvement of social workers and other professionals in their lives. Some of the interview discussions that follow illustrate how practitioners sought to find ways to resolve ethical dilemmas within the requirements – and sometimes perceived constraints – of job roles, availability of time and other resources in their workplaces.

Successive reports and inquiries about social work practice have emphasised the importance of a sound evidence base for practice. While the precise nature of that evidence is contested and defined in different ways (see, e.g., Parton, 2000; Pawson, 2003), the need to develop and use evidence to inform positive outcomes is not (Scottish Executive, 2006; Munro, 2011). One of the tasks of the Munro review was to find ways to reduce bureaucracy in child protection work and increase the space for professional judgements. Munro concluded that 'children need and deserve a high level of expertise from their social workers who make such crucial decisions about what is in their best interests' (Munro, 2011, p. 84). This includes the ability to make critical use of best practice from research to inform professional judgement and decision-making. The degree to which our practitioner participants explicitly referred to research findings in the interviews was variable, and Munro has identified improving the use of research to inform practice as a key area for development of the social work profession in England. However, there was no doubt that these social workers drew on a wide range of different forms of knowledge. These included their knowledge of the law, ethics, organisational procedures and processes, and, perhaps most prominently, their direct experience of working with children and families in different contexts. This breadth of evidence accords with Research in Practice's definition of evidence-based practice as 'practice that is informed by the best available evidence of what is effective, the practice expertise of professionals and the experience and views of service users' (Barratt and Cooke, 2001, p. 2). The particular forms of evidence discussed in these interviews were inevitably determined by the unique nature of each practice context described. The illustration of 'best' practice in practitioner accounts comes through the social worker's capability to use evidence for practice in a flexible and creative way, through their use of observation, analysis and reasoning. Munro (2011) also highlights the importance of challenge by others, highlighting the pitfalls of reasoning that relies too heavily on intuition. Unless practitioners are well supported with opportunities for supervision and reflection, there is a danger that excessive reliance on intuitive reasoning will, in uncertain and anxiety-provoking situations, generate an unrealistic sense of certitude (Payne and Betman, 2007, cited in Munro, 2011, p. 91). The importance of possessing the confidence to be open to challenge and debate in relation to decision-making about risk is evident in all four of the interviews. In Jock Mickshik's case the challenge initially comes from other professionals and from David's foster carers, while for Clive Rosenthal this emerges from his own critical reflection on his work with Myra. In contrast the interview with the social services team working with baby Grace, and her mother, Amy, provides an opportunity to hear how they worked together, negotiating their sometimes rather different assessments of risk to Grace to make decisions about her care. This focus on the context in which risk decisions are made is picked up again in Chapter 11 when Marie reflects on the importance of a supportive organisational culture to her work with adopted and fostered children in Scotland.

Four stories of risk

The narratives about working with children at risk of harm introduced over the next four chapters provide an opportunity to gain an understanding of how social workers grapple with the tensions and dilemmas about risk explored in this introductory chapter. They are about 'the actual work in trying to protect children' (Ferguson, 2011, p. 2). Their focus is therefore on what happens when social workers engage with children and their families in homes, schools – and what happens back at the office, in meetings and discussions with multi-disciplinary colleagues. They also offer insight into how the social workers felt about the work that they did, including how they managed feelings of anxiety, and sometimes frustration, as they worked with children and families to make both small and major decisions about intervening (and not intervening) in their lives. The chapters explore different kinds of risks to children at different ages and stages, living in a range of different family contexts. Three of the chapters are about social work practice in local authorities in England, and one relates to an independent social work agency in Scotland.

In Chapter 8, Suzanne Lyus and Wendy Whitehouse (with their colleagues Jane Strange and Becky Hopkins) illustrate a team approach to assessing the parenting capacity of a young mother with learning disabilities. Amy was suspected of having harmed her first child who was subsequently removed from her care, and anxieties were high, and optimism low about her ability to parent her baby, Grace. The need for 'defensible' and well-documented practice is especially evident in this case, balancing the wish to empower Amy to parent her child with the need for tightly evidenced assessment that she could do so safely. The case also illustrates that assessing and managing risk is not only about the big decisions but is often composed of ongoing everyday decisions about, for example, how to offer and when to begin to withdraw support.

Jock Mickshik is a specialist worker who provides service to adults and children in England who exhibit sexually harmful behaviour. Chapter 9 explores his work with David, a young man in his mid-teens in foster care, who has been both vulnerable to abuse because of a traumatic childhood history and profound learning disability, and has presented a risk of sexual harm to others. A key feature of this practice example is the dual challenge of simultaneously working with 'risk from' and 'risk to' David. Jock came to this work very much as 'the expert professional' and his account provides a powerful illustration of the importance of maintaining a critically reflective stance in which the social worker is able to hear alternative explanations and understandings, and respond to these in an open and flexible way. The role of the multi-disciplinary 'team around the child' is a significant one, drawing in a range of expertise and experience of this particular young person. Jock also illustrates the way in which good practice relies on an understanding of, and an ability to select from, a range of different forms of knowledge about practice, including alternative theoretical models, relevant research and ways of engaging creatively with children with profound communication difficulties.

Clive Rosenthal was also working with an adolescent, a young woman at risk because of the breakdown of her relationship with her mother. Myra, at 14, was actively engaged in a range of risk-taking behaviours, including drinking, drug use and underage sex. Clive's dilemmas, discussed in Chapter 10, centre on the right of public authorities to intervene in family life, and the uncertain outcomes arising from intervening or not intervening. The case also picks up earlier questions about what we mean by 'risk' in the context of adolescent experimentation, and how the social worker's experience of and orientation to those kinds of risks may influence practice decisions about thresholds for intervention. Clive's work with Myra also involved some difficult decision-making about parental rights and responsibilities and what was 'good enough parenting' in the context of this case.

Finally, in Chapter 11, Marie Brown, who works in Scotland, discusses risk enablement in the context of her practice with Alannah over a period of eight years. Alannah, who is 13, has had a permanent and very settled home with foster carers since she was five. Marie debates the risks of a 'safety first' approach in relation to contact between looked-after children and their birth parents. Drawing on the concept of resilience, Marie describes some of the organisational challenges involved in enabling a looked-after child to benefit from positive risk-taking.

Conclusion

Working with risk goes right to the heart of some fundamental questions about social work practice – about the balance between individual autonomy and protection from harm, between standardised responses to perceived risk and creative personalised practice, and between conflicting perceptions of risk. Risk is, by its nature, difficult to define. Not only can risks be perceived positively or negatively but understandings of risk are also culturally and historically determined. 'New' risks are constantly emerging, such as the internet and childhood obesity, generating different ideas about what is 'safe' or 'dangerous' for children and their families. Stalker suggests that, faced with what might seem an impenetrable quagmire of ambiguity and uncertainty, social workers need to regain their role as 'experts in uncertainty', making fine judgements about risk and daring to work 'creatively and innovatively' (2003, p. 228). In the rest of this section we explore how four social workers and their colleagues set out to do just that – and some of the challenges along the way.

8 Assessing Risk of Harm: A Team Approach

Suzanne Lyus, Wendy Wyatt-Thomas and Jean Gordon with Jayne Strange and Becky Hopkins

The team in question consists of members of an assessment and support Team[1] in England. It employs social workers, support workers and foster carers and works closely with a range of other organisations including adult community care and legal services. Its aim is to enable parents to parent their children 'in a safe environment with a view to supporting and encouraging them to develop a better understanding of their child's needs and how to adequately meet these independently and on a consistent basis'. The placements are provided by foster carers as near as possible to families' local communities.

Questions to ask yourself as you read:

- What makes for an effective assessment?
- What are the advantages and disadvantages of group decision-making?
- What skills do social workers need to communicate and negotiate understandings of risk to colleagues, children and families?

Introduction

Social work practice usually takes place in the context of some kind of team. Sometimes that team is made up of social workers, but it is increasingly the case that teams include people with a range of different roles and backgrounds. Typically social workers will be part of several kinds of overlapping teams and networks with different purposes and accountability mechanisms. Expectations from successive UK governments that services will be 'joined up' and 'integrated' is not a new one, but has run through policy, research and practice in relation to children and families for more than 50 years (Rose, 2011).

There are few who would argue with the idea that good team work is at least desirable – and probably essential – to providing effective and efficient services that meet the needs of children and their families. Bringing together practitioners and managers with a range of different expertise and perspectives into a collaborative team enables knowledge-sharing and mutual learning. Chapter 7 highlighted the social construction of risk and the influence of personal risk histories, professional training and societal norms. Teams provide practitioners with opportunities to consider risk together, hearing different perspectives, seeing different ways of working and debating questions of risk with colleagues with a variety of different perspectives. The benefits of a team approach to risk seem self-evident. At the same time the kinds of differences that play out in any team – different experiences, roles, accountability, levels of power – inevitably create a degree of conflict. Finlay and Ballinger suggest that, though difference can cause tensions,

> the greater the difference the more we stand to gain from the expertise of others. It is really only on this basis that we can really work together. (2008, p. 166)

Some teams are multi-disciplinary, but in this chapter we explore the work of a team of social services practitioners with different roles and backgrounds. Unlike other chapters in this book, this was a group interview which provided an opportunity to explore the ways in which sharing and debating different constructions of risk can contribute to critical best practice.

'The Team'

The Team is unusual in that, although its staff are employed by the local authority, it operates at 'arm's length' from the Council's children and family social work teams. This arrangement enables the Team, when requested, to conduct independent assessments of parents' capacity to care for their children, and so to provide information to the courts to inform decision-making about their future care. This assessment is a service that is generally carried out by privately employed independent social workers in England, at some cost to the local authority, so the introduction of this separate but in-house service is seen as a way of reducing costs to the local authority.

The role of the Team in the example of practice described later was to assess the ability of a young woman, Amy, to care for her baby daughter, Grace, while providing mother and child with intensive support and supervision in a foster placement. In early discussions with Suzanne Lyus, the Team's manager, she was very clear that the work with Amy and Grace, like all work that the Team does, was only achievable because of their collaborative approach to practice. Interviewing just one of the Team members that worked with Amy and Grace, would, Suzanne suggested, provide only a very one-dimensional view of how the Team assesses and responds to risk. The interview on which this chapter is based was therefore with four team members that worked with parent and child. All team members were employees of the local authority, and part of the social care workforce. This practice example does not therefore address the inherent complexities of multi-agency working, rather focusing on the potential for teams of all kinds to achieve to achieve 'something more than the sum of their parts' (Hallett and Birchall, cited in Rose, 2011, p. 4). The interview offers a window on the process of team collaboration and the importance of discussion and debate when making crucial decisions about levels of acceptable risk.

The first of these team members, crucially, since she provides day-to-day support to the family, is Amy and Grace's foster carer, Jayne Strange, a very experienced carer who has been with the Team since it was established. The second is Wendy Wyatt-Thomas, the 'Senior Assessing Social Worker'. Her role was to work closely with the child's allocated social worker from the local Children and Families team, co-ordinating and undertaking an assessment of Amy's ability to care for Grace Suzanne herself is also a social worker, and she manages the Team. Becky Hopkins, as Children's Services Manager, supervises Suzanne and the work of the Team. This role is quite a complex one, since it involves supporting the Team's relative autonomy and independent status within the council at the same time as managing staff who are part of that service.

Amy and Grace

Amy is 25, and has a learning disability. Amy's first child was removed from her care because of safety concerns. These included an unconfirmed allegation that she had shaken and injured the child. Amy has regular contact with the child who lives with Amy's ex-partner. When Amy became pregnant again, by a different partner (whom she is no longer with), there were considerable concerns from social work and other services about her ability to care safely for another child. Care proceedings were initiated when Grace was born, and she became the subject of an Interim Care Order (s.38, Children Act 1989). Amy and Grace were referred to the Team to allow an assessment of Amy's parenting capacity. The local authority's legal department issued a 'Letter of Instruction' for the Team setting out the need for an independent assessment of Amy's ability to care for Grace and to safeguard her welfare. At that point anxieties about Grace's safety were very high, and the Team was initially asked to provide intensive day- and night-time supervision to ensure Grace's safety. For example, Jayne was required to have Grace in her bedroom overnight, and to be awake to supervise her night-time feeds.

Early days – beginning the assessment

From the start of the placement it was apparent that Amy's self-care and independent living skills were very limited. She was unused to managing her money or planning her day, and lacked practical skills or knowledge about caring for a baby. Jayne's role was particularly demanding with potential to be pulled in two directions; she provided support to Amy while safeguarding Grace's welfare, and contributing to an assessment of Amy's parenting capacity and ability to care for Grace in the longer term. This involved enabling Amy to develop generic independent living skills so she could look after herself, as well as parenting skills so she could provide care to Grace.

The group interview started with a reflection on Amy's first days with Jayne:

> *Suzanne (team manager):* I think we came with an open mind to start with. We came into this work, thinking – how can we make it happen? How can we support Jayne to enable Amy to look after Grace?
>
> *Jayne (foster carer):* Amy was cared, had to be cared for 24 hours a day and supervised 24 hours a day. Grace didn't leave my sight at all – where I went, baby went. Which meant that Amy came as well – to most things – apart from the bathroom! But she came on family visits and shopping outings and things. It became very apparent right from the start that Amy couldn't do anything for herself; she had never been allowed to be who she was. She didn't know how to bath herself, she didn't know when

to wash herself. She didn't know how to cook, she didn't know how to clean, anything. She had no idea of the level of her own intellect really. She wouldn't hold a conversation, she couldn't look you in the eye. She would always walk around shuffling her feet with her face to the floor; a very sorry sight was Amy.

Wendy (Senior assessing social worker): I think with Amy, she found it very difficult didn't she? Because she had to learn completely independent living skills as well as learning to look after a baby – as well as being assessed.

It was evident from the start of the assessment period that there was a steep mountain for Amy to climb. There followed a period of slow, painstaking work to support Amy to develop life and parenting skills. At the same time as Amy was being supported very intensively, the Team was building up a detailed picture of Amy's ability to meet Grace's needs for, for example, food, comfort and stimulation. Wendy, the Senior Assessing Social Worker was visiting Amy, Grace and Jayne every week. She spent time with Amy and Grace, and discussed Jayne's detailed recordings of events over the previous week. These visits established the extent of progress as well as plans for coming weeks.

The assessment required a multi-disciplinary approach with medical and legal involvement as well as the expertise of the Team. Amy also had an advocate who could support her to express herself at meetings and through decision-making processes. The team draws on a range of assessment tools to meet the needs of different parents and children. In this case the Parenting Assessment Manual (PAMs) (McGraw, undated), a systematic, evidence-informed framework for parenting assessment used in the United Kingdom and internationally, which is attuned to the needs of vulnerable families, particularly parents with learning disabilities, was particularly useful. PAMs is designed to present complex information in a format that, at the time of writing, interfaced with the Common Assessment Framework (CAF). This framework has been used in England and Wales to assess children and young people's needs and to develop shared understanding of how to meet those needs (Children's Workforce Development Council, 2009).[2] The Team's approach was also informed by the work of Bentovim et al. (2007), who have built on the ecological approach provided by CAF, to set out a staged approach to assessment, planning and intervention to support interdisciplinary, child-focused and evidence-based practice.

While all Team members brought a range of complementary skills and knowledge to the work with Grace and Amy, these explicit practice frameworks provided a broad consistency and a level of confidence in the evidence base on which their practice was based. This evidence base does not, of course, stand still, so the Team's commitment to ongoing training for all staff was also important. Members of the Team working with Grace and Amy needed to draw on a wide range of skills in, for example, observation, listening, recording and critical analysis. Often the Team needed to be creative and think 'out of the box' to adapt the model of assessment to this family's particular needs. For example, Amy's reading skills were limited so the Team had to be proactive about finding alternatives to the written word. A bank of pictures was identified that allowed Jayne to help Amy create shopping lists and plan day-to-day activities with Grace.

Managing risk, supporting increasing independence

The aim of the placement was to provide a protective environment for both Amy and Grace in which assessment could take place, and at the same time give Amy the opportunity to focus on building a secure, nurturing relationship with Grace in the early months of her life. We go back to the Team now, as they discuss the progress of the assessment:

> *Suzanne*: With Wendy and Jayne working with Amy as closely as they were, they were able to identify very quickly what might help her learn best and what would support her to parent Grace satisfactorily. And you know, clearly the way that Jayne was working with Amy every day was giving her confidence as well.
>
> *Becky (Children's Services Manager)*: Something really important, Jayne, I think is the relationship that you have developed with Amy and that in itself has been a safeguard for Grace.
>
> *Jayne*: …all of a sudden Amy bloomed. She realised I wasn't going to do it for her and she had to get on with it, and she did. She has just gone on learning. She still has problems: she can't read, she is not very good with her times. She is not that brilliant at feeding Grace solids, but hey ho, she does it, and Grace survives and Amy survives and she does it brilliantly. She loves her, which is what we were all worried that she wouldn't do, that she would retaliate [by hurting Grace] like she had before.

These changes were clearly very positive ones, and satisfying for the team as well as Amy. However, as Jayne's use of the word 'survives' suggests, the team had to do some hard thinking about what this progress meant for Grace and her welfare. Amy's past difficulties in caring for her older child – and an allegation of physical abuse – meant that protecting Grace from harm had be to the team's number one priority. At the same time a response to Grace that was too protective might be counterproductive, and indeed might create new risks, including potentially reinforcing Amy's lack of confidence and skills in relating to others and, crucially, to her ability to parent Grace:

Becky: You can hear now the progress that everybody thinks that Amy's made and that's absolutely right, she has. We have seen that and assessed that. But it was quite difficult wasn't it, to change other people's views and to be able to move the plan on and make changes for Amy and Grace along the way? There was one point where you as a team were really clear that actually it was time to reduce the level of supervision that Jayne was providing. But for other professionals [outside the team] that hadn't been working so closely with you it was frightening. And I think it's perfectly understandable in light of Baby P and Victoria Climbié, that child protection teams will tend to be risk averse. For you all it was a risk – but a risk that you felt confident in managing

Jayne: I was worried that if they made all the supervision stay [in place] Amy was going to go back down to the way she was before.

Wendy: Jayne and I had quite a few debates about risk when Grace was still sleeping in Jayne's bedroom. We were beginning to talk about the possibility of Grace going into Amy's bedroom because she'd reliably got up to attend her at the first squeak – and she had always handled her appropriately at night. So we thought that we could look at Grace going into Amy's bedroom. But I was saying, well, what if something happened?

Suzanne: We would review the placement every month and there would often be these difficult discussions because we needed the evidence that Amy could safely take more responsibility for looking after Grace before we could move things on. So we began to test Amy out more and find out more about what support she was going to need, how long the placement maybe needed to last. Grace was subject to an Interim Care Order, so we were very mindful that the child care team needed to agree and be comfortable with everything that was going to happen in placement, and they weren't for a very long time.

Jayne: No, they kept harking back didn't they?

Wendy: I think, to be fair, Amy's previous child was about five weeks old when she said that she'd shaken her and I was very keen to get past that stage before I felt confident that that was less likely to happen. Though, at the same time, she wasn't attached to her first child – she was inundated with lots of telephone calls from her partner at the time and from her family and just completely overwhelmed.

Suzanne: She wasn't ready to be a parent when she had her first child. I think that's what's come out.

Wendy: No, she wasn't ready... But I was able to talk with her about how she felt about Grace and how that was different to her previous child and our conversation went round and round for quite a long time, didn't it? Amy said she found it really difficult, she knew what she thought and felt but she found it difficult to find the words that I would under-stand. So I said, 'Well, you know, lots of people find it difficult to talk about how they feel, you know, it isn't just you'. And then I asked her what she thought when she looked at her because, you know, I'd seen her making eye contact, stroking her face, talking to her, smiling at just everything that she did. Amy said she thought she was lovely and so then I asked her, 'So how would she know that you think she's lovely?' and she started then describing what she did. She said, 'Because I talk to her all the time in a silly, kiddy voice and stroke her face and I kiss her and I tell her, "I love you Grace"'.

So that was just really, really lovely to hear and I felt a bit more confident because Amy was clearly developing an attachment to Grace and she was responding to her. Amy and I had some long conversations about what had happened previously, what was different now. She talked about not being in an abusive relationship anymore, not getting lots of phone calls, family members making demands on her time and her emotions and so she had all of that to give to Grace. So it's only then that I think I felt a bit more reassured about Grace going into her bedroom and decreasing that supervision.

Becky: But it's been a gradual letting go, hasn't it? We usually start off with, you know, an hour at a time and then build that up and once we know that a parent can work with us and everything's going smoothly, then, maybe a fortnight later, we are increasing the level of independence again, so it's always the small step approach really.

This 'small step approach' is a key to the way that the Team works. Stories about risk and social work that make the headlines very often relate to major decisions about risk, which, if people get them wrong, can lead to injury, neglect and even death. Making decisions about risk is, however, part and parcel of day-to-day social work practice, where each 'small' decision, like the decisions the Team was making, with Amy, about the level of responsibility she could take for Grace, helps to contribute to more major and visible life-changing decisions about children's welfare. Crucially, as Becky suggests earlier, this step-by-step approach enabled the professionals themselves to take risks: risks that they felt '*confident in managing*' based on systematic collection and analysis of evidence from working so closely with parent and child.

Risk and change

A long-established tenet of social work practice is that assessment is not a single event but instead is a continuing process. The assessment of Amy's capability to parent Grace was necessarily a dynamic one, as Grace rapidly developed in the early weeks and months of her life, and Amy began to take on increasing responsibility for her care. Communication between Team members, and with Amy, was crucial, to ensure that Amy was having sufficient opportunities to consolidate her learning, and respond to Grace's changing needs. Sometimes, as Wendy explains below, this meant pausing to take stock and to consider different approaches:

> And you can always pause then and say, 'Right, OK, we will stay there for a while, because actually to do any more feels too risky', or you can pull it back if it hasn't worked well. If the child has been put at risk, then you would pull it right back again.

An important strength of the Team's approach is that assessment happens in context: in the place where parenting actually happens, through observation of and support with the day-to-day business of parenting of children during bath times, night-time feeds and changing nappies. Here the Team reflects on the benefits of this approach, and their future plans for work with Grace and Amy:

> *Suzanne*: I think maybe we can come to a view more quickly about risk to a child because we see the whole day and we see it in context. We are seeing the whole routine of the parent and child when we have got them in a placement. If there have been things that haven't gone so well you can put them in context, and Wendy can report on them alongside all the things that have gone well. So we can see possible risks to Grace as a point to work on and developmental rather than thinking Amy's never going to succeed in caring for her.
>
> *Wendy*: Now I think it's about how we support Amy though Grace's different developmental stages as well and how she manages that because every time she changes, she needs a little bit more support.
>
> *Suzanne*: Thinking in terms of the future role, we have had those discussions haven't we, because Grace is being reviewed by a paediatrician

now because her development does seem to be delayed. If Grace has got special needs of her own Amy's parenting is going to need to be better than 'good enough'. And then, if Grace was intellectually brighter than she was, and much more able, what is that going to mean for them? I think by the time the placement finishes we'll have a bit more information about Grace and how her needs will need to be met, but they're difficult discussions aren't they?

Wendy: But we are able to have those discussions aren't we? I know you and I certainly do in supervision and at other times as well, you know, just over a coffee, because they are dilemmas for all of us.

These final quotes bring us full circle to where this chapter started, a reminder of the importance of articulating different understandings of risk, and engaging in active debate to find the 'best' way forward, based on the most current knowledge of what's right for that child and that parent at that time. The stakes were high in this case; the bottom line was Grace's safety. It was essential that the perspectives of all Team members that were working with Grace were heard and taken seriously. While the group decision-making processes described in this chapter seem to have been productive ones, the outcomes of decision-making can be distorted by group dynamics. The group ethos can be one of conformity, in which the overwhelming aim is to reach consensus without conflict between team members (Beckett, 2007). Munro (2002) has described this phenomenon as 'groupthink'. Groupthink can be responsible for extreme decisions, informed by excessive caution or dangerous risk-taking. The work with Grace and Amy was certainly cautious, but, by being open to reviewing the evidence from a range of different perspectives, the Team was able to help Amy to move on and take increasing responsibility for Grace without sudden changes that might have put her at risk. Another danger of groupthink is that teams themselves can become too complacent about their group's decisions. A sense of 'us' and 'them' can develop, fuelled by negative perceptions of other child protection professionals (Munro, 2002). This may mean that the views of others outside the immediate small team are discounted or ignored. This underlines how important it was in this case that this team was outward as well as inward facing in its debates and decision-making processes.

There were still many uncertainties about the future for Grace and Amy. Looking ahead to the future, the Team was cautiously positive about Amy's progress and ability to parent her child in the longer term, and was anticipating that she would, with agreement from her Guardian and the Courts, be able to move to supported accommodation with Grace. Uncertainties about her potential vulnerability, about her ability to parent a lively toddler or a school-age child, and about Grace herself, and concerns about possible developmental delay, were not going to go away, but, for now, all the signs were promising.

The context for practice

The model of intensive support and assessment that the Team uses is not a commonplace one, and when it was first established there was no 'blueprint' for its operation. It has taken time for the Team to develop its own way of working, and to ensure that its foster carers and other staff have access to the level of ongoing training and support they need. As we have seen, Team members are encouraged to participate in decision-making, and there are a range of opportunities for formal and informal support, discussion and debate. For example, there is a weekly meeting for all staff and regular individual supervision with opportunities for reflection on practice. There is mutual recognition of what different team members bring to their roles. For example, as the interview suggests, Jayne's role as foster carer was a central and valued one, in which she supported, modelled and encouraged Amy to grow and develop, both as an individual and as Grace's parent, but did not disempower her as a parent by 'doing for' her. It was evident too that Wendy's relationship with Amy, her support to Jayne, and her ability to draw in a range of knowledge – about the law, policy, up-to-date research, child development and attachment, for example – was crucial to the assessment process. Working to a shared framework, including the PAMs model, helped to ensure that the assessment process was systematic, structured and evidence-based. At the same time it was evident that the Team was able to respond in a very flexible way to changing circumstances when necessary. Munro (2011) has argued that child protection in England has become too heavily weighted towards complying with prescription, including limited timescales for social work assessments, which she suggests distort practice. One of the features of the Team approach is that it is less hampered by targets and bureaucratic practices than the majority of social work teams. All staff have a level of autonomy and there seems to be respect for each other's capabilities, as well as a supportive management structure and a 'hotline' to management support in a crisis.

The Team's approach might be perceived by some, especially perhaps social workers in hard-pressed social work teams with relatively little opportunity for the kind of intensive engagement with service users described in this chapter, to be 'a luxury'. The Team and its managers, however would argue that their intensive approach that focuses on the individual support needs of the parents as well as the needs of the child or children, is a necessary one if a realistic picture of people's needs, strengths and difficulties is to be achieved within the lived context of their day-to-day lives. Austrian (cited in Aldgate, 2011) emphasises the importance of tailoring assessment to the individual through a process that recognises the uniqueness of the person and their particular circumstances. There are no shortcuts; the process of assessment, including the development of trust and confidence between parents, children and workers, is critical to the outcome. Here 'best practice' is not about the practice of a single social worker or other professional, but what can be achieved through collaborative endeavour.

Notes

1. The 'Team' is capitalised in this chapter to distinguish it from other teams that it works with.
2. The recommendations of the Munro Review (2011) prompted plans to revise the Common Assessment Framework in England and Wales. Scotland's framework, the National Practice Model, has some similar features, including the My World Assessment Framework.

9 'Trying to Get It Right' with David: Addressing the Risk of Sexually Harmful Behaviour

Jock Mickshik and Jean Gordon

Jock has worked with sexual abuse since 1994: with children at risk of harm and, as a probation officer, assessing, supervising and treating adult men with convictions for sexual assault of children and adults. This dual perspective supports him in his current role as a specialist risk assessment and treatment worker for a local authority, working with adults suspected of, or with historical convictions for, child sexual abuse, and with young people who display sexually harmful behaviour.

Questions to ask yourself as you read:

- What tensions does Jock encounter when balancing David's right to choice and independence against the safety of other children?

- How can social workers best address potentially sensitive issues, such as sex and sexuality when they are working with children and families?

- How do you respond to challenges to your expertise and authority?

Introduction

Working with risk, while always challenging, is very much part and parcel of social work practice. Assessing and managing the risk of sexual abuse, and particularly child sexual abuse, is an aspect of practice that many practitioners and managers find particularly daunting. The topic is an emotive one, which can cause strong reactions, from anxiety and fear to revulsion, feelings which are often fanned by sensational media coverage. Jock's considerable experience, and, in particular, his understanding of the multi-faceted nature of social work with both victims and perpetrators of sexual abuse, might have made it difficult for him to select a single example of practice to explore for this section on risk. However, his choice to tell David's story was an easy one, as he explained:

> [Iif] I look back on my career, I will think of one thing that I tried to get right and feel proud of that, David would be right up there. It is just that sense of moving from a professional task that I have the skills and the specialism to help with, to a personal commitment to this kid.

Jock's reference to 'trying to get it right' is a key one in terms of his stance as a critical social work practitioner. As he goes on to explain there are no easy 'rights' and 'wrongs' when it comes to working with children with complex needs who pose a risk to other children. Working with David also tested his personal and professional values in ways that have had a lasting impact on his social work practice.

David

David was initially referred to Jock by his social worker, Helen, when he was nearly 13. His foster carers, Yvonne and Jim, had become very concerned about his obsessive masturbatory behaviour which included using objects such as cuddly toys to masturbate with, sometimes in public places. David's early years were traumatic. His early childhood was characterised by his mother's drug and alcohol misuse, and a succession of violent and sexually dangerous men who visited or lived in his home. He has learning difficulties resulting from brain injuries caused by an assault in the first year of his life. These resulted in significant brain damage, including partial loss of sight and impairment of his verbal language abilities. It seems very likely that David continued to witness and experience significant emotional, sexual and physical abuse and neglect until his eventual removal from his mother's care to his foster carers when he was 12 years old. David came into local authority care under s.20 of the Children Act 1989[1] which conveys duties on the local authority to provide accommodation to children when their parents are unable to care for them. He is accommodated with the agreement of his mother, although there is no realistic prospect that he will ever return to her care. Jock explained that a fuller picture of David's early years had only begun to emerge since David went into foster care:

> David really required one to one, 24/7, in terms of his needs. It is rather like having a five or six year old in a twelve/thirteen/ fourteen year old's body as he is growing older. And his mum certainly didn't have the capacity to look after him... David was a challenge because he brought with him a huge amount of behavioural issues, that were not just around his learning difficulties, it was particularly the sexual issue, a very difficult thing for the foster carers to get their heads around.

Responding quickly to heightened risks

The concerns highlighted by his carers about David's potentially harmful behaviour suddenly intensified after an incident at David's special school. The school reported that David and a younger girl with learning difficulties had been observed engaging in what appeared to be sexualised behaviour together. David and the other child were interviewed but neither made any disclosure. As Jock explained:

> [W]e weren't able to have a good clear narrative of what happened, whether they were playacting, whether it was led by David, or led by the girl, but there was demonstration that, given the opportunity, David out of supervision would be able to behave in a sexualised way at the very least, even if he wasn't perhaps sure what he was doing... It's a big issue and it brought back into focus David being around much younger children and what he could do.

A rapid response was clearly required and Jock instigated a 'Strategic Risk Management Meeting', a forum similar to a Child Protection Conference. His explanation of the rationale for this collaborative model of risk management used in his area is one that picks up some key aspects of best practice working with sexual abuse, and, indeed, risk of all kinds:

> [W]e know what goes wrong with social work, there is different information held by different people that doesn't get shared, and the idea of those meetings is to get all the information put on the table so everybody knows what it is, and it is shared. From that we then develop a plan, how to intervene and then we set a review day, so you plan your timescale to do the work.

This all sounds quite logical and straightforward, but, like many encounters in social work, this meeting brought some surprises and unexpected learning, not least for Jock himself.

Jock approached his role as chair of the risk management meeting confidently. It is one that he had carried out many times before, and he has developed a style of facilitation that has worked well, often in very fraught circumstances. He started by going round the room and getting everybody's viewpoint about David. Jock aimed to gain a picture how he was functioning at home and at school, and to begin to assess potential and actual risk of harm. When, however, he came to sum up these perspectives and to name the risks that David might present to others, the meeting began to take an unexpected turn:

> I said to the group that we know from past experience that, if we didn't intervene effectively to manage David's behaviour, should he attack sexually a three or four year old boy or girl, it would be unlikely we would be able to keep him in the community, that he would perhaps spend the rest of his life being very restricted within a mental health unit. He wouldn't ever go to prison but we would be talking about some very restrictive secure accommodation because of that.

> Now, to me, that just seemed obvious, that we can't allow anybody with learning disabilities to sexually attack little children, it can't happen. When it does, the state steps in. So I said that as a matter of fact and the school teacher and the carers burst into tears. I felt dreadful. It really affected me, and I was just stating what was obvious. What I had underestimated – in both a bad way and in a good way – is just how much the school and carers loved this boy.

> On reflection I realised I come into the meeting with that 'professional hat' on and looked at it logistically: 'we have an issue here, we need to plan and have an intervention strategy to manage this behaviour. If we don't, the outcome will be this, this and this'. I hadn't realised just how dedicated these people were. They had a personal commitment – which was very good for me [to hear]. I think in hindsight that I would have been much gentler, saying, it is in David's best interests we do this because he is a lovely kid and we really want him [to do well]. So I think I would have spun it in a different way so that it could have been heard without that level of distress.

Jock's reflection on what happened at this meeting is a reminder that workers need not only to 'know' practice, in the sense of Jock's ability to use, for example, relevant theory, research and legislation, but also be able 'not to know': to be open to other ways of seeing the world.

Glaister (2008) suggests that acknowledging 'not knowing', accepting that uncertainty is part and parcel of social work, is a core principle of critical practice. Jock's willingness to really listen to what other people were saying at the meeting was a turning point in the work with David, the school and his carers. It involved an acceptance that, while professional knowledge of the kind that Jock carries with him is essential to effective, evidence-informed practice, there are lots of other kinds of knowledge which are as valid. The other participants at the meeting brought knowledge of David and his potential, as well as their own experiences of working with and parenting children. At the heart of Jock's ability to cast off the mantle of 'professional expert' are core social work values about developing respectful, empowering relationships which value 'the equality, worth and dignity' (International Federation of Social Workers, 2012) that everyone – service user, carer or professional colleague – brings to the table.

A united approach

The response to Jock's concerns about David's future at the meeting was such a strong one that this effectively united participants in a shared commitment to addressing risk:

> what I then got was this wall of dedication, care and commitment … so my guilt was balanced by this admiration … there was a team there, who – come hell or high water – would support this guy … and I was thinking, 'Yes! With that in place we should be able to get there'.

Jock was able to draw on this strength of feeling at the meeting, and, with the participants, developed three parallel strategies for managing the immediate risks that David potentially posed to others. There were also risks to David's longer term well-being and stability because some of the possible responses to reduce this risk (e.g. a move to secure accommodation) might result in him having to move from his foster carers who were highly committed to caring for him, and with whom he seemed very settled and content.

It is worth, at this point taking a step back and exploring Jock's thinking and decision-making about how to intervene to reduce the risks associated with David's behaviour. Throughout the interview Jock reflected on the complexity of making judgements about risk, especially when that risk is posed by a child such as David who is himself highly vulnerable. The rights movement has helped to challenge the once taken-for-granted assumption that people with learning disabilities who expressed their sexuality were either 'asexual or promiscuous' (Morrow, 2003, p. 148). In David's case, his emerging sexuality was, as for any adolescent, part of growing up and becoming an adult, but the impact of his behaviour on himself and others clearly had to be addressed. Jock's starting point for his work with young people who display sexually harmful behaviour is that children *show sexual behaviour because they are acting and showing us what has been happening to them.* Framing David's sexualised behaviour in this way suggested that the primary aim for intervention was a therapeutic one, to try to address this problem in the context of childhood experiences. At the same time, as Jock had made clear at the initial meeting, sexually harmful behaviour, whatever the cause of the behaviour and whether the risk is posed by an adult or another child, must be responded to urgently and action taken to minimise the risk of harm. The age and maturity of a child displaying dangerous behaviour also has to be taken into consideration. David was now entering adolescence, when *the line becomes much more blurred between acting out that behaviour and beginning to perpetrate against others.*

Jock's role involved negotiating a delicate balance between these two inter-connected aims of intervention: therapy and risk reduction. How 'a presenting problem' – in this case, David's sexualised behaviour – is viewed can result in very different trajectories, both in terms of how social work practice takes place and the potential outcomes for children and families. Jock explained how he teased out the evidence that informed his decision-making in relation to David. First, Jock's work with David was informed by his day-to-day practice experience of working therapeutically with children, simultaneously aiming to maximise their potential and taking action to protect others from harm. At the same time he was incorporating his understanding of a number of theoretical approaches: the importance of attachments to primary care givers, how children learn and how they develop resilience. A familiarity with relevant research findings was also important. For example research findings furnished Jock with the evidence to challenge a prevalent view that all young people who show sexually harmful behaviour will necessarily go on to become adult sex offenders (Vandiver, 2006; Worling, 2004). Another thread of knowledge that Jock drew on was about the possible impact on David and on those he might put at risk by *not* intervening to address the problems being identified by Yvonne and Jim. The finding that sexually harmful behaviour by adolescents can have a disproportionately negative impact on their adult self-esteem and relationships (Hackett, Phillips,

Masson and Balfe, 2011) gave further strength to Jock's conviction that professionals and carers should intervene as soon as possible to manage David's sexualised behaviour. This was to protect others from potential harm *and* to try to ensure that David himself did not suffer these kinds of adverse consequences in adulthood. Sometimes labelling the breadth of evidence that social workers may base their decision-making on as 'eclectic' can be regarded as a way of avoiding difficult questions about 'why' the practitioner has made a particular decision. Jock's 'eclectic' account, however, was about his engagement in a creative and iterative process involving the teasing out different evidence forms and testing out their relevance for this particular service user in this particular practice context. Pollio (2006, p. 231) suggests that this acknowledgement of 'the real world messiness' of social work practice is essential to the 'art of evidence-based practice'.

So how was the knowledge gained from this assessment to be used to intervene? Jock weighed up the advantages and disadvantages of using different 'off the peg' intervention models. Jock has had training in and made use of a number of well-evaluated programmes to address sexually harmful behaviour. He had seen positive outcomes with these kinds of interventions but also knew that it was vital that the programme had a good 'fit' with David's particular needs and the contexts that might trigger concerning sexualised behaviour. His assessment, with the multidisciplinary team, was that existing programmes were unlikely to match David's particular needs and unpredictable developmental pathway. It was rapidly becoming evident, with high levels of concern about David's behaviour and future risk of harm to others, that no single intervention was going to be effective. Jock instead worked with David, his carers and the school to develop three linked intervention strategies. These strategies harnessed the motivation and energy of the 'team' of adults around David, so developing a collaborative and highly consistent approach to the risks that David might present to himself and others at school and home.

Two interventions were designed to address immediate risk through behavioural change, based on the application of learning theory. First, school staff agreed to work together to prevent David from going to the toilet at school to masturbate when he wished to. Instead, they were to use a distracting technique, involving him in a classroom activity, or taking him for a short walk in the school grounds (a strategy later to be christened by school staff as the 'wank walk'!). The second was an intervention focused on directly changing David's behaviour at home, and required Yvonne and Jim to give David a very consistent message, that masturbation *is fine, but it's **not** public, and it **would** cause offence.*

Therefore David was told that he could masturbate in private in his bedroom or private shower/toilet, but not in public spaces.

The third approach was led jointly by Jock and by David's social worker, Helen. It took the form of work with David to try to support him, not only to change his sexual behaviour, but to understand the need to moderate this behaviour. Jock, while extremely experienced in this field of work, now found himself in relatively uncharted territory. He had undertaken direct work in the past using a cognitive behavioural approach, a talking therapy that aims to change maladaptive emotions and behaviours by helping individuals to change established thinking patterns. However, he had used this approach with children who could engage with questions like, 'What were you thinking when you did that?' or 'What were your feelings about behaving in this kind of way?' David didn't have the cognitive or verbal skills to engage with this kind of exploration. Another method that he had used was to use drawing as a means of communication with children, but David's very limited vision closed off this route. They experimented briefly with using colour alone to help David express his feelings, but this was not successful. Again Jock found himself weighing up his clinical experience and his knowledge of the fairly limited research about addressing sexually harmful behaviour in children. He lighted on the possibility of using play as a means of therapy. Jock was aware that non-directive play therapy has been shown to have less positive outcomes than a cognitive behavioural approach in addressing sexually harmful behaviour (Carpentier et al., 2006). However, with the therapeutic options narrowing, he and Helen elected to try out a version of this approach. David himself was always eager to engage in imaginative play, and this method might just start to address not only the currently concerning behaviour – obsessive masturbation – but also help David to begin to find sustainable ways of managing his sexuality in the future without harming himself or others.

Through a process of trial and error Jock and Helen found that the most effective way to communicate with David was through play with a doll's house. The brief play sessions were introduced, each ending with tea-making and biscuit-eating as rewards for concentration. While the sessions did not lead to any detailed disclosures about the early childhood neglect and trauma that he had experienced, they did give David an opportunity to talk about some of the things that had happened to him. He was able, for example, to describe with great accuracy the mattress he slept on in his mother's house and the 'safe-place' he was put in when 'bad things' were happening to her.

Although David's play itself was not led by Helen or Jock, Jock was specific and directive in his communications with David about his sexualised behaviour, using the dolls to convey clear messages:

> Using the dolls I could explain, 'This is a little person…this is a big person…a little person doesn't have sexual feelings. You do, David. But you cannot bring sexual feelings to a little person'. So, just repeat, repeat, just going back reminding him every session doing that.
>
> For this work it was very important that I could talk about sex and sexuality in a really open and frank way that engages the young person. I think adults – and even therapists shy away sometimes from being very direct with young people, particularly with guys.

Helen and Jock worked with David in this way for about eight months. During this they were meeting regularly with Yvonne, Jim and school staff in regular risk management meetings, reviewing progress and fine-tuning the three interventions that they were working together on.

Making a difference over time

One theme that came over very strongly during the interview with Jock was the way in which he, and the rest of the team were committed to work with David in the longer term:

> With David we stayed in there – because of his learning needs, because of his disability, because of the risk issues, we stayed. That was really important to all of us. I got infected by the team – his carers', his school's dedication to him in the end, and it became a real issue of principle.

Over time, there was a steady diminishing of David's visits to the toilet to masturbate, and, by the time of the fourth or fifth risk management meeting, the school was no longer reporting significant concerns:

> [W]hat the outcome had been was that the school had hugely reduced their own anxiety…[they were saying that], 'We can manage this behaviour. He has sexualised behaviours, yes, but we have a strategy to deal with it. We feel confident about it.' David himself was now much more focused at school, he was in a group where he was making more friends. I think that might have happened anyway, that wasn't due to us and the therapy that we did, I think that was the peer group and the brilliant school he was in. It was just nice that friendship forming with other kids

with learning difficulties, boys and girls, had a much safer context to it, and much less issue of risk.

At the same time Jock saw David's foster carers, Jim and Yvonne, becoming a lot more confident about managing his behaviour. There were difficulties, and setbacks, and times when additional support and advice was needed, but the overall feeling of the group was that the risk to other children's safety was gradually decreasing. After about eight months Jock and Helen decided to end the regular direct work with David. It was not that they thought that this work was 'finished', or that David had no further potential for development, but rather that they assessed that they had gone as far as they could in direct therapeutic work, and that this work was now beginning to kick start changes in other parts of his life:

> You know, you love to go into therapy thinking, 'I am going to do a good piece of therapy work, it's all going to come out'. Well actually, I have been around way too long to believe that now! What we did is I think we just unlocked a door, that is all we did, we just turned the key of the door, and it was really for David then to open the door to tell his carers things that happened to him, then to shut the door again. And I think that process will go on for many years, many years before we get a better picture.

This insight provides an important reminder that, for young people like David, with traumatic backgrounds and complex needs, there are no 'quick fixes'. Jock suggested that it is only possible to look at the potential impact of the therapeutic work that he and Helen did with David if we also look at the how this interacted with other influences in his life. For example, the high level of support from school and growing attachment to Yvonne and Jim over time appear to have allowed David, in his own time, to feel safe enough to begin talking to his foster carers and school staff about past traumas in his life. As home and school addressed the specific risks related to David's sexualised behaviour, these risks decreased, as did his foster parents' anxiety. This in turn gave Yvonne and Jim the confidence to tackle new challenges as they arose.

Sustaining change

The risk management meetings continued for some time after the play sessions finished, with Jock providing support and advice in the background. Gradually the focus shifted from managing risk to broader matters of his welfare and, as he steadily approached adulthood, making plans for the future:

> It has been a privilege to see his confidence and skills growing in direct proportion to the care and commitment of the carers around him. David and the community have, I believe, become safer as a result of our intervention and team work...And it was team work, it wasn't me resolving anything, it wasn't the carers, it wasn't the school, it was **all** of us, joined up together working as a team, each with our own little team. You know I had a very powerful role in that but my role was to coordinate and to bring it together to review it to say, 'How are we doing guys? Is it working? Is this working with David?' And it was. It didn't have to be me, it could have been someone else, it just needed someone with the commitment and the experience to work with everyone and help this young person to manage his behaviour himself.

Looking into the future, Jock sees one of the key challenges for carers and practitioners will be how best to support David's right as an adult to have a safe, informed and consenting sex life.

Reflecting on practice

It was evident during our interview that, despite a long career in a challenging practice area, Jock remains fully engaged with his role as a specialist social worker. It is important to him that he continues to have opportunities to engage directly with young people and to motivate others to be similarly enthused by practice:

> I read up, I am still fascinated; I read about it, I am really interested in that academic side, so that appeals to me. I like the teaching of it, I like imparting the knowledge of it to other people, I like helping other professionals to be aware that this isn't [just] something out there, they can get their heads around it, they can do it. And you know, I still have the opportunity to be in a room sitting with a young person and a family and the minute that that stops is the minute I just stop doing my work.

Looking back at his work with David, Jock identified that one of the main areas of learning for him – one that he has continued to draw on in his work with other young people – was the importance of recognising that there are always many stories to be told by and about children. Jock's ability to listen to and respond to others' views about David and about risk in the initial meeting was, for him, not only a significant event in the decision-making in this case, but also powerful because it reminded Jock of how important it was to be open to these different perspectives. Had Jock, in the powerful role of the 'expert' chair of a risk management meeting, *failed* to hear or to respond to expressions of that commitment to support David to change his behaviour, then both the process and outcome of the helping process might have had a different, and possibly, from the perspective of David, his carers and the school a less successful one.

At the time of writing Jock still assists in reviewing David's progress. Eighteen months after our interview David was still at his school and feedback from the staff was very positive:

> He has a degree of independence – going to and from toilets safely on his own now – and is a popular and valued member of his student group. There have been absolutely no concerns about his sexual behaviour and he is treated like any other student, albeit with the necessary support to meet his learning needs. I again raised the question of whether we still needed the risk meetings and the consensus was that we should have one more final meeting in six months then conclude the process of risk management.

Jock and David's social worker have now designed a training programme that they are taking into specialist schools and colleges to help support staff to understand the complex issues of managing rights and risks in relation to sexual behaviour and learning disability. Their work with David, his foster family and the school has been the template for that programme.

Note

1. The equivalent legal provision in Scotland is s.25 of the Children (Scotland) Act 1995.

10 Myra: A Balancing Act

Clive Rosenthal and Jean Gordon

Clive is a senior social worker in a local authority Children in Need team in England. He has been a social worker since 1972 and has previously worked with children and families in a variety of different roles which have included a focus on advocacy, children's rights, training and family group conferencing.

Questions to ask yourself as you read:

- Why and how had social work with Myra and her family got 'stuck'?
- Are there tensions between supporting parents to care for their children and protecting children from harm?
- What was the role of reflection on practice in this case?

Introduction

Social workers make difficult decisions about risk to children and young people all the time. Some are day-to-day decisions about when to visit a family at home or pick up the phone to speak to another professional, while others are major decisions that will have a significant and often lasting impact on children and their families (Baker and Wilkinson, 2011, p. 13). This chapter is about one of those big decisions, about whether to support a young person, Myra (14), to remain with her family, or to seek to protect her from present and future harm by enabling her to move out of her family home.

The previous two chapters have charted a relatively well-defined social work process from first referral, through risk assessment, intervention and review. This is not to say that these examples of practice were straightforward, or that the future safety of Grace or David is completely secured, but both cases involved thoughtful, planned collaborative work, and, for the practitioners involved, a sense of progress towards agreed goals over time. In contrast this chapter provides a snapshot of social work with a family in an apparently constant state of crisis and dispute, and of service responses that have tended to be reactive and short term in their impact. Several assessments had been undertaken over the years, and there had been sporadic intervention in response to concerns about Myra, and, before that, her elder sister, Clara. A number of social workers had taken responsibility for the case, and the family had become 'well known' to services such as social work and education, with all the weight of professional fatigue and frustration that can accompany this expression. Practising social workers will recognise this description of a family with chronic problems, where both the family and professionals may share similarly pessimistic beliefs about the likelihood of achieving positive outcomes. It can appear that every approach has been tried and failed, and that none of the available alternatives for intervention are going to make a difference.

Clive's choice of this particular case example was not because it provides any 'easy answers' to how social workers actually go about improving children's lives. Instead his work with Myra and his family played out against a backdrop of complex family dynamics, high emotions and parental hostility, such that he doubts whether the word 'best' could ever be applied to it. However, as often is the case in social work, it is the most personally testing examples of practice that also provide the greatest opportunity for critical reflection and, ultimately, for learning.

Myra and her family

When Clive first met Myra she was living with her mother, elder sister and younger brother. Her father, Frank, left the family ten years ago after serious domestic violence towards his wife. Myra was 13 when she first came to the notice of social services because her relationship with her mother, Nicola, was rapidly deteriorating. Mother and daughter began to have serious confrontations, often ending with Myra leaving home and going missing, sometimes for days at a time. On two occasions Nicola contacted the social work emergency duty team to ask them to 'take it away'. These volatile requests could be sparked off by apparently quite minor lapses in behaviour by Myra. Myra visited her father from time to time, but the quality of the relationship was very poor, with Frank oscillating between a wish to 'fight his daughter's corner' (against Nicola, and, sometimes, against social work and other services) and outright hostility towards her.

A number of different approaches to support Myra at home and school had been attempted, including involvement of a Family Support Worker and additional educational support. Alternative accommodation with her father was briefly explored, but it rapidly became apparent that Frank could not provide her with a safe or stable home. Meanwhile concerns were steadily rising about Myra's safety. During her frequent absences from home she associated with individuals known to be involved in criminal activity. She often drank heavily, used cannabis and was candid about being sexually active. Alarmingly, Myra reported that on one occasion an unknown man had tried to abduct her in a car.

There were, therefore, considerable and well-evidenced risks to Myra. These included day-to-day risks to her safety due to her vulnerability, such as the possibility of pregnancy and of physical harm, as well as longer term risks, associated with the continuing rejection she was experiencing from both parents, poor school attendance and the absence of a stable and positive home life. However, it appeared that these risks had not, when her case was allocated to Clive, been considered sufficiently concerning to trigger a child protection conference, and there was no formal safety plan in place. Past records revealed quite a similar pattern of breakdown in relationships between Myra's elder sister and Nicola, and of poor school attendance. However, then, as now, there had been no major intervention, and these problems were thought by both to now be resolved. Meanwhile the hostility that was so evident at home was mirrored in family communications with social services staff, including a poor relationship between Myra and her previous social worker. Overall, when Clive was allocated this case, social work with this family was drifting, jolting from one unresolved crisis to another with little or no evidence of amelioration in the risks to Myra, or longer term planning for her future. Local authorities in England and Wales have a duty (under s.17 of the Children Act 1989[1]) to promote the upbringing of children by their families. Crucially, however, this duty has to be set against the Act's paramount consideration, the welfare of the child. During the six months Clive and other professionals were to work with Myra, Nicola and the rest of the family, it became clear that inaction was not an option: the growing risks to Myra's safety, welfare and future had to be addressed. The central question was, could Myra's welfare be promoted and safeguarded at home, and if not, was there an alternative plan that would meet her needs better than remaining with her family?

A fracas in reception

Clive's first contact with Myra and her mother took place in the reception area of his social work office:

> There was a fracas in reception and what had happened was there was a 14 year old young person and her mother having a rather animated confrontation and when I got out there they were literally fighting over a mobile: not punching each other but dragging each other around the room fighting over a mobile phone. They managed to get separated, Nicola left and I ended up with Myra, who had thrown all the information leaflets over the floor in the reception area. I obviously tried to calm her down, she was distressed following the argument with Nicola. I said, 'Shall we pick the leaflets up?', and to my amazement she helped me to tidy the leaflets up.

> Since then, we – the family support worker, the school, and I – have been working...to restore the relationship between Myra and her mother. I have done a lot of time with both of them, with the young person and the mother and with them together. Myra, when she is in a calm mood, which she is most of the time, is very articulate, palpably intelligent young person, perfectly capable of reflecting on her own situation and what behaviours might lead her to difficulties, and the dangers of being out late. When you can have a sensible conversation you have a very sensible conversation. When she's in the full of teenage angst, you can't have any sort of sensible conversation, it is just the world is against her, and she will snap your head off.

Clive's reference to 'doing a lot of time' with the family is a telling one; this was a case that demanded a great deal of time and energy from him, both in terms of trying to co-ordinate the existing plan of addressing risks to Myra through home support, and responding to frequent crisis situations as well as referrals from the police and the local authority's emergency duty team. Clive identified one of his strengths as a willingness and ability to engage with young people. He reflected in particular on the importance of being able to sustain relationships with young people through unsettled and traumatic times, and to work through hostility and negativity:

I like young people and their voices ... I think I carry on in this role because at the end of the day it's the welfare of the young person that is why we are here, and we are trying to make the best for that young person. I think I can value her for what she is and go through that just, live with the hostility for a while and relate to the person that's there. It's bizarre because she and the family cause me more headaches than almost any other young person I have had before and take up a disproportionate amount of my time. [But] you know, underneath it all there is a troubled young human being, who needs a bit of support.

Children and young people engaged in child protection processes are known to value trusting relationships with their social workers, which help to make them feel they are part of achieving positive changes in their lives. However, often the reality is rather different; significant numbers of children have minimal relationships with their social workers, with little or no face-to-face contact outwith meetings and reviews (The Office of the Children's Commissioner, 2011). Child abuse inquiries have repeatedly identified lack of direct engagement with children and young people as a major failing of professional practice. Prompted by the Munro report (2011) and other research evidence, safeguarding guidance in England and Wales is now unequivocal: 'Anyone working with children should see and speak to the child; listen to what they say; take their views seriously; and work with them collaboratively when deciding how to support their needs' (HM Government, 2013, p. 9). As emphasised in the Relationships section of this book, making effective relationships with children takes time, and a willingness to take opportunities for what Ferguson (2008) refers to as 'intimate' practice: in cars, parks, schools and indeed in social work waiting rooms. It also requires organisational practices that recognise the importance of these relationships 'so that social workers can get to know children, and are not viewed as remote but powerful figures' (Ibid., p. 15). However, as Daniel (2007, p. 121) suggests, even when time is pressured, skilled workers must be able to 'convey the message to the child that they take his or her views seriously'.

From fire fighting to re-assessment

Assessment practice in the United Kingdom is strongly influenced by an ecological model which considers the developmental needs of the child in the context of parents' or other carers' capacity to respond to those needs, and the impact of wider family, community and environmental influences (HM Government, 2013; Scottish Government, 2012). Use of a conceptual assessment framework, provides a systematic means of identifying and analysing the impact of both risk and protective factors in the child's world (Bywater, 2012, p. 52). There was evidently a plan in place, based on a previous assessment that the focus of intervention was to enable Myra to remain at home by providing support to the family. However, assessment is necessarily a continuous process that has to take account of changing needs and circumstances. To gain a current understanding of risk and protective factors for Myra, required Clive to have a good understanding of child development, and, in particular, to recognise the impact for her of adolescence:

> It's been important to understand the context of where Myra is at. First of all there is her developmental stage; I am aware that she's going through or reaching puberty and there's all the stuff, all the things physically, emotionally, that come along with the baggage with puberty. Generally people at her age are tempted to experiment. When we were young, we did the same, we weren't perfect in every way. Myra pushes the boundaries and is the kind of person that the press is all too happy to stereotype as a 'yob'. I think that kind of labelling is unhelpful and discriminatory. I don't think we should be too worried about a certain level of adolescent rebellion. But if she does behave in ways which put herself in danger – which she certainly does – then that **is** a concern and we need to act. But you have to understand why she is behaving that way and recognise what's in it for her. So the focus of my work isn't, 'You bad person for doing these things'. It's, 'We need to look at the safety of this. I understand why you want to go off doing that, but is it a safe environment for you?' And you have to keep valuing the young person at the centre of it all I think.

Here Clive identifies the importance of an understanding of how children develop, and particularly the impact of adolescence, as well as his commitment to social work values of respect for individuals and an anti-oppressive approach. Reder and Duncan (1999, p. 101, cited by Smeeton, 2012, p. 156) identify the importance of developing a 'dialectic mindset'; a way of interrogating the available evidence, being open to a range of alternative (and possibly contradictory) explanations for any given situation. One possible interpretation of Myra's behaviour was that it was 'just' teenage experimentation, a phase that would pass with time. The fact that her elder sister also had difficulties in adolescence, now apparently resolved, might encourage this assessment. However, a re-assessment of the seriousness of the danger that Myra – rather than Clara or any other hypothetical teenager – was exposed to was required. In this quote Clive drew on some of his own experience of adolescence to try to understand what might be considered to be 'normal' in terms of teenage experimentation. Care does, of course, have to be taken about using personal experiences of childhood and being parented to inform practice. On the one hand, a recognition of how our experience of being a child might affect our professional judgement is a key aspect of reflective practice. On the other, social workers have to be very careful that their decision-making is not clouded by their particular personal beliefs about the nature of 'normal adolescence' or a 'good parenting'. Wilson (2008, cited by Smeeton, 2012), while seeing the need to recognise 'the child within', emphasises that a central principle to effective ethical social work with children is 'the ability to understand what it is like to be *that child* within the context of *their family*' (Ibid., p. 155).

Complementary to his direct work with Myra alone, was Clive's engagement with Myra as a member of her family:

> For me, the dynamic between Myra and her mother is interesting: Nicola can't deal with Myra's attitude. Myra is very in her face and challenging, confrontational, and Nicola responds with more confrontation. Using confrontation with confrontation you get an escalation. But usually parents can take the adult role to try to step back and calm it down. Nicola doesn't seem able to. Sometimes it is clearly Nicola doing the provocation in the first place. Sometimes it seems to be like two adolescents together having a bit of a spat, rather than one adult and one adolescent... At the same time, some of the things Myra has done are seriously out of order, like going missing, which she has done very, very often, sometimes she runs off and she has been missing for up to two or three days and been found by the police, and any parent would struggle with accepting that. So Nicola's probably right to be angry sometimes, but, in terms of what comes first, I don't know, is it Myra's behaviour in some ways, that leads Nicola to reject her, or is it the constant rejection that make her feel the need to rebel? What is clear is that Nicola is clearly a very, very needy person and I think she finds it very hard to prioritise her child's needs, and she cries very often, she cries virtually at every meeting that we discuss the situation, she will end up crying.

At this time Clive was working closely with not only Myra and her mother, but also her school, a Looked After Children (LAC) educational officer, and a Family Support worker, whose remit was to provide home-based support to the family. In an attempt to formulate a more effective plan to address risks to Myra, he initiated a Family Group Conference to bring the parents and involved professionals together to collectively address the concerns about risk to Myra. This initiative was abandoned after a single meeting because neither parent was prepared to meet again. Meanwhile there was no evidence of reduction of the risks identified for Myra. Turney et al. (2011) suggest that practitioners can find themselves trying to manage 'contradictory imperatives': keeping their focus on the needs of the young person while simultaneously attempting to develop effective working relationships with parents. When there is a shared understanding between professionals and parents about the nature and seriousness of risks to young people, and a willingness to work collaboratively, then this tension is manageable. However, in a situation where Nicola, despite serious attempts to engage and work with her, was responding to rising professional concerns about Myra's safety with hostility and denial, Clive and his colleagues were quickly running out of alternatives for intervention. Looking back on his work with Myra and her family, he reflected that:

> A lot of time with this family I have been firefighting which wasn't really part of the plan. It seemed to be crisis after crisis after crisis: with [Myra] going missing, with Nicola saying, 'I can't look after her any more', with Nicola contacting us every time there was a nasty incident, which happened an awful lot, same with Frank, when she stayed there. So we have been reacting a lot of the time. Unfortunately, this isn't productive or positive in terms of any case plan.

A change of direction

It was becoming increasingly evident to Clive and other professionals working with Myra that decisive action was required that would, at the very least, give her some safe 'breathing space' away from the family. Throughout the weeks of crisis that preceded this point, Clive had been keeping a steady focus on developing a reliable and trusting relationship with Myra that would enable her to feel safe enough with him to speak about what mattered to her and how she saw her future. This direct work was often challenging and opportunities for engagement often occurred unexpectedly and at times of crisis. Describing a car journey with Myra, after Clive had gone to collect her after one of her many disappearances, she was *'full of attitude and talk, and hostility to everyone including me'*. Over time, however, it seemed that he was able to make himself a sufficiently reliable figure in her life for them to develop a productive working relationship. Clive's relationship-building skills appear to have been key to the development of his understanding of how damaging home life had become for Myra, and to convince him of the need for action.

This decision was evidently not Clive's alone, but one developed with Myra, and to some extent Nicola, although her feelings about whether she was able to parent her daughter at that time were often ambivalent. Other decision makers included the extended team of education, social services and health professionals working with the family. Nevertheless, it was Clive who took the initiative and 'called time' on a steadily deteriorating situation in which it was increasingly clear that Myra's needs were not being met. This is perhaps not atypical of multi-disciplinary practice with children and families where, while there is active involvement from professional colleagues, there is often a tacit understanding that the impetus for a change in direction in work with families will come from social workers and their managers.

A decision was made that Myra would be accommodated away from home on a voluntary basis (in other words, with both her parents' agreement since they had parental rights and responsibilities for Myra) under s.20 of the Children Act 1989.[2] This would, it was thought, provide very necessary 'time out' for Myra and her mother, and make it more possible to start planning with Myra for the future. After a brief, and unsuccessful, foster placement, Myra moved to a residential Assessment Centre for a 12-week assessment period. At the time of the interview, Myra had been at the Centre for five weeks, and her first review, shortly before our interview, had been, from Myra's point of view a positive one:

> We had a meeting with Nicola, Myra, residential staff, myself, the LAC education officer, the Family Support Worker.. Everybody there thought there had been progress apart from Nicola who was very angry that we were congratulating Myra for attending school. Why should we do that, when every child should?
>
> According to Nicola it was one step forward and five steps back and I said, 'I think that the truth is the opposite, that we have made several steps forward and she shouldn't be absconding yeah, but she is doing it less regularly so I think we are moving forward'. Nicola has made a complaint about [that], that nobody was there for her and we were all hostile to her. ...because she was like, total rejection, total criticism, total hostility, and actually, the young person in the meeting did very well, knowing the history between them and the dynamics of the way they work. I think on balance that the placement is working because Myra can't cope with the intensity of family life at the moment. To me the

rejection by both parents seems overt, continued rejection, and is very damaging to Myra's self-esteem. I am guessing that the space away from both her parents is allowing her to be more mature and more reflective about her behaviour.

We need to keep Nicola on board, she is her mother and she does have parental rights, although working with her is not the easiest task in the world. But throughout we must recognise that Myra's welfare is paramount — as the Act says — so I tread very carefully. Myra is a vulnerable young person and her situation won't be solved today, or tomorrow, or next week or next month.

The benefits of hindsight

The interview with Clive took place at a time of great uncertainty in Myra's life — would she return home after the assessment period with an effective plan to support her and her family? Or would a return to her mother catapult her straight back into the high emotions and risk-taking behaviour that had dominated the previous year? It was too early to say what the outcome of the assessment would be or what kind of risk management plan would be put into place in the longer term. This was, for Clive a good time to take stock and review his work with Myra and her parents. What aspects of his practice, and collaboration with other professionals had worked well? What had been personally and professionally difficult, and was there anything Clive would, with hindsight, now have done differently?

At the centre of Clive's reflection on his practice was, for him, a central question about the timing of the decision to accommodate Myra away from home. The outcome of doing so seemed, at least in the short term, a positive one for Myra. However, reflecting on his practice, Clive concluded that he had been slow to act:

> I think with hindsight maybe we should have looked at accommodating Myra earlier. There are a lot of reasons, such as poor educational and other outcomes, to believe that we should avoid accommodating young people. However, the harmful effects were so severe and so corrosive for Myra that she was unsafe and she was being psychologically damaged by the continuous rejection. I always want to work with the family to try and heal any issues, so I was saying, 'We'll work with you, to try and look at the issues, but we're not going to take her away'. I think at first, when I took over this case, her voice wasn't being listened to and I think because of whatever is in Nicola's background, and because of Nicola's

own needy status, she is incapable of putting a child's needs before her own.

Here Clive is identifying a central tension for social workers, achieving the 'right' balance between everyone's right to have their perspective attended to, and to be actively involved in decision-making, and the need, sometimes, to take decisive action to halt or prevent harm. At the same time as exercising those key skills of empathy and relationship-building 'in the moment' social workers have to be able to stand back, to analyse complex information and to draw on the best available knowledge of how best to promote and safeguard children's welfare. Turney et al. (2011), reviewing messages from research into assessment of children, found evidence of an unwillingness to intervene when adolescents are at risk. They identified a range of possible reasons for this, including, perceived or actual pressures to ration scarce resources, a belief that teenagers, in contrast with a younger child, will somehow be able to 'sort things out for themselves' and concern, that mirrors Clive's, that a move into the looked after system might be damaging to the young person. However, this understanding has to be set against a growing body of research that suggests that the negative impact of care for children and young people has been over-stated, so that the potential of effective use of the care system as means of improving the lives of vulnerable young people may not be realised (Brandon and Thoburn, 2008; Hannon et al., 2010). This snapshot of influences on decision-making about care proceedings is a reminder of the range and complexity of knowledge that underpins safeguarding children and young people from harm. Fine judgements have to be made about applying research and other evidence to practice to ensure that they are not only used to confirm a course of action ('confirmation bias'), but also to seek out evidence that challenges those assumptions (O'Sullivan, 2011).

Clive's work with Myra and her family, though brief, stands out for him because of the opportunity it afforded him for reflection on his practice and for learning that has informed his continuing work with children and families. It might seem paradoxical to see making, owning and learning from mistakes in child protection as part of 'best practice in social work', especially in the context of an increasingly managerial, and sometimes litigious, working environment. Clive's account of practice is, however, a reminder that assessing and responding to risk is, like people's lives, complex, with outcomes that are often difficult to predict, or to explain, even with the benefit of hindsight. It is crucial for social workers to be aware of how their feelings and responses to children and families can influence their judgements (Bywater, 2012, p. 63). Munro argues that it is also essential for social workers to be willing to perceive their judgements and decisions as wrong, and to engage in the kind of critical reflection that Clive describes in this chapter:

> Taking a more critical attitude to one's work is not simple. It takes time, intelligence and effort. Realising your first judgements are wrong can be an unpleasant experience and social workers need to be supported and encouraged in subjecting their work to more rigorous scrutiny. (Munro, 1996, p. 806)

Notes

1. The equivalent legal provision in Scotland is s.22 of the Children (Scotland) Act 1995.
2. s.25 Children (Scotland) Act 1995 in Scotland.

11 Taking Risks with Alannah

Marie Brown and Jean Gordon

Marie works as a Senior Supervising Social Worker for an Independent Fostering Agency in Scotland. The Agency provides placements for children who are 'Looked After' by the Local Authority; placements can be short-term or permanent.

Marie qualified in England and worked as a Local Authority child care social worker for about five years, including periods working in Duty, Permanence and Long Term Children and Families Teams. She also undertook independent adoption and fostering assessments and Family Group Conference Coordinating. For the last seven years Marie has been working for an Independent Fostering Agency.

Questions to ask yourself as you read:

- Should social workers take risks with children?

- Why did Marie think that contact with her birth family was important for Alannah?

- How can social workers work constructively with risk in their organisations, and with other agencies?

Alannah and her family

Marie first met Alannah eight years ago when she was five years old. Marie had recently assessed and approved Sophie and Iain, her foster carers. Alannah settled very well into the family, and about a year later the couple asked for the arrangement to become a permanent one and they were assessed to be her new parents. Their application was subsequently approved by the local authority. Marie, in the role of supervising social worker has continued to support Sophie and Iain, monitoring Alannah's care and liaising with other professionals, including Alannah's local authority social worker (LASW). There are, inevitably, many stories that Marie could tell about her work with Alannah and her family. This particular story is informed by Marie's particular interest in and long experience of working with children who are 'looked after' by the local authority:

> I have an interest in social justice for looked after children who are already a discriminated group – and there is strong evidence that they are further discriminated against by the way the system works. Most children have consistent and caring adults who are part of their everyday life, but for some looked after children this is not the case and we fall back to protocols and unworkable procedures that tend to be 'defensive practice'. This is not only true of the local authority but also within the Agency which also has a duty to comply with legislation – there can be issues about how to interpret guidance and what is appropriate for that child in practice.

Marie's focus on the welfare of looked-after children mirrors that of 'Extraordinary Lives', a report that set out the Scottish Government's intention for looked-after children:

> We must have the same hopes, expectations and commitment to looked after children as we have for all our children. In a Scotland where every child matters, we want all our children to achieve their potential and to be able to celebrate success in their lives. (Social Work Inspection Agency, 2006, p. vii)

That children need to be 'safe', and that this may involve protecting children, many of whom have had previously harmful experiences, is hard to contest. At the same time, as discussed in Chapter 7, children need opportunities to *take* risks to grow and develop in confidence to enable them to achieve and grow into responsible, included citizens. This chapter examines some ways in which Marie has addressed dilemmas about potential risk to Alannah posed by contact within her new family, and with members of her birth family. We describe two of these challenges and how they were resolved, and finish with Marie's reflections on her practice and what has informed her approach to decision-making about risk. The main focus is on how Marie has worked within the context of her organisation and the local authority, and in partnership with her manager, social workers and other colleagues rather than the detail of her direct practice with Alannah and her family.

Alannah, who is now 14, has given Marie permission for her story to be used for this book, as has her new family. The name, 'Alannah', is her own choice of pseudonym. She has read this chapter with Sophie and said that she is happy with the content. As in other chapters in this book, key details have been changed to protect the anonymity of others involved in this story, such as other social workers and members of Alannah's birth family.

The context: social work and the law in Scotland

Since Alannah lives in Scotland, the policy, practice guidelines and legislation referred to are also Scottish. This is not to say, of course, that the practice issues discussed are not relevant to social workers in other parts of the United Kingdom, and indeed other parts of the world, but there are some important differences between practising social work in Scotland and the rest of the United Kingdom. While legal principles, including the paramountcy of the child's welfare, are broadly similar in the four UK nations, some of the legal provisions, terminology and processes are markedly different. Although there is not room in this chapter to describe these divergences in any detail, it is important to explain this local authority's continuing role in relation to Alannah conveyed by a Parental Responsibilities Order.[1] Parental Responsibilities Orders transfer decision-making powers from birth parents to the local authority. They were introduced to promote a sense of permanence and security for children who are unable to live with their birth families. The Order transferred all parental rights and responsibilities, including the right to decide where Alannah lives, to the local authority. Since the implementation of the Adoption and Children (Scotland) Act 2007 these Orders have been superseded by a more flexible alternative, the Permanence Order, which shares parental rights and responsibilities between the local authority and, for example, foster carers (see Adoption Policy Review Group, 2005 for a full discussion of the reasons for these changes).

Marie finds that the local authority's role of corporate parent presents some tensions that affect her in her role as supervising social worker for an independent sector organisation:

> The local authority becomes the legal parent of the child but ironically their social workers will have less contact with the child and their new family because the child is deemed to be safe and their well being is

ensured. Probably the only situation where once you become a 'parent' you see your child less!

In some respects this is right – the child should have a right to a family life with their new parents without interference under Article 8 of the ECHR.[2] But it is often a frustration around the times when decisions need to be made suddenly. The local authority – who have not had contact with the child for months – will have the final say in the decision. This is where the role of an independent agency social worker is quite complicated as you need to ensure that the child and family are advocated for whilst ensuring that there is a good working relationship with the local authority.

The importance of this relationship – and the ways in which Marie has sought to work effectively with the local authority forms an important thread in her story about working with Alannah, Iain and Sophie.

Nan and Grandad

Soon after Alannah moved to her family she began to get to know members of the extended family, many of whom lived locally. Over time she expressed a wish, like many children, to have overnight stays with 'Nan' and 'Grandad', Sophie's parents, who lived nearby. Marie saw this wider family network as a real strength of the family and wanted to encourage the relationships that Alannah was building. Iain and Sophie discussed this possibility with Marie, who consulted with Alannah's local authority worker and gained a positive response to the suggestion – but only if a criminal records check of both grandparents was undertaken. This was insufficient for Agency procedures, however which required a fuller assessment:

> [W]e were told that this was not possible without a full Form F2[3] assessment being done because any child who was placed with the agency could only stay overnight with assessed and approved carers. This felt like a sledgehammer to crack a nut. This was a permanent placement, the grandparents were not respite carers, they're not being paid to look after the children whilst the carers are away so why would we need a full assessment?

Regular contact with grandparents, including overnight stays, is a 'given' for many children. However, the initial plan to make this possible for Alannah might have ended here, with, in this case, a potential blanket ban on overnight visits to family members unless a full fostering assessment was carried out. Stories like these tend to provoke the despairing cry of, 'it's just bureaucracy gone mad'. Many professionals can also become frustrated with systems that appear to be rule bound and inflexible. But the Agency's concern with the safety of Alannah and other looked-after children they support on behalf of the Local Authority was not, of course, a trivial one. Risks to children's safety in residential and foster care have been well documented (Social Work Inspection Agency, 2006), and a tightening up of procedures to improve the safety of looked-after children has partly resulted from the disquieting findings of high profile inquiries into abuse. Marie was torn between her accountability to the Agency (and in turn its accountability to the local authority for Alannah's care) and her judgement of what was best for Alannah:

> It felt difficult for me as, given [Sophie's] parents' age and some health problems, I would not have been able to recommend them for approval as respite carers. But I did feel that they were able to offer Alannah a richer family experience. I felt that there were risks – of course – but that I could make an accountable decision here that I could stand by. My view was that, from my knowledge of Sophie and Iain I believed they had good judgement and would not compromise Alannah nor their family in any way so if there were any issues they would not allow her to stay. Alannah was seven by this time and was a really lovely girl who would be unlikely to be a challenge in her behaviour. For me personally it felt really scary – I strongly believed that it was wrong not to enable Alannah to be with the wider family – but what if I was wrong? What if something happened when she was staying there?

Despite these anxieties, Marie's confidence in this judgement, based on her knowledge of the carers, Alannah and their capabilities, prevented her from just accepting the status quo. She discussed her concerns in supervision with her manager who supported her to propose an alternative approach. The new plan took the potential for risk of harm seriously but seemed a more proportionate response to risk than the very detailed assessment advocated by the agency:

> From my relationship I had with the family and with my supervisor I felt I was able to change the decision. I undertook a formal assessment visit to the grandparents and to the cousin, undertook statutory checks and completed a written assessment which I felt ensured the decision that was agreed by myself and my supervisor was an accountable one. There is never a way to prevent risks but it felt that we had appropriately managed the risks in a way that did not compromise Alannah experiencing normal family life.

Alannah's birth family: maternal step-gran and birth father

When Alannah first moved to her new family she had no contact with members of her birth family. As she settled in, however, Alannah began to ask questions and to express an interest in meeting her relatives, including her birth step-gran. Marie raised these questions with local authority colleagues at one of Alannah's regular looked after children reviews:

> [A]nd it was kind of, 'Oh well, we've come across this before, actually [the birth family] weren't very consistent'. It felt that the local authority believed the risks would be that contact would not be sustained and this would be damaging to Alannah's wellbeing so best not introduce it.
>
> I could understand this position to some extent, but Alannah was well settled now in the new family, well supported and was interested in seeing these birth family members. So this has some bearing on how we could manage this risk – she had a strong supportive family to fall back on who would help them make sense of this. There could be a really positive spin off in that she may be faced with a disappointing and difficult experience, but through that the bonds to those around her could be strengthened... The understanding of how painful this could be could help her resilience at managing difficult times, building up her capacity to process difficult emotions.

Marie was taking the potential for risk seriously, but was also considering the protective factors that could enable Alannah to 'bounce back' from possibly difficult circumstances and events. These included intrinsic and extrinsic factors such as Alannah's secure base, sense of belonging to her new family and self-confidence as well as her access to wider supports in the extended family and at school (see Daniel and Wassell, 2002). A resilience-based approach has a close fit with the intentions of the Scottish Government's holistic and strengths-based approach to assessing children's needs, *Getting it Right for Every Child* (Scottish Government, 2012).

Marie thought that Local Authority's concerns about contact had once been well-substantiated, but that these potential risks needed to be explored again in the light of Alannah's stage of development and the strong roots she had put down with her new family. Marie also recognised that a significant factor for Alannah's LASW was the time to think about exactly what the risks for Alannah were, and how these might be managed:

Given I felt quite strongly about this and felt that I needed to advocate on behalf of Alannah, we pushed a little more for this. Recognising that it was difficult for the local authority to have the time I asked, 'Do you want me to go and talk to her? I'm happy, I'll go and collect Gran, I'll meet her, I'll do an assessment. I know you are really busy, I'll go and do that'. And actually we did, we went and got step-gran, and brought her down to the office. And it was lovely, because then she did actually give that commitment to Alannah. After a couple of supervised contacts then the LASW agreed that the foster carer could take over organising the contact and it became a naturalised contact for Alannah with her birth family that was supported, appropriate.

Marie's strong relationship with Iain and Sophie as well as Alannah was a significant factor in making this contact happen, giving her confidence that they would be able to be honest with her about how they were feeling:

I knew from my contact with them that Alannah was settled enough and was able to make sense of her contact through the discussions she could have with Sophie and Iain. I also knew that the carers were supportive of the contact but able to be clear about their role and that they would always put Alannah's needs first.

When she was about 11 Alannah became curious about her birth father and wanted to meet him. In consultation with her local authority colleagues Marie met her birth father to determine what his motivation for contact was:

He gets it, he's pleased that Alannah's where she is, he's pleased that she calls Sophie and Iain 'mum' and 'dad'. Yeah, he's sorry for what happened, but actually a one off contact would be supportive because it would let her see him... It may be a bigger risk in the long run not to let her see him as [later on] she may be at a more vulnerable teenage stage where some of his lifestyle could hold attraction for her. Whereas at the 11 or 12 years stage Alannah is mature and sensible enough and very much part of her family as she hasn't moved into the stage of wanting independence from them.

The Local Authority had reservations due to her birth father's drug and alcohol difficulties in the past, and there were related concerns about his reliability. They proposed a slightly complex assessment process which again felt 'too big' for what Marie and the family were looking for – an initial 'one-off' contact for Alannah to meet her birth father:

> I know there's a bit about parents needing to show their motivation and capacity to provide care for children – and this is appropriate where you are considering rehabilitation but for this case it did not feel like it was a model that should be used. It felt quite punitive and almost set up not to work. The purpose of the contact for Alannah was for her to gain a sense of birth family to help her development. She was a child who was very reflective of her situation, quite amazing in her insights on her life, so I was confident that she would manage this contact. If it was emotionally painful for her she had very strong relationships with her mum and dad to be able to talk this over with them.

Again, Marie was weighing up risks and protective factors for Alannah, including the risk that *not* making this contact could itself be damaging. This was, she pointed out, a time in Alannah's life which Erikson (1950) has identified as being crucial for resolving tensions between identity formation and role confusion. There was also a question for Marie about the purpose of any assessment, and she argued for clarity about Alannah's needs:

> In order to enable contact which can feel risky you need to be aware that families change, children grow up and are at different ages and stages so will have different needs in respect of why they want contact.

Marie's advocacy on Alannah's behalf was eventually successful, and a single and well-supported meeting with her birth father was arranged. Marie's ability to 'look round the corner' to see what might be important to Alannah as she grows and develops was an important part of enabling this ultimately valued contact with her birth family to take place.

Taking risks with children

The title of this chapter is a deliberately provocative one. In Chapter 7, we discussed the way in which risk has come to dominate the practice of early 21st-century social work. On the face of it 'taking risks' with any child, perhaps particularly a child who, like Alannah, for whom the local authority is partially acting as a 'corporate parent', is a potentially alarming notion for any social worker, manager or policymaker. At the same time it's impossible for any of us to imagine a life without risk or uncertainty. Risk, Titterton (2011, p. 32) argues, is 'an essential part of the subjective experience of being human'. Each of the proposed contacts – with her grandparents, her birth grandmother and her birth father – *could* have been harmful to Alannah. For example, her grandparents might not have been able to cope with caring for a young child, or Alannah might have been distressed by contact with her birth father or step-grandmother. Marie took these risks seriously, but knew that they were only part of the picture:

> There is also a real need to focus on children as able and competent. The resilience model is a strengths based one that is hopeful and can recognise transitions can allow change and help develop resilience.

In both of these brief vignettes of her work with Alannah and her family, Marie recognised that the risk of inaction, for example, not acting on Alannah's curiosity about her birth family, could itself cause harm. However this potential and longer term harm was, to a large extent invisible to social work and other agencies, when compared, for example, to responding to a child protection emergency:

> In permanence the risks aren't generally big blue light flashing risks – is this child in danger of immediate harm? It is less dramatic risk decisions but these often have significant lifelong impact for looked after children and that is sometimes not appreciated.

As Marie's discussion about each of these risk decisions makes clear, none were taken lightly, in the sense that the outcome was seen as an obvious or common sense one. It is well recognised that adopted and fostered children face 'additional tasks' that other children do not have to negotiate (Triseliotis, 1997). Depending on the child and his or her particular circumstances, these tasks include making attachments to new parents, coping with separation and loss, and searching for a sense of personal identity: finding out just *who they are* (Neil, 2003, p. 278: author's italics). Contact with birth families is known to assist with these tasks for some children, but research findings, especially in relation to long-term outcomes, have been equivocal about the benefits for children. Neil et al. (2003) have emphasised the importance of practitioners thinking through each child's needs in relation to the benefits and risks of contact in a systematic and evidence informed way. This assessment is by its nature situated in the context of this child in this new family; there are no shortcuts to deciding whether contact is 'right' or 'wrong', or how best it can be facilitated. In Alannah's case this assessment was reliant on knowledge of her needs, capabilities and support networks as well as the aim and nature of the contact proposed. This knowledge was held by several people – Alannah herself, of course, her parents, and by Marie as well as a number of other professionals:

> If I have a good sound working relationship with the carer and the children then I am in a stronger position to make accountable arguments when asking people to make decisions.

Marie's long contact with the family was highly significant in allowing her to take risks *with* Alannah and her parents, giving her the confidence both in the assessment and her ability to monitor the outcome of any decision. However, this eight-year relationship with a child and parents is unusual. Children and young people's evidence to the Munro review emphasised the importance to them of '*trusting and stable*' relationships with social workers and other professionals, yet for many this was not achieved (Munro, 2011, p. 129). Often Marie would be communicating about Alannah to an LASW who had had negligible contact with Alannah, Sophie and Iain, and therefore little to base any risk assessment on other than past records. Marie's relationships with Alannah's social workers have generally been effective and collaborative ones, in which her knowledge of the family was valued, and, as in the vignettes above, LASW colleagues have trusted her judgement. However, this is not always the case in Marie's experience. Sometimes time pressures present stubborn barriers to good quality risk assessment – and the potential for risk enablement:

> It is really difficult when social workers are so very busy that they use a very heuristic type of model to make decisions – really because they don't have the time to think about, here's a risk, how do we manage it? It is quicker to say – too risky!

Heuristics are mental shortcuts – 'rules of thumb' which help us to speed up and simplify everyday decision-making. However, as with any child there was no quick 'rule of thumb' that would enable Marie, her local authority colleagues and her family make on-the-spot decisions about contact. Instead, as Marie demonstrated in her interview, the assessment involves a careful analysis, based on an ecological understanding of Alannah's current situation. That assessment is informed, in Scotland, by the National Practice Model's My World assessment framework and well-being indicators (or SHANARRI[4] outcomes) (Scottish Government, 2012). At the centre was Marie's relationship with and knowledge of the family, underpinned by her understanding of the impact of, for example, attachment and identity on Alannah. Knowing that the sensitivity, empathy and involvement of foster carers and adoptive parents are crucial predictors for successful contact (Neil et al., 2003) was another important piece of knowledge in the jigsaw of this assessment. Her ability to bring together knowledge from theory, research findings and direct experience of this family enabled Marie to question and help to change decision-making that limited the potential for life-enhancing experiences and relationships for Alannah. Without Marie's advocacy the assessment of risk in each case might have been solely based on the precautionary principle – that it was 'better to be safe than sorry' (Kemshall, 2007, p. 207). This required Marie to be both confident, and able to accept that change and progress are often slow and painstaking:

> I think you have got be quite, not strong in yourself, but you've got to be able to know you won't solve everything... I think you have got to have confidence in yourself.

Taking risks with organisations

In contrast with earlier chapters in this section, this chapter is mostly about 'back office social work': the thinking, recording, one-to-one discussions and multi-disciplinary meetings that lie behind the public face of social work. The rise and rise of managerialism in social work, and the proliferation of policies and procedures that seem to attempt to address every eventuality are well documented (see Chapter 7). Although it is easy to dismiss policies and procedures as unnecessary 'red tape', organisations would come to a standstill without them. 'Bureaucracy' has many detractors but does help to ensure that notions of legal accountability, equity and equality are integral aspects of service provision, even if organisations do not always operate as effectively as they might. One response to the plethora of detailed and prescriptive guidance is for social workers to 'put up and shut up' with organisational decisions that they do not agree with. And, indeed, as Marie described earlier, this strategy, if hardly good practice, may well arise as a coping strategy when social workers are working in highly pressured working environments without sufficient time for relationship building, reflection, critical analysis and quality supervision. However, if social work is, as Marie suggested at the start of this chapter, informed by a sense of social justice and improving, in her work, outcomes for looked after children, then this is dangerous doctrine. Jones and Watson (2013, p. 68) propose that the best social work combines 'a fundamental pragmatism about what can be achieved in the here and now with a critical engagement with how things could be better in the future'. Marie's pragmatism, her forward looking 'can do' approach to making things happen within the often tight timeframes in which she works is evident in her negotiations with others:

> I would try not to be moaning at a social worker about what they have not done. It is more constructive to try and help find a way to get it done. The absolutely vital thing is that the decisions made are accountable and they are openly discussed and agreed this is more likely to happen if there is a network of good professional relationships between the workers and with the carers.

In Chapter 6, Mike made a very similar point, in relation to his role as a manager of a Children and Families Team in Wales. Seden (2008, p. 178) emphasises that social workers have to be articulate with those with delegated authority and power in organisations about the impact of organisational practices on service users. Marie saw this as a two-way street: she was an active in expressing her views and advocating for policy and practice change to benefit service users. She also saw herself benefiting from working in an organisation that provided her with a secure base from which to be, when the time was right, a risk taker:

> I think there is an attachment focus for me in thinking about risk enablement. If I am feeling secure in my team and with my supervising manager then I am more able and confident to make decisions and manage the emotional content of them. The sense of 'being held' is really important in social work for practitioners to be able to continue to give people a service that will develop their potential to meet the challenges they face...multiple adversity – which social workers will experience in their day to day work – can overwhelm workers which means they lose the emotional capacity to make risk decisions – as anything that is different will be regarded as dangerous.

Marie finds ways to sustain herself – and she uses the support available from within organisation and her colleagues in other organisations. Like Ferguson (2011), she emphasises the importance of emotional thinking space provided by peer support, regular supervision and opportunities for critical reflection on practice:

> You need to develop an emotional resilience yourself. Where does this come from? Partly it is emotional experience you have had in social work. It is really important to have support in order to be confident in the risks you are enabling. It should not be a solo activity. The reflections

that can happen in supervision, the questioning by a competent leader who is able to question your hypotheses about a situation, get you to look at the other side. This type of leadership cannot be underestimated as it gives you an emotional security that will encourage and develop you as a practitioner.

Notes

1. s.86 Children (Scotland) Act 1995. There is no precise legal equivalent in England, Wales or Northern Ireland: the Order should not be confused with a Parental Responsibility Order.
2. European Convention on Human Rights.
3. In this case, a detailed assessment of the grandparents as respite carers for Alannah.
4. SHANARRI outcomes are for the child to be: Safe, Healthy, Achieving, Nurtured, Active, Respected, Responsible, and Included.

Part 3

Power, Negotiation and Problem-Solving

12 Power and Negotiation in Practice: From Problems to Solutions

Barry Cooper

Introduction

The stories of practice in this section of the book illustrate some of the shifting patterns of power and negotiation in social work. In many ways these can appear to be 'hidden concepts' in practice as they are often tacit or unspoken about. In talking to practitioners for this book it was noticeable that, although the use of power and the processes of negotiation were rarely named as such, they nonetheless influenced the courses of events that were being described in subtle and complex ways. These links between power and negotiation are placed into perspective by examining another ever-present and debatable pair of concepts, that of problems and solutions. The rest of this chapter introduces these three themes to further explore and explain why the use of power is an inescapable aspect of social work. I will argue that although the purposeful use of power and negotiation is under-recognised in social work, these are not ends in themselves. The constructive, ethical and expert use of professional power and negotiating skills are only the means through which social work addresses the reasons for its involvement: identifying problems and finding solutions to those problems. The three stories of practice in this section and the narrative comments that accompany each story will help to ground these ideas in three very different practice examples.

Working with power in practice

Social work has its jargon words like any other profession. However, it also uses everyday words in very specific ways and an understanding of this helps to detail some of the complexities inherent in social work practice. A good example is the sociological concept of 'power'. Power is found within social work literature (Smith, 2008) although it is often in different guises through concepts of empowerment and anti-discriminatory or anti-oppressive practice perspectives. Understood sociologically, power is an abstract and complex concept. But it is also an everyday word that people recognise, use and can implicitly understand. However, despite being in common usage it seems resistant to easy or agreed definition. In social work, there can sometimes be a tension in the acknowledgement of power by practitioners as it often appears to conflict with the deeply held values of anti-oppressive practice and service user empowerment (Beresford and Croft, 2000). These are complex professional debates and it is not always clear as to what extent practitioners are aware of their power – in practice. There used to be a saying in social work:

> Social workers have more power than they think they have; but not as much as others think they have.

This neat aphorism tries to capture a feeling in the profession that social workers were insufficiently self-aware of their own power potential afforded them by their roles, tasks and duties. At the same time there was an unrealistically inflated perception among the media and public commentators outside of the profession that social workers were either power-crazed (removing children from families) or incompetent in their use of power (failing to prevent child abuse). Some of this can be explained by the complexities of power and the often hidden differences between espoused values and values in action. In other words, it is easy to 'talk the talk' and write about professional principles and values, which social work does very well. But it is much more difficult to 'walk the walk' and maintain principled consistency in action among the pragmatic compromises and ethical dilemmas of complex social work practice. In order for power to be shared and for processes of empowerment to be created, or disempowerment to be challenged, there has to be an understanding of how power works and how power accrues both personally and from a professional worker's position with the welfare network. A major avenue to achieve this is through processes of negotiation.

Talking about negotiation

The vehicle for the workings of power and influence in social work is through its major professional tool – 'talk'. Whereas power can be argued to be a ubiquitous aspect of social work, the same cannot be said of negotiation. It's not always clear as to what extent practitioners actively negotiate with people in an open and transparent process. Talk, at its basic level, is an everyday mode of communication. But in social work, everyday talk has the potential to be transformed within a professional working relationship into focused and purposeful processes of change. The ways in which talk is used, the values that inform it and the ways in which service users experience social work communication depends upon how power is used by practitioners. In other words, negotiation as a social work process recognises that power differentials in a relationship may be far from voluntary and proceeds on the basis of as much transparency as possible in the different circumstances of interventions into the lives of parents, children and families. Three practice principles can be identified as underpinning the ongoing processes of negotiation. First, there needs to be an open sharing of perspectives. A practitioner has the power to be clear about their assessments and how they see given situations. They also have a professional responsibility to facilitate service users to express their view of things. This is easy to state but it demands confidence and a high level of skill and sensitivity in practice. Second, the sharing of perspectives should lead to the identification of areas of agreement and disagreement. An essential aspect of clarity about what people can agree on and disagree about is to identify those areas that are negotiable and non-negotiable. Third, in child and family social work, a negotiative approach will prioritise the maintenance of working relationships but will ensure that the safety of children is never compromised. All three principles are part and parcel of an open, negotiative use of professional power. But to what end? Power and negotiation are the means by which social work should operate. However, the reason for any social work involvement is always about problems and solutions.

Problems and solutions

Cooper (2009) has suggested that social work can be characterised as 'the problem profession' and argues that there is a tendency for practitioners to become shaped by the problems they help to define rather than by the solutions they should be of assistance in creating. As Chapters 13 and 15 illustrate, social workers get involved where problems become seemingly intractable and vulnerable people are at risk. The danger for a problem-oriented profession is that the too much time and energy can become focused upon problem definition at the expense of what O'Sullivan (2011) describes as 'solution building'. In a strengths-based approach to social work the emphasis switches towards practitioners becoming involved in trying to help people find their own solutions to what have become defined as problems of living.

'Social work problems' are uniquely complex in being located within social behaviour. The boundaries between public policies and private lives are fluid and contested territories (Bauman, 2005). As a result, the 'problem' itself, often a complex package of competing perspectives, is rarely defined solely through an uncontested objective reality. There may be elements of irrefutable 'fact' in the objective conditions of a situation but a large part of a 'social' problem is made up of complex social and interpersonal perspectives from a number of different people involved. The social work problem, therefore, needs to be defined. This definition can only be socially negotiated and agreed, or, in many cases, the areas of disagreement agreed. For this kind of professional activity in these circumstances, there can be no 'instruction manual' or map of how to proceed (Lester, 1999). A way forward has to be created by social work practitioners through detailed and often-contested negotiation. This task frequently needs to occur in collaboration with multidisciplinary colleagues and these days, almost universally, it is expected to involve children, young people and their families as a central part of the process. In order for this process to fully involve the necessary range of people, it has to be participative within shifting territories and situations. Lave and Wenger (1991) argue that such participation is a process of negotiation:

> Participation is always based on situated negotiation and re-negotiation of meanings in the world. This implies that understanding and experience are in constant interaction – indeed are mutually constitutive. (p. 51)

The insight of solution-focused approaches (De Shazer, 1988; Macdonald, 2011) helps to shift the focus of power and negotiation away from a fixation with the problems of the past to look forward towards ways in which things can change in the future. An emphasis upon change is crucial to understanding social work. It is not just about changes in people's lives as 'improvements' although these are essential for any measure of effectiveness. It is more fundamental than that. The core uncertainty and ambiguity of social work interventions in fluid social situations means that practice needs to be understood in different and conceptually challenging ways. These different insights into social work problems, through power, negotiation and a new emphasis upon solutions, are further analysed and explored in the remainder of this chapter.

The use or abuse of power in social work

Power in social work is a very difficult concept to capture and convey. As a professional activity, the power of social work arises from its historical development in the United Kingdom as the way in which the state intervenes in the private relationships of families, parents and children. In this sense, 'social work' is well named as its locus of application on behalf of the state is the 'social' between private and public (Rose, 1996). Individual acts of social work intervention, therefore, are carried out within a detailed framework of legislative duties and obligations. But, as any lawyer will confirm, legal fiats are rarely unequivocal. Social workers operating within this field carry enormous potential power through the authority of the law. However, the authority is not clear-cut. The social field is one of great indeterminacy and the application of social welfare law depends upon professional assessment and interpretation. So, publicly sanctioned interventions into private and interpersonal arenas require the professional social worker to not only assess and arrive, with colleagues, at a judgement of the behaviour of others but at the same time to also seek to change that behaviour (Howe, 1996). A similar insight was proposed by Satyamurti (1979) in what has become an enduring explanatory leitmotif for statutory social work with children and families. In this case the double perspective was of both 'care and control'. This juxtaposition of potent, but potentially conflicting, professional mandates creates in children and families social work, especially, a core ambiguity of purpose and activity (Okitikpi, 2011). Many of the stories in this book illustrate how practitioners struggle successfully to make and maintain relationships in risky situations while balancing a professional desire to help and support against the professional duty to exert control and keep children safe.

This core balancing act renders the power of the professional social worker as essentially latent and ambivalent. The implicit nature of professional social work power that seems both 'virtual' yet is legislatively manifest is thereby all the more influential through not only its invisibility but also its apparent negotiability. These complex ambiguities of social work power are persuasively explained through the seminal writings of Foucault (1972, 1975). Central to Foucauldian analysis are the ideas about 'discourse' which, in social work, can be understood as inseparable combinations of knowledge and power. Such 'regimes of power' are exercised by professionals through, for example, the specific technologies of assessment and care planning (Gilbert and Powell, 2010). The potential to lock individuals within oppressive practices is something that individual practitioners and the systems within which they operate have to be aware of and constantly guard against. However, as the stories of practice in this book illustrate, it is rarely straightforward to be clear about the often necessary exercise of power and authority in complex social work interventions.

The interpersonal aspects of professional power, exerted within the 'social' field, are incisively critiqued through the notion of the 'psy' complex (Ingleby, 1985; Rose, 1985). Ingleby's ground-breaking work examines the micro-practices of everyday social work in both adult psychiatry and social work interventions with children and their families. It illuminates and highlights both the ambiguity of social interventions, and by clear implication, their potential for open negotiation. This analysis of power highlights psychological ambiguity as an inherent aspect of publicly sanctioned interventions into private lives. The notion of ambiguity (Parton, 1998), in turn, helps to recognise how the inherent power of the social workers position offers the potential to either use or abuse this power. Social work assessments are the central activity through which this ambivalent power is sustained. A social worker's evolving assessment is often reactive to a family history of past problems but, at the same time, to have a plan for change it must also be conducive of future solutions. It is from this awareness of the power of assessment that anti-oppressive practice analyses originate (Dominelli, 1996; Turney, 1999). The ability to negotiate is a vital core skill if awareness is to be developed into practices.

Critical best practice and the value of negotiation

An explicit 'anti-oppressive' practice requires skills of open negotiation within the values of an open-eyed awareness of the unequal power dynamics within social work relationships with service users. But, the analysis of Ingleby (1985) highlights the danger of professional workers in these social fields exercising tacit power to defend their assessments and interventions through what he describes as 'selective self-vindicatory readings of situations':

> For the professional's account is strongly biased in the direction of justifying their own actions: it rationalizes the present and rearranges the past into a triumphal perspective leading inexorably toward it. (p. 80)

Social assessments based upon a professional consensus view of the present and selective readings of the past are always vulnerable to this subtly powerful abuse of professional power. The assumption being targeted by this critique is, of course, that there is knowledge that leads to 'a truth', 'out there in reality' to be 'discovered' by the expert professional. The development of multi-disciplinary assessment processes that also involve service users is an attempt to guard against this and allow multiple perspectives. However, it remains unclear as to what extent a professionally driven conference process is able to achieve a re-balancing of power. Ingleby's argument identifies social field professionals as essentially 'socialisers' exercising power through ambiguous and unspoken cultural assumptions of consent to authority. In setting this out Ingleby explicitly reflects Satyamurti's (1979) 'care/control' double perspective and argues that:

> [T]he provision of care has become increasingly a matter of socializing people, so that it becomes difficult to think of 'help' as separable from 'control'. If we are hampered by our ambivalence toward the welfare system, I shall suggest that this is because of a fundamental ambiguity in the politics of intervention. (1985, p. 101)

However, this critique of 'the politics of intervention' rests upon an incisive but rather limited binary analysis of power. Recognising the ambiguous combination of care and control in social work is an important stage of becoming aware of professional power. But it doesn't fully reflect the multi-faceted nature of complex practice that can be explored through a critical best practice (CBP) perspective. Social control and the ethical use of 'good authority' (Ferguson, 2012) are vital constituents of relational power in social work. An empowering professional relationship strives to place the power, where possible, with the service user through an emphasis upon the negotiation of solutions, ideally within a helping relationship. This has to include both the practitioner's and the service user's perspectives and views of the situation with any differences and areas of agreement clearly identified.

This analysis needs to be understood within a broader critique of the evolution of modernity with its core assumptions about progress and perfectibility. The combination of a positivist science and its influence on social work can be identified as part of such developments within the field of social policy and social welfare. However, social work is not compellingly constituted purely as a disembodied, theoretical perspective. A CBP approach argues that social work is created, enacted and sustained as intricate activities within complex, situated, interpersonal and cultural organisational environments. A key process in the creation and maintenance of such environments are the largely taken-for-granted assumptions of negotiation and reaching agreement. Critical and constructive approaches to social work are an important part of the debates in social work (Parton and O'Byrne, 2000; Witkin, 2011; Fook, 2012). They have a commonality of interest in critical reflexivity through the power of language; and the structuring of relations between people and institutions through the language of power. However, if there is a key difference of emphasis in practice that moves social work from being critical to being constructive; it is the distinction between problems and solutions.

Beyond problems – constructing solutions

Fook (2002) argues that a key issue arising from 'uncritical' practice is that of problem reification within disempowering discourses. In other words, a professional fixation with problems within an uncritical use of talk that doesn't move beyond problem analysis is, in itself, a problem. A problem that is likely to get stuck. The criticism is aimed at positivist epistemological assumptions; that is, a clear subject and object division, leading to a naïve process of linear 'fact' and information gathering as a precursor stage. The resulting processes of assessment, planning and intervention flow from the definition of the initial problem and reflect the earlier critique by Ingleby (1985), above. Problems, on this uncritical approach, are conceptualised and located within individuals and groups because of some characteristic of that individual or group. Assessors within this approach are uncritical collectors of enough facts to help discover the essential 'truth' of the problem. Such a process is essentially disempowering for both assessor and assessed as it assumes what Fook terms a 'static identity category' (p. 117) with no recognition or allowance made for changes in people's lives and personas within different contexts and existential engagements. This is clearly not a realistic process for social work in dealing with changing situations.

The alternative critical approach put forward by Fook therefore acts to recognise and negotiate around the dominant discourses of power relations through what she calls narrative diversity or the construction of different meanings within situations. She puts it like this:

> A new approach to the understanding and practice of assessment making involves a broad recognition that the act of assessing involves creating a set of meanings which function discursively. [therefore] ... we need to allow for multiple and changing understandings which are contextually based and may be contradictory. (Fook, 2002, p. 118)

The recognition of different perspectives is a key aspect of a CBP approach to social work. CBP opens up the possibilities for recognising the structures of power and exploring alternative ways of practicing. This renewed focus upon different individual service users' ways of making sense of their situation is an important aspect of a 'constructive' approach to social work.

Constructive social work, as set out by Parton and O'Byrne (2000), is an important contribution to visions of the future of social work. It usefully draws upon related approaches such as narrative and solution-focused therapies and reflects the critical professionalism theme taken by Fook [op.cit]. In so doing it recognises that the emphasis upon assessment in social work is central to what sets it apart from other personal service professions within the wider social care field. Social work is 'essentially the work of *making judgements, so that decision-making can be better informed* (Parton and O'Byrne, 2000, p. 134) [original emphasis]. However, there are in the constructive approach no underlying assumptions of linear processes leading to a basis of certainty for judgements or decision-making. In fact, Parton (1998) has re-examined the ideas of Rojek et al. (1988) and argued persuasively for the recognition of ambiguity and rediscovery of uncertainty as the only defensible approach to the demands and expectations of social work. This argument constitutes a serious challenge to the prevailing modernist assumptions of risk management underpinning some recently conceived purposes of assessment (Crisp et al., 2005, p. 63). Parton argues, importantly, that it is only within a recognition of the 'under-determined' nature of social realities (Searle, 1995) that scope can begin to be discerned for a more creative and honest approach to assessment in social work. The constructive approach to assessments of problems and possible solutions shares the same focus upon language as being indicative of structures of power as other 'critical' approaches. There is also a similarly critical attitude to what is viewed as the 'naïve realism' of traditional assessment approaches. A key difference is in its view of problems and solutions and in its assumptions about human agency in creating a future. The de-emphasis upon problems is a radical one for social work. The profession has become virtually synonymous with problems as its *raison d'etre*. The constructive approach therefore has much in common with the solution-focused work of De Shazer (1988, 2007).

In a solution-focused approach there are no assumptions about behavioural causality. Instead, there is an emphasis upon the ability of people to create their futures through a sense of purposeful agency. This emphasis questions the assumptions of certainty underlying attempts to explain the causality of 'problems'. In this approach, problems are seen as besides the point of any possible solution. Any attempt to understand the problem is seen as not only a waste of time but actually counter-productive. The solution-focused approach, therefore, depends heavily upon an assumption that individuals can and do envision and create images of themselves and their wider circumstances. The social workers task, as Chapters 14 and 15 illustrate, is to try and gently move people beyond their safe familiarity with the problem and towards an increased, and inherently much more risky, appreciation of change towards a potential solution. So, in this renewed focus upon future solutions, individuals are being invited to examine the totality of their experiences and thereby place 'the problem' in perspective. The approach asks people to recall a time when 'the problem' was not there and then to envision how things would be if the problem once again was not there in the future. They are being invited to be actively selective and decide to choose those elements of their experience that are relatively problem-free and begin to think and feel more about what this was or would be like. This refusal to be constrained by habitual and normative pressures is based within the constructivist theoretical position with regard to human agency (Kelly, 1991; Butt, 2008) and recognises the many ways in which language powerfully constructs personal experience. The under-determined conception of language in use means that the understanding of situations, and the words and meanings attributed to those situations, are open to 'invitation'. In this approach to practice, a social worker is inviting the service users to join them in an open negotiation about what can change. In the following three stories this 'invitation' in social work is sometimes, but not always, realisable.

Three stories: the power to negotiate solutions in practice?

The three stories of practice in this section of the book illustrate how the themes outlined above are complex, interlinked and sometimes absent! They are from three quite distinct practice settings and offer different perspectives on how, in social work, things are rarely predictable in the use of power, the scope for negotiation and the balance between problems and solutions. In each story, however, there is a case to be made for the practice illustrating aspects of how practice is often the best that can be achieved in the specific and unique circumstances of particular people and places in time.

The first story is from Naomi, a local authority childcare social worker in England. Her work with Linda is in some ways an easily recognisable example of child protection, statutory intervention and contested care proceedings. But some of the specifics of how the case progressed and the impact this has upon Naomi, Linda and her foster-carers are unique. It is an example of professional power in action and a vivid depiction of what has to happen despite very limited opportunities to constructively negotiate with parents who are opposed to the social work view of their situation. The story vividly illustrates the balancing act of 'care and control' where the need for care of a child has to be maintained alongside the need for there to be control through legal proceedings. One interesting thread is that in 'upping the ante' by issuing a public law outline[1] the local authority social work team can be argued to be precipitating a 'crisis' within a family. Naomi's story is an example of the necessary use of social work power with little or no scope for negotiation between opposing views of the situation.

The second story is from Jenny, a post-adoption support social worker in England. Her example of practice within a complex network of birth family members and adoptive families illustrates the huge part played by processes of negotiation. In this story, compared to Naomi's, there is no power afforded from legislation in the social work role and duties. The power of persuasion in Jenny's story is advisory only and derived from long-standing relationships and the status that arises from the use of 'good authority' over many years. The facilitative processes of talking with people, helping them to cope with changes and to understand the perspectives of others and different ways of seeing things are central to best social work practice. There is, in this story, an equal recognition of how problems can arise and be perceived and yet, in the absence of explicit power and authority, people are empowered to find their own solutions over time and work things out for themselves.

The third story is from Pat, an independent social worker in England. Pats work mainly derives from the Family Courts and has a statutory focus upon particularly entrenched and contested 'problem' situations within families that cannot easily be resolved without specialist help. Pat uses a solution-focused approach to her work and the story helps to set out how and why this is so important and effective in her work. In many ways, solution-focused theory and methods of social work are the essence of constructive and empowering practice. The simple, skills-based techniques that Pat uses with her family are based upon the ethical use of power within the authority clearly set out by the court process. The story illustrates how negotiations based upon a solution-focus are simple but radical challenges to the traditional social work preoccupations with problems.

Note

1. In England, the duty to issue a 'public law outline' is a method by which the local authority gives notice of its intention to initiate statutory care proceedings. It is intended as a transparent process that informs all parties of their concerns and allows for legal representations to be informed.

13 Negotiation and Resistance: It's All About the Child

Naomi Gillard and Barry Cooper

Naomi qualified from University in 2007 and intended to work with adults with severe and enduring mental illness. Throughout her degree she concentrated on studying mental health and did not consider working within children and families teams an option. However, upon qualifying, there were few social work positions in mental health and so began in a long-term Children and Families team. Her experiences of working with children and their families were positive as her interest and experience increased across the range of child protection, children in need and the youth courts through working with teenagers who were remanded to Local Authority care. Naomi completed a Postgraduate Diploma in Working with Children, Families and Carers in February 2013 as part of her continuing development and is now a relatively experienced practitioner taking on complex cases and care proceedings. However, her work with Linda Smith and her family arose early in her professional development. The story is an illustration of best practice within an English local authority child and family social work team.

Questions to ask yourself as you read:

• What is most important in maintaining a child-centred practice?

• Why should you be clear about statutory powers and duties in social work practice?

• How does it make you feel in situations of conflict and resistance?

Case summary – Linda Smith

This story centres on Linda who is 13 years old and her social worker, Naomi. Her parents are Mr and Mrs Smith and she has a much older sibling. The background history of a family, leading up to statutory social work services becoming involved, is always likely to be partial and incomplete. In cases where there are parents that avoid welfare services involvement it is often necessary to piece together the past in order to make sense of the present. The complexities of childcare welfare services mean that this task involves other agencies and often other workers within the same social work service. In this case, information had been available earlier as the records showed an older referral from a health service professional who had been treating Linda's older sibling. The referral expressed concern for Linda (then age 6) but was not pursued as the information was given 'in confidence' and no formal complaint had been made.

Some years later these concerns resurfaced. Linda's school contacted social services as they were increasingly worried about her. She seemed to have difficulty controlling her behaviour and would shout out during class, throw pens at people and seemed unable to form friendships. She would often arrive at school hungry and dishevelled and suffered at school from bullying. The problems for Linda had been long-standing enough for her to have an 'educational statement' of special needs and part of this agreement was that she should be escorted on and off of the school bus as an attempt to protect her from bullying behaviour.

A joint investigation between social services and the police revealed that Linda lived with her parents in a house that was in need of extensive repair. The home was cluttered throughout and there were structural problems with the building. This damage caused Mr and Mrs Smith to live out of their bedroom with Linda sleeping on the floor. The home had no cooking facilities other than a microwave and no heating. Mr and Mrs Smith owned another property locally and the living conditions were still poor but much better than the original house. As part of the negotiation to avoid the use of Police Protection Powers, the parents agreed to live out of their second house and work with social services to improve the living conditions for themselves and Linda. The concerns led to an Initial Child Protection Conference and the case was transferred to the longer term team and allocated to Naomi.

Over the following year of Naomi's intensive involvement the 'picture', that began developing of what was actually going on with this family, went through dramatic changes. At the beginning it seemed to be a case of offering help to parents who were experiencing a number of problems in living and seemed to be unable to cope. However, the nature of the intervention changed to become a statutory duty to protect a young person despite the resistance of the parents. The central rationale and driver of this change in power perspectives was Naomi's social work focus upon and resulting relationship with a young person. This is the story of Naomi's social work practice experiences, in her own words, and what happened to safeguard the well-being of Linda.

Initial phase: working with the 'grey'

I think it was the amount of greyness of the case. It was too grey. When it is in every aspect you need to dig further to find out why. Which is another kind of alarm bell really isn't it?

In this early stage my idea of what the problem was kept changing. The father had health difficulties and could not work, and the mother was working full time. I looked at her stressors; full time mother, working, looking after Linda and looking after the father and I initially thought that the housing situation and poor finances had got the better of them. It seemed at that time that they needed the right support to live in that second home and so what we tried to work with was for Linda to go to foster care for 28 days under a voluntary agreement. We were arranging for an agency to go in and clear out the home. This was 'preventive community services' as an approach; this was let's get in, help improve their situation and let them live their life without services.

But as time went on, the resistance and non-engagement of the parents worsened and I would get strange telephone calls from them to say that I wasn't allowed to have Linda in my car. An identified area of need was for Linda to have an adult to talk to in a safe environment, and that would be met through me meeting with Linda at school. The parents seemed to have accepted that as part of the plan so that is how I got my access to her. But something kept niggling at me and I think sometimes you have to go with your instincts when you are a social worker. School thought Linda had a form of autism, but could not start an assessment due to the parents not agreeing. I did not believe, from my own experience, that Linda had some of the 'typical' traits of autism.. Linda demonstrated great empathy for people. I spoke to Linda about feelings, for example, Linda was able to articulate that if someone hit me, I would feel pain and be upset and would say, 'I hope nobody ever would do that to you'.

There were too many little bits of information leaking out from our discussions among the workers involved that told me something wasn't right. The core groups consisted of myself, the school nurse and education; parents did not attend. The core groups were held in the school. On the second core group, I was walking through the school and Linda saw me and started to follow me. I allowed Linda to come with me and she sat down with the school nurse and teacher. Linda appeared to be enjoying the attention, she was beaming. My concerns increased due to Linda having two blisters between her thumb and forefinger and she stated it was from riding her bike a lot, I was not so concerned about this, as the grips on bikes can be tough on hands, until Linda stated, 'I have to go out for three hours, I have to get out of the way.' This is when information started coming through that told me something was not right.

Interviewer: So it was from you making the effort to spend time with Linda, slowly you started to see what life was like for her.

Yes, it is an example of the importance of relationship based practice; it is so easily forgotten, because we are busy, it is almost like we have to see that child, we have to do these home visits to tick a box – but you need to remember why you are going there. Because she had a teaching assistant, it was a lot easier, she didn't engage in classes because she was getting one to one with the teaching assistant. So I was able to just pop in and out, I didn't need to book appointments. It started as simple as talking about what she enjoyed, cars and art. Linda was really interested in cars and due to my limited knowledge, Linda was able to tell me all about cars. I believe it built a trust and she got to know me a little bit. I think if I had not done that, she probably would have been living as she is and we would not have got the disclosures as she was so shut down.

Phase two: 'upping the ante' – public law outline and disclosures

[T]hat is when the negotiation becomes difficult I think, because I know what I have seen, and I know what I have heard, and I know that the child has told me that – but I have got to relay that and convince my senior management of the same thing but they haven't seen it, they haven't met the child, they don't know what she is like, they don't know that when she is stressed she looks at the ceiling and moves her hands and they don't know any of that, so I think that's when I started struggling, it was almost trying to convince everybody of what I heard and what I saw and that it was true.

We had made a decision to go into the public law outline process; the evidence being, parental non-engagement, Linda's continuing school behavioural problems and the evidence of her still sleeping on the floor in the home. So I had written them a letter, outlining the reasons why and arranging a meeting and advising them that they needed to now involve a solicitor in the process.

I sent the letter and tried to discuss the action with the parents. They were angry but with the child protection plan not working and no change occurring, the action was necessary. From that pre-proceedings letter, within a few weeks in May, I received a call from the school to say that Linda had arrived at school in a foul mood, angry and upset. Linda was eating crisps in a classroom and she was told off, and they described Linda looking at them and I remember them saying 'it was absolutely desperation, she'd just looked at us and pleaded, I just have to eat'. They could see it was a genuine need. They took her out and gave her some toast and spoke to her. Linda stated that she needed to talk to me, and that she can't go home anymore.

I went along and she sat down and yes, she just started to talk about the physical harm, being beaten by a clothes brush, the reason why she was so angry at school was because she wasn't allowed to eat all day the previous day, and that night and that morning, because her Dad thought she was naughty about something, but Linda wasn't able to identify what she had been naughty about. She had been woken up throughout the night, because it was for her own good and she was talking about her mum getting beaten nearly every day, she was kicked in the side, other times, it's worse. And that was the start of the disclosures.

I felt very strongly, we had to take action at that point. We applied for an Emergency Protection Order and I had to gain the service manager's agreement. I remember there was a discussion about Linda going home while we issue care proceedings – I think the idea was to make sure that what she was saying was correct. But because of the months of non-engagement and the information that was coming through; myself with the support of my line manager consulted the legal team, and we stood our ground with regard to stating Linda should not return home. I just felt very strongly, that if you could see the difference, as she was talking, I would be very shocked if she was lying, because that would be an incredible story to make up and to be so real about it. I had to go back to school after the management meeting while legal was preparing the paperwork for court, and explain to Linda that we were going to apply to the court for her to go to foster care immediately – and to check 'is that what she wanted?' and to check again her understanding of why I was applying to court for her not to return home, and to ensure she understood.

Phase three: working with everyone despite resistance

Throughout the proceedings I continued to write to the parents with information about Linda, any assessment, or contact issues, I continued to be the one to sign off that letter because it felt like it was important, because I was still the social worker, they might not have wanted me to be, but I was still there, I was still working with their daughter and I was also trying to acknowledge with them that they were still her parents...

The scope for negotiation between local authority and the parents was virtually nil because they wouldn't engage in discussions with us. Their solicitor was very much saying, 'I feel like the social worker they are coming to me with queries that they need to be phoning your office to ask'. But they wouldn't do it; they would not have anything to do with the local authority at all. You can't force people, they need to know that she went to the dentist last week, or she had this done, or she had a day out doing this, and I often wrote to them, because what I was trying to do is to get some sort of communication back with them.

Interviewer: But how did it feel for you, because you are basically being rejected there aren't you – they are seeing you as the baddy, they are putting you in that box, and for a lot of people that makes it easier doesn't it, it makes them feel better. How did it feel, what was it like being the baddy in this?

I felt frustrated, I suppose it upset me a little in that I questioned my skills as a social worker, I felt under-confident, 'what can I do differently, how can I change this situation?' But then, through regular supervision, actually, I recognised that I did all that I could in the situation. But, when they started making accusations and threats towards me and particularly accusations linking me to their daughter; I felt very angry about that. Not only for myself but for Linda because she was so humiliated. And what was happening was that Linda was becoming concerned about me, saying, 'they might hurt you, they might shout at you, I don't want them to do that to you' and that is the wrong role. I had to reassure her, with support from the foster parents. The foster carers would often joke with her saying, 'she is made of harder stuff than your parents, and she'll be fine', and that helped soften it for her and they managed to help her laugh, which helped me to feel better about it. Linda's parents would always phone them up and say, 'that bloody Gillard', so in the foster-family, every time I visited, they had a joke going, every time I visited; they would roll their eyes and say, that bloody Gillard! They used humour, and it helped Linda and helped me as well. Because it was a case of, what have they gone and done now, and as the proceedings went on the more bizarre the accusations were becoming and the more I felt stronger and able to kind of think, what's next.

Reflecting on the experience: social worker and young person

Linda had to give her perspective throughout the court proceedings and it was hard and I think starting to border on traumatic for her and emotionally harming. Linda originally spoke to me, and then to the foster-carer, the Guardian, an advocate, a paediatrician and also the school. This is an immense amount of people and by the end of a nine-month court case she had enough and needed it over.

Linda went through various stages of separation. Linda's perspective at first was hope that her parents would make changes as she felt she should live with them. Then anger that they were not making changes and would phone and be horrible to her and her foster-carer. Linda continued with her view that she should go home. Linda was embarrassed to be in care and didn't want anyone at school to know. Linda did not always agree to the plan, as sometimes she would insist on returning home to care for her mum (she worried for her), it was then I would have to say 'no' and that I would not allow that. Linda would try to argue but then understood and accepted this. Linda's behaviours were very challenging at times and separation anxiety became very challenging for the foster-carer. If they went out for a night and had her 'baby-sat' she would stay by the front door waiting their return and then be angry with them for going out. Linda's perspective changed throughout the proceedings and after about six months she started to settle more and realised that nothing back at home had changed and that she would likely not be returning.

Linda's experience has been hard and tough, due to her age and being the main subject of a court case. However, she started in an emergency placement on the Friday until the Monday. That was over a year ago and she is still there! Linda formed an attachment and the foster-carers bonded with her and provided her with stability and a nurturing home. They believe in her and they support her and will always fight for her rights. Linda has many social difficulties which result in her needing extra help in school or to attend special group activities and sometimes it can be a battle to gain this extra help. The foster-carers do not give up on her and will not allow her to go without the support she needs. They have accepted Linda into their wider family and so wider family members step in for respite care without Linda feeling rejected as she is staying with 'Aunt Julie' – normal within their family and perfectly acceptable. They are determined for Linda to not feel like she should be treated differently, but also accepting her social limitations and keeping her safe. They did put up with verbal abuse from Linda's parents which not many would do. As time has progressed they no longer hear from the parents.

I would say at the time of being shouted and screamed at and followed in my car by the parents, I felt irritated by this. There are self-doubts in how to manage the situation, but due to their extreme behaviour it only ever confirmed that I was doing the right thing. It does add emotional pressure to an already emotionally charged job. I believe pressures from that case and other cases, plus threats and witnessing Linda still being emotionally harmed, made me feel under-confident and at times like I can't work at that level of anxiety. Social work is a stressful job, but sometimes there are releases of the anxiety; this was not the case at this time. I found myself emotionally charged for the majority of the time about all cases. I don't think it could have gone on. Eventually this eased, anxiety eased and the parents stopped harassing so much. I think it caused me more anxiety with the foster-carers and Linda being on the receiving end of it all, and me not having the power to stop it – that was frustrating. I didn't lose sleep (that takes a lot!) but I don't think the quality of sleep was that good as I would often wake in the morning having dreamt of the case or another case!

When I compare the anxiety and pressure of how I feel today with the cases I have, I can look back at this and honestly state I could go back and manage that much better now. What has happened since is that my cases are very complex and I am managing more risky situations. Linda's parents were verbal and were not very good at following me – I knew what was happening and I had a sense of control. It is much worse when you don't know what they are going to do and you know they are able to do harm. This is the importance of supervision and support. I had very good support at that time.

Personal reflection

I worked with Linda at a time when I was still learning about the court process and what role the social worker plays as part of this. I worked closely with Linda prior to her being accommodated in foster care and my aim was to build up a relationship with her so that I could understand her life, her views and how she lived day to day. I remember being cross examined on the day the local authority applied to court for an Emergency Protection Order and I was able to describe Linda and talk about her in detail. This knowledge proved invaluable and has proven to be essential in other care proceedings cases. In addition, it enables the practitioner to be child-focused and able to keep the child at the centre of any care planning. Once Linda was placed into foster care, we had the responsibility to promote contact, despite it being emotionally harmful towards Linda. At times, contact with her mother was positive, other times she would whisper to her, or the father would turn up shouting. Linda was often very upset about this and as proceedings went on, Linda started to choose not to attend. Parents felt she should be 'forced' to have contact and it felt at times that the planning in court around contact was to suit the parents needs rather than Linda's needs. On reflection, as the social worker, I should have limited contact early in the proceedings, although this would have led to a contested hearing. I believe now with the benefit of hindsight that is what I should have done. As a result of this, when planning for contact during care proceedings I now create a plan that puts the child and their needs in the centre. Contact continues to be a difficult issue in court and the care planning is not always clear. This case has shown me that the work does not stop at the final hearing, and in fact more intervention is needed after to help settle the young people and to help put in protective measures to ensure the young person and carers remain safe and feel secure.

Discussion

It is a truism of social work that every case is different. This is undoubtedly correct in the unique, particular details of people, places and the dynamics of interactions over time. But it is also true that there are larger scale patterns of similarity and familiarity through which the practice wisdom of social workers and their supervisors can develop. This story of an apparent case of child and family support that on closer scrutiny turns into high priority child protection is unique but will be recognisable to anyone that has worked on the front-line in a local authority children's service. Undertaking this close scrutiny and enquiry is, we would argue, the job of a social worker. In complex and puzzling situations it is the social worker's role to pull together the strands and form a judgement of what is going on and determine, with others, whether and what form of intervention is needed. In this story of practice the social worker climbed many learning curves of knowledge, skills, values, resilience and practice capability. It is the sort of practice example that experienced social work colleagues often knowingly reflect upon and identify with a degree of British under-statement as 'a good learning case'. As Naomi explains, this case came quite early in her career and she needed to develop a coping capacity to deal with the demands of a situation that quickly spiralled into a statutory obligation to intervene. Harry Ferguson argues that to 'enable the core tasks of child-centred practice to be carried out requires personal resources, a capacity for deep reflection and a highly skilled performance' (2011, p. 74). Naomi's story is an example of all these three qualities.

A central factor in the direction that this case took was the time that Naomi gave to Linda in growing a relationship of trust. As she put it:

> it is an example of the importance of relationship based practice; it is so easily forgotten, because we are busy, it is almost like we have to see that child, we have to do these home visits to tick a box – but you need to remember why you are going there.

In Scotland the 21st Century Review, *Changing Lives*, emphasised the importance for service users of 'a reliable, consistent relationship with a single worker whom they trust' (Scottish Executive, 2006, p. 37) and this key message has been repeated in the Munro Report recommendations for England (Munro, 2011). There has been much criticism of 'care manager' developments in social work that have led to practitioners spending more time feeding the recording system in front of a computer screen than they do in working with children and their families (Garrett, 2005). Naomi recognised that she needed to fulfil the target obligations and 'tick the box' but it was about much more than that. The driver for Naomi was getting to know Linda and for Linda to get to know and develop some trust in her as a social worker. That was why, in facing the resistance and hostility to her involvement by the parents in Linda's home, she prioritised seeing Linda at school on a regular basis. Naomi was able to work with the teaching assistant and other welfare colleagues at the school to develop a secure place to develop her relationship (Gilligan, 1998). Her connection with Linda became an epicentre of importance from which flowed case direction, case decisions and case priorities.

Early in our discussions I was struck by a part of what Naomi said:

> ...something kept niggling at me and I think, you know, sometimes you have to go with your instincts when you are a social worker.

This 'niggle', this feeling that something is not right, speaks to the complexities of how people make sense of what is happening on a number of different levels. The role of intuition or 'gut feeling' in professional practice is recognised through an understanding of what is called tacit knowledge (Atkinson and Claxton, 2000) and its important role in guiding more explicit and evidence-based decision-making. Naomi's story illustrates why it is so important for social workers to be open to and to listen to 'the voice within'. Maintaining an independent view of situations that has to be persuaded is what professional judgement is about. As Naomi said, over the initial phases of her involvement and developing assessment of what was happening, *'There were too many little bits of information leaking out from our discussions amongst the workers involved that told me something wasn't right'.*

In this story, Naomi had very little opportunity to negotiate with the parents because of their resistance and hostility. However, with her supervisor's support, she still needed to actively negotiate with a senior service manager and persuade them that an Emergency Protection Order under Section 44 of the Children Act 1989[1] was needed in this situation. In a local authority statutory service, the lines of management accountability demand that decisions are approved and for this Naomi needed to back her own judgement. This takes courage, resilience and a determination to stay child-centred. Naomi was able to do this because she had spent time with this young person, had developed a relationship with her and as a result 'knew' that her account had to be believed. This story is an example of why listening to the voice of the child (Ofsted, 2011) remains the central message of child protection. If child protection is about any one thing, it is all about the child.

Note

1. The equivalent provision in Scotland is s.37 of the Children's Hearings (Scotland) Act 2011.

14 Negotiation Without Power: Mediating Post-Adoption Contact Arrangements in a Facebook World

Jenny Jackson and Barry Cooper

Jenny recently retired after a social work career of over three decades spent entirely within local authorities. When generic practice gave way to increasing specialisation she worked with children and families and then moved into the field of adoption and fostering. For the last 16 years of practice she worked within a local authority adoption service which pioneered the provision of a range of support services to all parties to adoption – adopted children and adults along with their birth as well as their adoptive relatives. For much of this time she took the lead role for contact issues which included responsibility for the service's Letterbox scheme. This is a means whereby, if agreed to be in the best interests of the child, adoptive and birth families can exchange letters, usually once a year, without compromising the confidentiality of the adoption.

Questions to ask yourself as you read:

- How much power and control do social workers have in practice?

- Why is it important to negotiate with people and include their different perspectives?

- What aspects of your practice do you feel could be more negotiative and how would this make improvements?

Case summary

Jenny's story focuses upon some of the issues arising from trying to negotiate post-adoption contact arrangements for families in the aftermath of complex historical care decisions. 'Letterbox' contact, where an adoption agency mediates the exchange of communications between birth and adoptive families, is the most common method of contact for children that have been adopted (Neil, 2004). An earlier survey by Lowe et al. (1999) estimated that 95 per cent of adoption agencies provided some kind of letterbox service.

This story involves a family group of four siblings, aged 11 (Adam), 12 (Bea), 14 (Carie) and 16 (Di). One of the historical complications in this story is that two children were placed for adoption with one couple, and two with another couple; the two families had been introduced to each other and they lived quite close to each other. The original plan was to enable the siblings to continue having the face-to-face contact they'd had up until then. Not all of them had been in the same foster placement, but they had maintained regular personal contact while they were in foster care. So, this was a good arrangement in the beginning. Unfortunately, by the time Adam and Bea were adopted, Carie and Di's placement had broken down, before any adoption order had been made and they had gone back into foster care. After a period of about two years they were placed back with the birth mother. So that meant that the planned face-to-face contact between the siblings couldn't continue as there is usually an assumption of non-disclosure of identity and whereabouts for adoptive families. The contact arrangements had to be changed to being indirect via Letterbox. The repercussions of this have only become clearer over time.

Some years later the children's birth mother unexpectedly arrived on the adopters' doorstep saying Adam and Di had been in touch via Facebook and she thought the parents ought to sit down together and discuss what to do. The adoptive parents told her to contact Jenny and several telephone discussions were had with both sides. A 'cooling off' period was agreed upon where no further contact was to take place between the children until a meeting between the adults could be negotiated and arranged. Jenny wanted to meet with the adoptive parents to explore how they felt about this and what options there may be for managing this new era of contact. However, this arrangement turned out not to be sustainable.

The discussion about this case took place at the beginning of these developments and highlights the issues that arise from complicated contact arrangements where there is a presumption of confidentiality and non-disclosure of identifying details. However, in an age of near universal availability of mobile social media, the rules that apply to adults are difficult to enforce with children and young people.

Power to the (young) people!

An 'open' model of contact between adopted children and their birth relatives after adoption is now the norm rather than an exception (Lowe et al., 1999; Parker, 1999). This move towards facilitated contact can be seen as a significant shift in practice away from the far more 'closed' model that prevailed in adoption practices from the 1940s to the 1980s (Triseliotis et al., 1997). However, the 'rules' of contact through schemes such as Letterbox are not entirely open. They are designed to preserve confidentiality and are a tightly controlled and monitored form of communication in order to avoid identifying data being released about where adoptive families live. The result is a restricted and infrequent form of contact that is the absolute antithesis of the immediate, spontaneous and very frequent social media contacts that are ubiquitous in their use by young people through mobile phones. The dilemmas arising from this technological revolution have only begun to be addressed in recent years (Fursland, 2010, 2013).

> What had happened apparently, according to the birth mother, was that Adam had sent a Facebook message via a friend's account to Di. Di then messaged him back and of course was saying, this was her dream come true. It turned out that Adam's friend's brother was at school with Di so that enabled the birth family to discover where the adoptive family live. But an additional complication is that, we had discovered that the birth family had moved to a house, close to the adoptive family. So at first we were alarmed and thought, 'they know something'. But it was just a coincidence. So we made the adoptive family aware of that. I also discovered which school the girls were going to and it wasn't the secondary school where Bea was due to start. And the adopters actually coped very well with all this. But the birth family didn't know anything about how close they were living to the adoptive family until Adam and Di linked up through Facebook. And that then enabled birth mother to go and knock on the adopters' door. As the adoptive mother said to me…'it's every adoptive parent's worst nightmare, you open the door and find your children's birth mother on the door step.' But in talking to the birth mother I do believe her in a way when she says, 'Well I thought that was the best thing to do, to go around there, parent to parent and say….'

Because what she was saying was 'This Facebook contact has happened, I don't know if you know about it, but you need to know. It's happened and I think we should all sit down together and talk about it.'

Working with decisions that people do not accept

The popular conception of adoption is that it is a final decision, taken after extensive due process, that children can't live with their birth parents and they are going to be adopted. But it is often the case that very few birth parents will agree to the decision and sign the legal order because, in Jenny's extensive experience of working with birth parents, to them it is like saying, 'here, take my children'. They may have to accept that in reality the child is never going to come back to live with them. So it becomes a passive acceptance by not actively opposing the order; but they don't agree to it in the emotional sense – 'I never signed away my child, I never agreed to the adoption'. So in a legalistic sense, it's been irrevocably decided but in the reality of people's emotions and, these days, the actualities of people's ability to contact each other, it may not make as much difference as it did in the past.

> Before, social media like Facebook we could pretty much guarantee confidentiality. I mean, there was always the outside chance, but we could pretty well guarantee it to adoptive families. But I think what Facebook is doing and what is so worrying for us is that that's really blowing it all out of the water. Within the Letterbox I can guarantee that there are all sorts of mechanisms which make it hugely unlikely that we are ever going to disclose the surname of the adoptive family to a birth family, their whereabouts or anything like that. But the spread of social media means that confidentiality in adoption can no longer be guaranteed in the way it was in the past. In many ways, it surprises me that these sorts of scenarios aren't happening more often. It remains to be seen whether Facebook will mean the end of confidentiality in adoption but I am dealing with a steady trickle of situations. Sometimes it feels like a bit of a flood, like two in one week, you know. What do you do? All I can do is try and contact people and encourage them to actually have a dialogue with me.

Helping to negotiate different perspectives

The happenstance of these two families being geographically close and the increased contact that Facebook offers to users of the service meant that actual meetings became more likely. It was perhaps inevitable that it would be engineered between the two pairs of siblings. Carie, who is very articulate and quite a strong character, feels very angry about the fact that she feels it was never made clear to them when choosing to return to their birth mother, that the price they would pay would be not to see their siblings again. Similarly, Di was absolutely determined that she was going to see Adam and talk to him.

> So the adopters had rung my team in a bit of a state and one of my colleagues had spoken to the birth mother on the phone and re-negotiated that this won't happen again until Jenny comes back; she'll pick this up. Now again, interestingly, birth mother's take on this was that she actually behaved responsibly and sensitively; she did what she thought was the best thing in the circumstances. She said she stayed in the background and she didn't try to talk to Adam because she thought she ought to leave that up to him. Whereas from the adopters' perspective, they felt angry and upset that the birth family had engineered a meeting but they were also angry and upset that birth mum had just stood there and not said a word, that Di was the only one who spoke to Adam. So they were as aggrieved by that as by birth mum breaking her word, which was how they saw it. They said she should have kept Di under control and to an extent they may be right, but on the other hand...birth mother's explanation was 'well, we went because we thought it was better than not going but we didn't speak to Adam because we thought that would make things worse'. And as the worker – and as someone who wasn't actually there at the time – how much weight do you give to this? Do you side totally with the adopters' view of the situation? For most adopters, when confidentiality has been the expectation, there's already quite a bit of wariness, of anxiety for them when thinking about any contact – even via Letterbox – with their children's birth mother because of the history. So again I'm trying to understand the adopter's feelings and as we would say, validate those feelings, accept them and then try to present alternative scenarios to them, 'have you thought about this; you see it that way, she sees it this way and actually I see it another way, you know, partly your way and partly her way; can you think about it from that angle too?' I try to present an alternative explanation for people to the one they might immediately seize on.

Negotiating to work directly with young people

In the complicated circumstances of a sibling group being split up and two living separately with adopted parents and two with birth parents there can be issues that arise where a post-adoption support social worker will find themselves mediating across differences. Negotiating with children and young people calls for particular skills and insights as there is often the acute awareness that, in many ways, the children are on the receiving end of decisions taken that are beyond their control.

> Sometimes the things that are most stressful are also the things that are intellectually challenging, which is what a large part of what the job satisfaction is. These four children it seems to me, have all suffered enormously because of things that are completely outside their control, because of the actions of adults; either the adults have failed to do things they should have done, or they've done things they shouldn't have done and the children pay the price for it. It's bad enough that the siblings are separated through adoption but it's been compounded by the fact that these two have gone home to mum. But there is a price to pay for that, which up until now has been the children not being able to see each other face to face.

In social work there are increased expectations that social workers must involve children and young people as participants in assessments, plans and decision-making (Wright et al., 2006). In principle there can be no argument against this although in practice working with children should be started through a negotiation with their parents. This is particularly the case in adoption where social workers have been extensively involved in helping to legally create the adoptive family. But in situations where children are older and increasingly seen as young adults and able to make their own autonomous decisions, the power to influence events may be limited for both parents and social worker. Nonetheless, in this case, Jenny needed to begin her next steps by negotiating with the adoptive parents.

> It was quite difficult actually when I got back to work. I had several phone conversations with adoptive dad and I was finding it surprisingly difficult to get to see the family, either the parents on their own or the parents and children. Usually parents who've got a problem are very keen for you to go round and see them rather than simply talking on the phone and on other occasions this has been my experience with this family but when I got back to work it wasn't like this. He wanted me to go and see the birth family first whereas I said to him, I would far rather come to you first because I need to understand how you're feeling and what your thinking is, and what the bottom line is for you, because it's for you to call the shots. But I had to do it that way in the end; to see the birth family first and then go and see the adoptive parents, and I felt he was keeping me at a distance which surprised me somewhat because normally when adoptive families are under some sort of stress, the first thing they want is a social worker sitting on their

settee and some face to face time. So it took quite a while and I think he just didn't want to engage with this, he was feeling very angry with birth mother. They've had a lot going on with the educational side about helping Adam manage this move to secondary school because he's not found coping with primary school at all straightforward either. So it took a while, but I did eventually get to see the adopters and they agreed that I should see the children. So I went to talk to Bea and Adam.

Negotiating with young people

In working with young people to ascertain their views and wishes it is important to avoid the assumption that they will be similar simply because they are in a category of 'sibling' or 'young person'. Most parents will know from experience that young people are likely to be very different and unlikely to want the same thing. Jenny needed to talk to the different siblings and find out how they saw the situation and what it was that they wanted to do. In Jenny's position of 'mediator' she had no power to make anything happen and was reliant upon her negotiating skills to find out what scope there was for influencing a sustainable outcome.

> So you know, we were doing various things, chatting, talking. Bea and Adam actually wanted to get out their life story books; that was their idea. They asked me a couple of questions about their past and I said I wasn't sure and did they have a life story book and ooh, they were away...so we also looked at their life story books and their 'later in life' letter and talked a bit about the situation and where they're at. Bea is saying, she'll be thirteen in March and she will be old enough to use Facebook then, officially. But she is anxious about seeing Di and Carie again without getting to know them first so her idea is to use Facebook to get to know them, which seems a sound idea. She's not in a rush to have face to face contact; I think she is quite anxious about it, because she said, 'how would I know what to say to them if I saw them?' So I acknowledged that and we talked about how she wouldn't be on her own, mum and dad would be there, I could be there, if that was helpful to everybody, when the time comes. And how the other important thing is that it doesn't happen for her until she wants it to, and that that is difficult because Di and Carie want one thing and feel one thing; but brothers and sisters don't necessarily feel the same about it. But it was clear from the way Di and her birth mother and partner talk that for them, the way they feel is the way everybody else must be feeling. I often encounter that from birth parents: 'Well, X must feel like that. X is my child so of course I know how they feel!' Well, yes you know them well,

in many ways you might be right, but actually maybe not always. Or, you know, 'They're brothers and sisters, they were always very close...' so it is almost impossible for the birth family to think 'Actually, Bea and Adam might not feel as keen on this as Di and Carie do.' So part of what I was doing was trying to uncover that sort of thinking and starting to feed in new thoughts and I'll do more now that I have met Bea and Adam.

Relationships as the foundation for negotiation

It can be easy to overlook the part played by an established working relationship when social workers are engaged in complicated discussions and mediation. In this particular case Jenny had been supporting both sides with the existing contact arrangements and associated issues for almost ten years. This had enabled the building of long-standing relationships. Social work practice, especially in situations of stress and conflict, is always easier if the practitioner and the service users know each other and understand something of how each view and handles various issues. It was particularly important for the birth mother that she perceived Jenny as someone who treated her with respect and acknowledged that she had an ongoing worth and role to play as a birth parent even though she did not have care of her children. Jenny recognised that birth mother wanted her children to be happy and growing into stable, achieving and well-rounded young people. However, her position as mediator meant that there would still be a need to challenge her at times and be very clear about the fact that the adoptive parents, not her, were Bea and Adam's legal and psychological parents and that this meant they were the ultimate decision-makers in matters regarding the children. Negotiating with all these different individuals with their different attitudes, all of different ages, living in different places and a birth mother who probably wants them all back together again is a complex and probably unique set of role and task demands.

> Birth mother still regards her children as her flesh and blood, and would find it very hard to begin to imagine that they might not at some point want to see her. Although in fairness to her I have to say, and I said this to her too, she does talk very positively about the adopters who she has met. They had a meeting during the introductions and birth mum says she's always felt very, very positively about the adopters and feels that they're doing a fantastic job. She says she recognises that they are and will remain the children's parents... you know, they're the ones who are there day in, day out and as I have said to them, I think she genuinely means that. In my judgement – and I've met a lot of birth parents over the many years

I've been working as a social worker – while you always learn to keep a degree of scepticism because the proof of the pudding is in what people actually do rather than what they say, nevertheless, I do feel birth mum genuinely means that. So as I have said to the adoptive parents, that is a positive platform to build on and it is quite unusual – I don't get that very often. The other thing is, she does accept the part she played in this situation arising…. I was talking to the birth family and at one point, I asked Di 'Who do you see as responsible for the fact that you and Carie and Bea and Adam weren't able to go on seeing each other?' What I was wanting to tease out of them, what we got to eventually was, it's not the children's adoptive parents' fault, it's not their responsibility and birth mother said 'It's my responsibility, you know, I take responsibility for what I was like at that time. Removing the children was the right thing to do at that time.' And it's unusual to find a birth parent that's actually willing to own up to something like that.

Discussion: negotiating complex problems with few clear solutions

In this story, Jenny's role involves skilled negotiating and problem exploration where different perspectives are accepted, examined and new ways of thinking about things offered up for consideration. What is 'a problem' for the adoptive parents may not be seen the same way by the young people who simply want to make contact and try to make sense of why they are living separately. The complex questions about contact between adopted children and birth families have been subject to much debate (Ryburn, 1996, 1998, 1999; Quinton et al., 1997, 1999; Quinton and Selwyn, 1998; Neil, 2010), but the widespread availability of the potential for instant contact through social media has somewhat sidelined the discussion in order to focus upon pragmatic responses. There can be few, if any, clear guidelines about the best courses of action beyond the patient, sensitive and personalised mediation that makes up much of Jenny's role and tasks in this story. As Elsbeth Neil (2002) succinctly concludes, 'In these kinds of situations, what is needed is greater than just emotional support – it is helping people to *think* and to develop a framework for understanding the dynamics of adoption' (p. 37). This 'framework for understanding' has to be created between the parents and children participating in a unique network of personal histories and interpersonal circumstances. Jenny is able to help both children and parents adapt to and prepare for complex and changing situations where there is little power to control events and even less benefit in trying to do so. The negotiations are much more about, as Neil says, helping everyone to *think* for themselves and take responsibility to be sensitive and responsive to the needs of others. In this respect Jenny is modelling best behaviour as an integral part of her practice. The young people in this story are, rightly, at the centre of importance and Jenny illustrates the detailed negotiations of her practice in raising their awareness:

> I'm trying to get them to think through different scenarios, you know, 'Have you thought about this...? What would happen if...? What would happen if you bumped into each other when you were out in the neighbourhood? What might that feel like? What do you think you might say? What do you think might do?' So I'll be trying to do some of that with both sets of children, the adopted children and their birth siblings if possible. Giving the birth siblings the message that it's best if you don't do that (initiate further contact), I understand that you'll be very, very tempted to, but it's best if you don't because what your brother and sister are saying is 'Not just yet' and 'It feels a bit uncomfortable to us.' But if you do find yourself in that situation... I'm trying to feed in ideas about the most helpful ways of doing things if they do actually find themselves encountering each other.

The skills of negotiating and of advocacy, of representing different sides to the others and of getting people to see things in slightly different ways, are fluid processes that social workers develop and creatively employ across situations. It can be rare for a clear consensus to emerge about problems which makes obvious solutions difficult to identify and attain. In some ways, in constantly dealing with new situations over which there is no real control and having to adapt constantly to changing situations, there is space for creativity where the only viable practice approach is to call upon reserves of knowledge, skills and experience and 'make it up as you go along' in responding to the unique aspects of changing lives over time.

> It isn't clear what the solution is because it's their lives and from now on we are in a new situation that's got to be managed. We'll have to go on doing the best we can at each stage, negotiating, renegotiating, continuing to interpret each side to the other, trying to help them understand each other's views and feelings. You've just got to keep on and on doing that.

15 Negotiating Solutions

Pat Barrow and Barry Cooper

Pat is an independent social worker and is appointed by the family court to assist in private law cases when parents or other family members are in dispute regarding contact and residence arrangements. Her career began in youth work after which she qualified as a social worker, first in the Probation Service, then Youth Justice and then in Family Court Welfare and the Children and Family Court Advisory and Support Service (CAFCASS) while also contributing to training and practice teaching. After almost 30 years Pat took the opportunity to continue her work independently and during the last four years has specialised in working exclusively with families and individuals entrenched in the acrimony and bitterness that can follow separation and divorce and have such a detrimental impact upon children.

Questions to ask yourself as you read:

- Why is it important to see beyond presenting problems?
- What are the advantages of a solution-focused approach to practice?
- What do social workers need to do to empower service users?

Case summary

Joe (7) and Susie (3) and their parents are typical of many families that Pat is appointed to work with. Mr and Mrs Potter had separated when Susie had just been born and Joe was four. Mrs Potter had moved away with the children to another part of the country and, having no knowledge of their whereabouts, Mr Potter had made an application to court to trace the family. It took several months to locate her and then it remained in a court not local to where Mrs Potter had relocated to in order to preserve her confidential address. CAFCASS was appointed and suggested monthly contact at a Contact Centre nearest to Mrs Potter's home and a round trip of 120 miles for Mr Potter. The aim of this arrangement was to give an opportunity for Mr Potter to re-engage with the children and to test his motivation. All too often there is an expectation that the non-resident parent (usually the father) will bear the financial cost of travelling to see their child. While this undoubtedly tests motivation sadly the financial burden can prove too much for some separated parents.

The matter was reviewed in court after six months. Mrs Potter had failed to turn up on three occasions insisting that the children had been unwell. The court decided to reconsider the matter after a further six months. By then Mrs Potter had missed two more visits and reported that while the children enjoyed seeing Mr Potter they needed her presence throughout the contact. Mr Potter felt frustrated by what he considered to be Mrs Potter's unnecessary presence and the court's reluctance to challenge her. He wanted contact to take place away from the Contact Centre. Mrs Potter would not consider this as she believed that the children were at risk if she was not present. CAFCASS advised that they could do no more to assist the family with what seemed an intractable dispute.

The court made the children party to the proceedings. Their solicitor instructed Pat to analyse the family dynamics, explore the possibilities for future contact away from the Contact Centre and identify what, if any, steps needed to take place to ensure that the children's safety remained paramount. The court realistically expected that progress would be in stages and could, in this case, take up to 12 months to resolve. The underlying principle that minimal intervention is always best for a child had to be balanced with an outcome which worked and was sufficiently flexible to avoid future returns to court. Judges can be prepared to re-timetable if, for instance, a two-month delay can mean a final resolution with the parents agreeing to ongoing arrangements.

Constructively engaging the parents

I arranged to meet both parents separately; Mrs Potter at home and Mr Potter initially after a scheduled contact and at home on a subsequent occasion. I always prefer home-based meetings; they set the scene and although I stress the need for a professional relationship it makes a helpful distinction between the work we will do together and the formal proceedings of the court.

Mrs Potter's anger and hostility towards Mr Potter were given full vent at that first meeting and it was important that I allowed her space to express some of how she felt. At the same time I had to prevent myself being labelled as 'the expert' with the expectation that I came up with the solution within a problem-solving model. I did what is referred to as the scaling exercise, scoring how life was for her right now – nought for truly awful and ten for perfection, or alternatively to choose from a selection of faces the best that fitted how she felt. Not surprisingly she scored three and selected the saddest face possible. 'Okay, so can you imagine life being any different? What would have to change?' Her response – 'well I don't want this court process to go on, I want it all to stop; I want it all to go away, him to go away'.

I encouraged her to imagine the reality of that and then, taking a more feasible approach, imagine what she could achieve and what would help to make her feel less helpless, more confident and in charge of her life. The crucial thing for her was to feel in control and not, as she felt it, manipulated by Mr Potter or dictated to by the court and a judge who did not know her or her children. It was clear that Mrs Potter was surprised by this approach; it almost stopped her in her tracks. Immediately conversation became more positive. I encouraged her to see that she could remain in charge and needed to identify clear and specific goals; and that I would support her to use her own skills and strengths to achieve those goals.

My first meeting with Mrs Potter was very difficult but she did agree that I should return later to meet the children. Although I often talk to children at home a more neutral venue enables that child to feel more able to talk frankly. I always seek the parents' permission to see a child in school and although Mrs Potter was somewhat reluctant she finally agreed that after meeting both children at home I could see Joe at lunch time at school. It is important that each family member feels listened to and given attention but knows that I have a similar relationship with each of them.

I met Mr Potter and took a similar approach with him. I initially listened to him expressing frustration and anger that there was so little contact, that his efforts seemed to be getting nowhere and how Mrs Potter's reluctance was being condoned by the court. I encouraged him to consider what he could do to make things easier. He suggested that I should visit him at home and see how his life had changed. He had a new partner and family and felt he was now responsible and a 'hands on' Dad. He wanted to include Susie and Joe and be a Dad to them too, not just a weekend Dad, but actively involved in their development.

I arranged a home visit to see Mr Potter and his family. A Mum who is nervous and worried needs first-hand reliable information. My discussion of Mr Potter parenting his young family and demonstrating a steady relationship with his partner made a big difference to his credibility with her. Both children were keen to hear about Mr Potter. I had taken photographs during my visit and on some occasions I may make a DVD. Tangible evidence is a step towards building trust for parents and children. I was pleased to hear that the pictures went in to school with Joe and that there had been a reduction in the negative comments he had been making about Dads and families.

Joe and Susie

Joe was pleased to see me when I went to visit him at school. I soon gained the impression that he loved to draw and also to act. He drew pictures of the Contact Centre showing exactly where everybody sat. He told me that he enjoyed seeing Mr Potter but 'Dad was bad', 'Dad had left' them, 'he's nasty and I'm scared'. Joe could not actually describe any specific times when he had been scared of Mr Potter and in fact it became clear during our discussion that his memories of him were quite vague and based on what Mrs Potter had presented to him. Since contact had taken place at the Contact Centre they had had a good time together. Joe responded to my invitation to act out a typical contact meeting. He instructed me to be Mrs Potter and as the enactment continued Joe wanted Mrs Potter out of the door so that he and Susie could be with just Mr Potter. However he quickly added that he would be scared if Mrs Potter was not present. Afterwards talking to his class teacher she expressed concern that at every opportunity Joe would tell the class how bad his Dad was and how scared the family were of Mr Potter and how they had to hide from him and keep their address secret in case he found them.

I encouraged Joe to consider what would need to happen for him to be able to see Mr Potter without Mrs Potter being there. His sensible suggestion was that I could be there instead. At his request I took this idea back to Mrs Potter, who perhaps not surprisingly was initially horrified at the suggestion. She was full of alarm and fear and I encouraged her to consider what would make that a bit easier. I asked her to remember the first day that Joe had gone to school, how had she coped with leaving him on that first morning? By enabling her to consider the strengths and strategies she used successfully in the past I was able to help her consider using them in a different situation.

Susie was a little girl with some health problems and congenital difficulties which hopefully in time would improve, but at the time she was more vulnerable to infection and susceptible to cold. While it is essential to take genuine needs into account it was clear that Susie's fragility was something which Mrs Potter could cling to and impede progress. Again I encouraged a solution-focused approach; how could she ensure that Susie was warm enough and her needs were being met? It was surprising how quickly Mrs Potter's mood changed when I put her in the driving seat and empowered her to take control and consider solutions. It is important to avoid providing advice and attempting to tell people what to do. The risk is that it may have tapped into her reservoirs of resistance and negativity.

Progress towards solutions

We went back to court a few weeks later for the court to review progress. It was agreed that the next stage should be contact observed by me away from the Centre. The order was agreed by all parties and put both Mrs Potter and Mr Potter in a positive frame of mind. It is always difficult if something is ordered by the court against a family's wishes as this hardly encourages co-operation.

As the arranged day of contact without Mrs Potter being present came nearer her text messages to me demonstrated that she was struggling to give the children the support she knew that they ought to have. We spoke at length on the phone. I encouraged her to take control, reassure the children that I would be there and everything would be fine. When I arrived at the Centre where I was meeting the children it was clear that she had given them support and the encouragement they needed. They were both eager and waiting to go out with Mr Potter. Our visit to the park was a huge success with me able to report to Mrs Potter that Mr Potter had been attentive, safety conscious and entirely appropriate with both children, giving them an equal amount of attention; and in fact both children had been reluctant to leave the park.

A few days later Mrs Potter reported that Joe was unable to sleep and was upset and having nightmares. We talked about divided loyalties and how, being aware of her negative feelings towards Mr Potter, he would be confused. He was now experiencing positive time with Mr Potter and the inner turmoil that would cause would most likely trigger his unsettled behaviour. Once again I encouraged Mrs Potter to identify what she could do to make it easier for Joe. She admitted that she had been somewhat reluctant to allow Joe to talk about the contact with Mr Potter, almost as though for her own sanity she needed to keep it separate from the rest of her life. Of course this was not helping Joe.

I suggested that encouraging Joe to draw pictures would capture the essence of his confusion and recognise that young children need alternative ways to articulate complex emotions. I have explored a variety of different ways of communicating with children; in particular, using story stems when a variety of family scenarios are presented using dolls and animal figures as well as language and inviting the child to complete the story (Emde et al. 2003). Encouraging a child to draw pictures invites questions such as 'tell me more about that' which for the child promotes a feeling of me being approachable and listening to them. Mrs Potter suggested that she would encourage Joe to draw pictures too. I saw Joe in school the following week and he was clearly looking forward to the next meeting with Mr Potter when I would no longer be there. He was quite sure that he and Susie would have a good time and wanted to draw a picture for Mrs Potter so she would not worry about them – the pictures had worked then!

Moving towards a sustainable resolution

Over the next couple of months contact took place on a regular basis with the children seeing Mr Potter away from the Contact Centre for a limited time. It was time to move on to the next stage and understandably Mrs Potter found that a scary prospect. She initially reacted angrily to the suggestion that contact should progress to a point where the children could be introduced to Mr Potter's new family and plans made for them to visit his new home. She was horrified at the idea and it was tempting for me as the practitioner to step in and provide the answer through 'advice'. In order to avoid disempowering the family I continued to encourage them to see that this was a joint enterprise and that we had to work together to reach achievable goals through clear and specific steps.

It's about breaking progress into little steps. You might say, 'well I can't possibly do that, the kids can't go and stay with their Dad'. Okay at the moment you haven't even left the room when they have been there with him. Can you imagine how you could perhaps begin to think about doing that? Not even how are you going to do it but how are you going to think about it? So the steps might be minute and you might feel as though 'good grief I'm not making any progress with this at all'. But you are because you are beginning to help that person rethink the solution; you are re-framing the problem so they can see a solution and a way that they can achieve some success and make some progress. Not doing this risks just getting bogged back down in the problem again going round and round in an endless circle.

It is never easy to predict the course that individual cases will take but there is no doubt about the powerful 'model' provided by a solution-focused approach. The day after a meeting, in which Mrs Potter had shouted and yelled and accused me of trapping her, she telephoned with an unexpected proposal. After a sleepless night she had considered the situation and thought it best if she met Mr Potter's new partner first so that she could reassure the children what she was like. She would travel down on a school day because Susie was starting nursery during the next few weeks and they could meet at a cafe and talk over coffee. Before meeting the other children she wanted Joe and Susie to meet Mr Potter and his partner and her family. Her step-by-step plan would enable her to support Joe and Susie so that their time with Mr Potter and his family would be a positive experience. On the first occasion they met the other children she would like me to be there too. It was a sensible solution-focused approach which Mr Potter and the court had no hesitation in adopting.

Concluding summary

Twelve months ago meetings between the children and Mr Potter were supervised by an anxious and angry mother. Now the children are having regular contact with Mr Potter and his new family fully supported by Mrs Potter. In addition they are enjoying the freedom in other areas of their lives which Mrs Potter was reluctant to allow. She has come to accept that as part of their development, the children need to test out new experiences and to be relieved of the responsibility of dealing with adult issues.

Both parents have begun to make some sense of the complexity of divided loyalties which any child coping with separated parents experiences. The court has kept a watchful eye on progress achieved. Mindful of the no order principle (an order should only be made in cases where it is likely to maintain the best arrangements for a child) it considered that a final order should establish the expectation of regular staying contact as a useful framework for future arrangements. These would of necessity allow flexibility to meet the changing needs of developing children.

A solution-focused approach has empowered the whole family. My role has been as catalyst towards change, encouraging clients to find their own solutions with minimal intervention. That intervention is designed to be brief but not time limited and supportive in a way that enables the client to initiate a process of ongoing change. I very much believe the saying that the more you talk about a problem the bigger it gets, whereas the more you talk about solutions the more likely you are to be able to find one. A solution-focused approach encourages the practitioner to see the client as temporarily unable to overcome a life difficulty because they have not yet found a way around it. Instead of focusing on pathology it seeks out and builds on what is healthy and functioning in people's lives. A client overwhelmed by their problems can lose sight of their strengths and resources. Giving credit for efforts made increases the sense of collaboration between the practitioner and the client and helps to motivate clients especially those with a long history of failure and isolation.

Using a solution-focused approach has been a turning point in my career. While being well aware of the limitations of clients it has enabled me to be more positive, optimistic and hopeful even when faced with apparently intractable situations. I can incorporate a rich array of techniques from other therapeutic approaches into the solution-focused frame. Experience supports my overriding conviction that clients' ability to reorganise interiorised experience is the route to overcoming problems (Dodd, 2003).

My way of working

My eclectic background encourages me to integrate a solution-focused approach with other models of working. The principle of solution-focused therapy is simple 'if it works keep doing it'. It is a practical and accessible way of working which empowers and encourages clients to take control of their lives and genuinely prioritise the needs of their children. However the apparent simplicity of practice belies the considerable relationship skills demanded of the practitioner.

High conflict disputes over contact and residence are not common; most separated parents reach amicable arrangements for maintaining their children's relationship with each parent. However a minority of separated parents cannot resolve their problems and initiate contested court proceedings. Within that group there is a small number which take up an inordinate amount of court time as judges and professionals attempt to find a way forward.

In my experience, previously intractable cases can only reach satisfactory resolution if the work is client-led and moves at the child's pace. I have learned when to hold back in ways that empower the client to find solutions that are right for them. My job is to coax clients in the right direction in order to achieve the realistic goals that we have identified together. For this, there has to be an understanding of the child's cognitive development and of patterns of adult behaviour; for example co-operation may be followed by accusations and expressions of anger. Children's wishes and feelings can be a minefield if taken at face value without appreciation of a child's ability to understand parental conflict. Parents often assume that their child understands the situation and sees it as they do; it is hard to accept that children can and do have their own individual views. It is important to help parents to have an appreciation of child development.

Exclusion of one parent is rarely the right answer, except of course where there is a genuine threat of violence which could mean an ongoing relationship would be unsafe either for the child or the resident parent. It can be tempting to suggest that it is simply not worth pursuing contact arrangements which will involve conflict. However, the counter argument is that denying an opportunity for contact and a chance to build a relationship with both parents is equally emotionally damaging to the child (Barnham et al., 2003). Research into this complicated area suggests that unresolved contact arrangements can impinge on a child's sense of their own identity and their ability to make and form their own relationships in the future (Flouri and Buchanan, 2002). For me closing the book without exploring the dynamics which play such a crucial part in how the family operate is the easy way out and also denies parents the opportunity to manage their own lives. A solution-focused approach is a life skill involving opportunities to use personal and social resources and to take small steps forward to the future that they prefer. As Gelatt states '... the future does not exist and cannot be predicted. It must be imagined and invented' (1989, p. 255). Even if the problem is complicated or long-standing it need not be assumed that the solution will also need to be complicated or take a long time to work. A solution-focused perspective argues that people can change without in-depth analysis of their problems; the solution construction process is very different from the problem exploration process. Of course the past should not be disregarded but the client is encouraged to recognise what worked and brought success in other areas of their lives and to repeat similar strategies and consider achievable goals. It encourages an optimistic view that the future can be different. As Bill O'Connell (2005) reminds us with an apposite metaphor, when driving a car it is helpful to look in the rear view mirror occasionally, but is advisable to spend most of the time looking forwards!

Discussion

There is no such thing as a typical case; each family presents a unique scenario but clear patterns of behaviour do emerge. This story has features common to entrenched marital family disputes where, perhaps at an unconscious level, one parent is angry and wants to 'punish' the other but their only 'weapons' are the children. These can be some of the most difficult situations for social workers to intervene and bring about change. Here, the impasse between the parents had led them to Court to try and find a resolution. However, Court proceedings and solicitors do not, by themselves, offer any magic wands. The difference in this story is that the Court context of structured power and authority set the scene for the productive involvement of an Independent Social Worker using her experience and skills in a series of constructive and sensitive solution-focused interventions. The history of well-established negativity was not avoided but it was turned on its head. Pat allowed Mrs Potter to voice her negative views whenever she needed but always moved this on to help her identify how her life could be changed to make it better for herself and for Joe and Susie. Service users can easily become disempowered when they feel overwhelmed by their problems and often wish to have all their problems solved for them. This is rarely a strategy for long-term success. A solution-focused approach is about helping people discover their own strengths and their own solutions as opposed to creating dependence. In this sense it is 'empowerment-in-action' and Pat's skilled use of flexible techniques fits well with the theoretical and practice-based perspectives of constructive social work (Parton and Marshall, 1998; Parton and O'Byrne, 2000).

Pat's experience and knowledge of child development at different stages during times of conflict enables her to explain to parents and children that children may adopt a strategy of survival by compartmentalising their time with each parent. One approach is to suggest to children that they shut the lid on Mum's box when they are with Dad; and when they finish contact with Dad, they put him in his box shutting the lid down firmly. This simple tactic relieves children of responsibility and parents are encouraged to begin to see the situation through their children's eyes. For example, after a while, Mrs Potter no longer insisted that arrangements had to be what Joe and Susie wanted. In high conflict cases it can be misleading to solely depend upon a child's wishes and feelings and yet, quite often, perhaps too much reliance is placed upon that. It can put children of a certain age in the invidious position of having to choose one parent over another. Children caught between warring parents face a terrible dilemma – should they be honest or should they be loyal? Pat's experience suggests that it is best, wherever possible, to negotiate arrangements that support the relationship between children and a non-resident parent. It relieves the child of the tremendous responsibility of having to get it right for both parents and it encourages parents to stop relying on events of the past and instead to begin to take control of the future.

Change can be very slow to achieve in social work, particularly where there may be entrenched attitudes and patterns of behaviour. Pat's careful work over a period of many months enabled the children's relationship with their father to slowly develop and for mutually acceptable contact arrangements to become established. Pat's role has been to act as the catalyst for change, engaging with each family member and enabling them to work towards what would be best for Joe and Susie. However, it would be wrong to assume that all solution-focused work requires long periods of time. In this story, the context of a Court Order within contested private law proceedings undoubtedly provided a timeframe wherein the Court was prepared to wait for signs of progress. The 'brief' aspect of solution-focused brief therapy (SFBT) can be used in many social work contexts including a social services intake team (Hogg and Wheeler, 2004). The assumptions underlying SFBT and the concrete applications that have been created have been systematically reviewed and shown to be moderately effective in a range of interventions with children and families (Department for Education, 2011b) although, as always, more research is needed.

Conclusion

Pat's story of practice brings together the key elements in this section of the book. The context for Pat's work for the Court is one of explicit and structured power and authority. However, by itself, this structure is relatively powerless to effect productive change within complex family life entanglements. The Court needs professional people to make working relationships. As an Independent Social Worker, Pat works within this frame of legislative proceedings and uses her professional power, of expertise and experience, to influence the attitudes, behaviours and relationships of the parents and the children. The underlying key to this change is the power of productive negotiating that accepts and contains anxieties and yet offers opportunities to move on. The problems that brought Pat into this family are not avoided but they are not seen as being helpful. So they are acknowledged and the focus moves on to helping people envisage and enact workable solutions. In this approach, the social worker is not 'the expert' who has the answer to solve the problem. Instead, they have a more constructive role as an expert facilitator of helping others to find their own solutions.

16 Conclusion

Jean Gordon, Andy Rixon and Barry Cooper

Critical best practice

We set out in this book to bring together examples of social work that can be described as 'best' practice. As our Introduction makes clear, this is not to suggest that there is only one way to do social work, or an 'ideal' outcome in any practice situation. Instead the best practice described is about doing 'the best' the social worker is able to do at that time and in that place, in the context of that child and family. Crucially, as the accounts of the practitioners in this book demonstrate, best practice requires a facility for critical reflection, and the ability to act on that reflection to practice skilfully and learn from experience. Naomi, reflecting on her work with Linda, concluded that she could *honestly state I could go back and manage that much better now*. And Myra's case was important to Clive precisely because of what he learnt about intervening with authority in a chronically harmful situation. This kind of reflection on the process of social work and learning from what goes wrong as well as right is as much part of best – and critical – practice as cases that have unequivocally positive outcomes.

We started out on the basis that there is social work practice that can and should be described as 'critical' and 'best'. Like many social workers, the practitioners who joined us in this project were often doubtful about describing their work in positive terms. This relates at least in part to the 'climate of negativity' (Jones et al., 2008, p. 1) that social work in the United Kingdom tends to operate within. But there is also perhaps an inherent tension here between criticality and confidence. A questioning, sceptical approach is fundamental to critical practice. Doubt can be a virtue when it comes to weighing up complex ᵗ contested evidence about the well-being of children. Conversely, ᶠidence and self-importance can be dangerous qualities in a ᵣ. Whatever the reasons for social workers' tendency to hide their lights under bushels, there is no doubt that much of what is good – and even best – about social work practice tends to remain hidden. This has several consequences, not least a lack of regard for the profession by the public, and sometimes other professions, and the risk that social workers internalise a damaging perception of their profession and themselves. While there is a burgeoning literature about social work practice written from a theoretical and relatively prescriptive standpoint, there is, as we highlighted earlier in the book, little written about the actual practice of high-quality social work. Reflecting on her role in this book, one of the practitioner authors, Pat Barrow commented on her frustration, as first a student and then a newly qualified worker, by *the dearth of literature which actually explained how I should engage, often with the most reluctant families.* We hope that this book, which joins a small, but growing movement (see also Ferguson, 2003; Jones et al., 2008; Howe, 2009; Gordon and Cooper, 2010; Ferguson, 2011; Jones and Watson, 2013) will make a contribution to shifting that balance and giving a louder and more influential voice to social workers talking and writing about their practice.

Talking and writing together

As well as listening to, recording and analysing practitioners' accounts of practice, we also wanted to involve practising social workers in the translation of their interviews into the written word. The reasons for this approach were partly ethical ones: social workers were talking about *their* practice so it was important to offer the opportunity to be part of making that practice visible, and getting (rare) public credit for doing so. This collaboration was also important because it allowed editors and practitioners to engage in a continuing dialogue about the relationship between what had been said and what was eventually written. This approach had its challenges, including time constraints on practitioners and knotty questions about how narratives can change in the telling, writing up and writing down (see Chapter 2).

It is notoriously difficult for social workers to gain sufficient time, support and credibility for writing about practice, and this sometimes made it difficult for them to be full participators in the writing process. There is also a tension between recognising the contribution of social workers and preserving others' anonymity. In this book this sometimes had to be resolved by anonymising the names of practitioners as well as any information that might identify children, families and colleagues. We have not attempted to evaluate the experience of participating practitioners in any systematic way. However, our perception has been that most of the social workers enjoyed the opportunity to talk and write about their practice. Early doubts (one practitioner, on first reading the transcript of her interview said that she was *amazed that anyone ever understands a word I say*) have tended to be replaced with positive responses to the written chapters. One social worker said he felt *very moved* after reading a first chapter draft; he already knew the learning experience described had been significant to him, but that seeing it on the page had been a powerful and confirming experience.

Towards the end of the writing process we asked the involved practitioners to tell us about their experience of writing with us for publication. All the responses we received indicated that the process had been an engaging one. On a personal basis the process of collaborative writing was variously described as *worthwhile, stimulating* and *a unique opportunity*. For example Jock Mickshik told us:

> On a personal level, I thoroughly enjoyed the opportunity to reflect deeply and extensively on a single piece of social work and to be able to reflect, in a very safe context, on those aspects of practice which I felt I had got right and those I had got wrong.

As made clear in many of the narratives in this book, opportunities to take an in-depth look at day-to-day practice are hard to come by, a point emphasised by Marie Brown:

> [It felt] Hugely indulgent! It is good to have the experience of unpicking what you have done and seeing how it makes a difference – sometimes on the 'hamster wheel' of social work we don't get the chance to do this.

The enduring impact of taking a critical best practice approach was also noted, as Pat Barrow explained:

> Critical analysis of my own practice has encouraged me to work innovatively and realistically with each family. It has reinforced my belief that every family offers a unique learning experience and that encourages me to refine and hone my skills.

We were also interested to find out whether practitioner involvement in this book would be likely to encourage authors to seek further opportunities to write about their practice. For the most part the answer to this question was a positive one, with two authors already engaged in further writing for publication or actively contemplating doing so, and others open to the opportunity to write, as Naomi Gillard told us:

> I love social work as a profession, and enjoy talking and writing about my cases. I hope this project will lead to further opportunities.

Our evaluation of the 'Practitioner Pathways into Publishing' initiative that enabled this book to be written was a limited one. A more systematic exploration of the benefits (and difficulties) of this kind of collaborative approach to writing about practice could tell us a lot about ways to facilitate practitioners to communicate their experiences of 'doing social work' to a wider audience.

All kinds of social work?

Given the very wide range of social work roles and contexts, just ten stories of social work practice with children and families are a drop in the ocean. We have explored some of the organisational contexts for social work – in local authorities, voluntary organisations, independent consultancy and the private sector in three of the UK's nations. The examples used include children of different ages, from Grace, who is just a few months old to Adam, Bea, Carie and Di who are in their teens. They include children living with their parents, foster carers and adoptive parents, and children, like Grace and David, who have disabilities. Some of the children, like Linda, are subject to compulsory measures of care, and in other instances families, such as Myra's, are working with services on a voluntary basis. Concerns about the welfare and safety of children inevitably take centre stage in many of the accounts as practitioners responded to a range of threats to children's welfare including physical and emotional abuse, neglect and substance misuse. There are of course many other aspects of social work that might be explored, such as practice in residential settings, hospitals or schools, and group and community work with children. Nevertheless, while this particular collection of social work stories can only provide a snapshot of social work practice, it does provide some intriguing insights into early 21st-century social work with children and families in the United Kingdom.

The practitioners accounts' serve as a reminder of just how varied social work practice is. In just ten case examples, social workers are found playing with children, negotiating with colleagues, on doorsteps and in sitting rooms, attending meetings, using legal powers, enabling contact with birth parents, challenging decision-making, reading up research, attending court hearings and writing reports. They run the gamut of emotions from Naomi's mixed anger and anxiety about Linda's parents' behaviour, to Niall's sense of impotence in the face of Dominic's argumentative family, to Jock's delight when carefully devised strategies to reduce risk to and from David begin to bear fruit. These emotions are not always recognised or acknowledged; their open expression in practitioners' stories offers opportunities for readers to reflect on the role of feelings and intuition, and how to respond to the strong feelings that can be evoked in practice. Emotions are 'part and parcel' of everyday social work, and need to be recognised, analysed and managed, as Marie and Mike emphasise in their chapters, by organisations and individuals, through reflection, supervision and other organisational processes (Senior, 2008, p. 279).

The child at the centre

Concerns about the rise of 'managerialism', of excessive paperwork/computer use and of a 'tick box' mentality are persistent themes in discourses about social work not least within the profession itself. The frequent conclusion is that social workers no longer have the time to actually see and relate to children and their families. This 'retreat from intimacy and face-to-face practice' (Ferguson, 2011, p. 37) is of course of considerable concern with potentially damaging consequences for children (Munro, 2011). It is striking then, the extent to which these accounts of best practice started and ended with the children themselves, and their families. From Michelle's careful preparations for meeting Emma and Charlotte with their mother to Naomi finding that Linda's love of cars provides a way into building a trusting relationship with her, the child is very much at the centre. Another common thread is what Ferguson (2008, p. 561) describes as 'liquid social work'. Of course some of the social work does take place 'backstage' in the office, but mostly social work is described as mobile practice on the go, from Clive's first interaction with Myra picking up leaflets in a waiting room, to Niall's car journeys with Dominic to KFC, to Pat's observation of contact arrangements in a local park. There is also a sense of optimism about the children the practitioners work with and a strong commitment to working in an ethical, strengths-focused way in complex and often uncertain circumstances, seeking to find ways to manage the often tricky balance between children's rights and adults' responsibilities and rights. These social workers think – a lot – about the quality of their practice, about the right balance between care, control and protection, and the impact of their interventions on children in the future, as well as the present. All this requires skilful use of themselves, the capacity for critical reflection and the ability to communicate their understandings and conclusions in an authoritative way. In this respect they met Ferguson's definition of critical best practice as being 'both skilful and deeply respectful of service users... while at the same time using good judgement and authority' (2008, p. 15). So, although every practice situation is unique, and there's no denying that social work often finds itself under pressure, these stories suggest that there are things to say about what good practice with children and families in the United Kingdom *can* look like. Jones and Watson (2013) came to some very similar conclusions in their exploration of best practice with older people, a reminder that these qualities and capabilities are just as important for social workers working, say, in the justice system, or with adults with learning disabilities or mental health problems.

The social workers had to be knowledgeable too – about the law, the organisations they work in, about theories of, for example, child development, family interaction and different ways of intervening in people's lives. Some social workers articulated this use of knowledge explicitly while others tended to weave these understandings into their narratives in more implicit ways. As a result the language of some of the key themes identified by the editors for this book – power, risk assessment, criticality – rarely appears in many of their accounts. There are also some intriguing gaps. So while, for example, Marie explicitly refers to social justice for looked after children, few practitioners touched on the influence of factors, such as poverty, gender, ethnicity and class, that may lead to families experiencing inequality and social exclusion. Without going back to re-interview practitioners it is hard to know whether this omission was down to the choice of case examples (which turned out to have little ethnic diversity), because we, as editors, failed to ask these questions, or because these structural factors were not seen as major influences on families by the social workers themselves. What social workers *didn't* say about their practice sometimes interested us as much as what they did say. Distilling social workers' implicit knowledge to reveal the 'concealed formal structure' (Pawson et al., 2003, p. 49) that lies behind practice is notoriously challenging. As interviewers were we asking the right questions? Or, is this conundrum more about finding better ways to build bridges between the different languages that practitioners and academics sometimes use to talk about practice knowledge (Marsh and Fisher, 2008; Gordon and Cooper, 2010)? In either case a critical best practice approach offers opportunities to research some of the enduring questions about how social workers draw on and make use of their knowledge.

Learning from best practice

'*At its most simple*', wrote Harry Ferguson (2003, p. 1005) in the first exposition of a critical best practice approach, '*the aim ... is to use critical theory as an interpretative framework and set out examples to promote learning*'. It has been heartening in a time of continuing anxiety for social work, with widespread cuts in public services, to be involved in writing a book that conveys how positive a force social work can be. It is important though that these stories convey more than a just warm glow to a profession often much in need of 'good news' – as reassuring as that may be. We hope that they also provide a stimulus for reflective and critical debate about the nature of social work with children and how it can be improved. Clive Rosenthal, one of the practitioner authors, continues to see *a vital place for practitioners regularly reflecting on their own and others' practice*, suggesting that, *without this it is hard to see how practice can improve*. A critical best approach has benefits for the individual practitioner but also lends itself to adoption by groups and teams, enabling collaborative debate about live practice experiences, with opportunities for impact on organisational cultures as well as individual practice and knowledge (Jones et al., 2008). It is also important to remember that social work students, as well as social workers undertaking post-qualifying awards, are regularly asked to write critically and reflectively about practice, and are frequently assessed on the final product. Many learners struggle to move from more familiar 'academic writing' to this reflective style. Access to a bank of stories of practice underpinned by reflective and critical thought has potential to support student learning about the nature of reflective writing and perhaps encourage learners and institutions to consider wider dissemination of some of this mostly hidden body of scholarship.

The kinds of skills, qualities and approaches described by social workers in this book also chime with the beginning of what appears to be a shift in the United Kingdom in thinking about what good practice is all about. In contrast with a broadly competence driven approach to social work training, we are seeing new professional learning frameworks that take greater account of the qualities that make a good social worker. Influenced by what service users and carers had been telling us for some time about what makes for good practice, the

Framework for Continuous Learning in Social Work (Scottish Social Services Council, 2008), and the Professional Capabilities Framework (Social Work Reform Board, 2010a) emphasised the importance of, for example, critical reflection and analysis, leadership, an understanding of power and social justice, and values and ethics. A critical best practice approach brings these capabilities together under one roof, and provides a way of visualising what these apparently abstract concepts mean in the context of day-to-day practice.

The critical best practice approach described and illustrated in this book is in its infancy. Like other writers (Howe, 2009; Jones and Watson, 2013) we have worked hard, with our practitioner co-writers, to unpick what 'critical' and 'best' mean in practice. How can what social workers say – their 'talking knowledge' – be translated into 'practice knowledge' (Gordon and Cooper, 2010) that others can in turn reflect on and learn from? There is still much to do to refine and develop the concepts that the approach is based on. There is also room for many more stories, set in different contexts, incorporating the perspectives of, for example, service users, carers and multidisciplinary colleagues. We have explored examples of social work practice in three nations of the United Kingdom. A critical best practice approach has potential to open up a much wider comparative discussion and debate about social work practice within the United Kingdom and internationally. What do, for example, social workers in Uganda, Chile or Sweden have in common with social workers in the United Kingdom, and how can they learn from using examples of their practice to gain a better understanding of both their own practice and that of colleagues from other countries? When we start talking and writing together about the practice of social work, who knows where our conversations will take us next?

References

Adoption Policy Review Group (2005) *Adoption: Better choices for our children.* Edinburgh: Scottish Executive.

Advisory Council on the Misuse of Drugs (2003) *Hidden harm: Responding to the needs of children of problem drug users.* London: Home Office.

Aldgate, J. (2011) 'The role of assessment in social work' in R. Davis. and J. Gordon (eds) *Social work and the law in Scotland.* Basingstoke: Palgrave MacMillan/ Milton Keynes: The Open University.

All Party Parliamentary Group on Social Work (2013) *Inquiry into the state of social work report,* Birmingham, British Association of Social Workers, http://cdn.basw.co.uk/upload/basw_90352–5.pdf (accessed 21 March 2014).

Altenberger, I. and Mackay, R. (2006) *What matters with personal narratives?* National Programme for Improving Mental Health and Well-Being, Edinburgh: Scottish Government. http://www.scotland.gov.uk/Resource/Doc/254267/0075279.pdf (accessed 21 August 2013).

Anning, A., Cottrell, D., Frost, N., Green, J. and Robinson, M. (2010) *Developing multi-professional team work for integrated children's services* (2nd ed). Maidenhead: Open University Press.

Association of Directors of Social Services (ADSS) (2005) *Social work in wales: A profession to value.* Wales: ADSS. http://www.adsscymru.org.uk/resource/m_E_Social_Work_in_Wales_-_A_Profession_to_Value.pdf (accessed 28 August 2013).

Atkinson, P. (1990) *The ethnographic imagination.* London: Routledge.

Atkinson, T. and Claxton, G. (2000) *Intuitive practitioner: On the value of not always knowing what one is doing.* Milton Keynes: Open University Press.

Baker, K. and Wilkinson, B. (2011) 'Professional risk taking and defensible decisions' in H. Kemshall and B. Wilkinson (eds) *Good practice in assessing risk: Current knowledge, issues and approaches.* London: Jessica Kingsley Publishers.

Barclay Report (1982) *Social workers: Their role and tasks.* London: NISW/Bedford Square Press.

Barnham, A., Lindley, B., Richards, M. and Trinder, L. (eds) (2003) *Children and their families: Contact, rights and welfare.* Oxford: Hart Publishing.

Barry, M. (2007) *Effective approaches to risk assessment in social work: An international literature review.* Edinburgh: Scottish Executive.

Bauman, Z. (2005) *Liquid life.* Cambridge: Polity.

Beck, U. (1992) *Risk society: Towards a new modernity.* London: Sage.

Beckett, C. (2007) *Child protection: An introduction.* London: Sage.

Beckett, C. (2008) 'Risk, uncertainty and thresholds' in M. Calder (ed.) *Contemporary risk assessment in safeguarding children.* Lyme Regis: Russell House.

Bell, M. (2002) 'Promoting children's rights through the use of relationship', *Child and Family Social Work,* 7, 1–11.

Bentovim, A., Cox, A., Bingley Miller, L. and Pizzey, S. (2009) *Evidence based assessment, analysis and planning interventions.* London: Jessica Kingsley Publishers.

Beresford, P. and Croft, S. (2000) 'Empowerment' in M. Davies (ed.) *The blackwell encyclopaedia of social work*, pp. 116–18. Oxford: Blackwell.

Beresford, P. and Croft, S. (2004) 'Service users and practitioners reunited: The key component for social work reform', *British Journal of Social Work*, 34, 53–68.

Bilson, A. (ed.) (2005) *Evidence based practice in social work.* London: Whiting and Birch.

Blom-Cooper, L. (1985) *A child in trust: The report of the panel of inquiry into the circumstances surrounding the death of Jasmine Beckford.* London: Borough of Brent.

Brandon, M. and Thoburn, J. (2008) 'Safeguarding children in the UK: A longitudinal study of services to children suffering or likely to suffer significant harm', *Child and Family Social Work*, 13, 4, 365–77.

Brandon, M., Sidebotham, P., Ellis, C., Bailey, S. and Belderson, P. (2011) *Child and family practitioners' understanding of child development: Lessons learnt from a small sample of serious case reviews.* Research Report DFE-RR110. London: Department of Education.

Briere, J. (1996). *Trauma Symptom Checklist for Children (TSCC) Professional Manual.* Odessa, FL: Psychological Assessment Resources. http://www4.parinc.com/Products/Product.aspx?Productid=TSCC

Buckley, H., Carr, N. and Whelan, S. (2011) '"Like walking on eggshells": Service user views and expectations of the child protection system', *Child and Family Social Work*, 16, 1, 101–10.

Butler A (2003) 'Book review of "The call to social work"', *British Journal of Social Work*, 33, 8, 1124–25.

Butler, A., Ford, D. and Tregaskis, C. (2007) 'Who do we think we are? Self and reflexivity in social work practice', *Qualitative Social Work*, 6, 3, 281–99.

Butt, T. (2008) *George Kelly: The psychology of personal constructs.* Basingstoke: Palgrave MacMillan.

Bywater, J. (2012) 'Working effectively with children and families in the safeguarding children arena' in M. O'Loughlin. and S. O'Loughlin (eds) *Social\work with children and families* (3rd ed). London: Sage/ Learning Matters

Cabinet Office (1999) *Modernising government.* London: Stationery Office.

Carpentier, M., Silovsky, J. and Chaffin, M. (2006) 'Randomised trial of treatment for children with sexual behaviour problems: Ten year follow up', *Journal of Consulting and Clinical Psychology*, 74, 3, 482–8.

Children's Workforce Development Council (2009) *The common assessment framework for children and young people: A guide for practitioners: Early identification, assessment of needs and intervention.* Leeds: CWDC.

Community Care (2013) *The Munro report two years on: Social workers find little has changed*   nhttp://www.communitycare.co.uk/2013/02/19/the-munro-report-two-years-on-social-workers-find-little-has-changed/ (accessed 24 April 2014).

Cooper, B. (2008) 'Constructive engagement: Best practice in social work interviewing' in K. Jones, B. Cooper and H. Ferguson (eds) *Best practice in social work; critical perspectives.* Basingstoke: Palgrave Macmillan.

Cooper, B. (2009) *The problem of assessment in social work: Practice, education and continuing professional development.* Saarbrucken, Germany: VDM Publishing House Ltd.

Cooper, J. (1983) *The creation of the British personal social services 1962–1974.* London: Heinemann.

Crisp, B.R., Anderson, M.T., Orme, J. and Lister, P.G. (2005) *Knowledge review 08: Learning and teaching in social work education: Textbooks and frameworks on assessment.* London: Social Care Institute for Excellence.

Croisdale-Appleby, D. (2014) *Re-visioning social work education, An independent review* https://www.gov.uk/government/uploads/system/uploads/attachment_data/file/285788/DCA_Accessible.pdf (accessed 3 March 2014).

Crown Prosecution Service (2001) *Provision of therapy for child witnesses prior to a criminal trial. Practice Guidance.* London: Home Office/ CPS/ Department of Health http://www.cps.gov.uk/publications/prosecution/therapychild.html (accessed 4 November 2013).

Daniel, B. (2007) 'Assessment and children' in J. Lishman (ed.) *Handbook for practice learning in social work and social care.* London: Jessica Kingsley Publishers.

Daniel, B. and Wassell, S. (2002) *The school years: Assessing and promoting resilience in vulnerable children.* London: Jessica Kingsley Publishing.

De Boer, C. and Coady, N. (2007) 'Good helping relationships in child welfare; learning from stories of success', *Child and Family Social Work*, 12, 32–42.

Department for Education and Skills (DfES) (2004a) *Every child matters: Change for children.* London: DfES.

Department for Education and Skills (2004b) *Every child matters: Next steps.* London: DfES.

Department for Education and Skills (2007) *Care matters: Young peoples' responses.* London: HMSO.

Department for Education (2011a) *A child-centred system: The government's response to the Munro review of child protection.* London: DfE.

Department for Education (2011b) *Systematic review of solution focused brief therapy with children and families,* London: DfE. https://www.gov.uk/government/uploads/system/uploads/attachment_data/file/184113/DFE-RR179.pdf (accessed 21 August 2013).

De Shazer, S. (1988) *Clues: Investigating solutions in brief therapy.* New York and London: Norton.

De Shazer, S. and Dolan, Y. (2007) *More than miracles: The state of the art of solution-focused brief therapy.* New York: Harworth Press.

Dodd, T. (2003) 'Solution-focused therapy in mental health' in B. O'Connell and S. Palmer (eds) *Handbook of solution-focused therapy*, pp. 74–83. London: Sage.

Doel, M., Allmark, P.J., Conway, P., Cowburn, M., Flynn, M., Nelson, P. and Tod, A. (2009) *Professional boundaries: Research report.* Sheffield Hallam University: Centre for Health and Social Care Research.

Dominelli, L. (1996) 'Deprofessionalizing social work: Ant-oppressive practice, competencies and postmodernism', *British Journal of Social Work*, 26, 153–75.

Dumbleton, S. and McPhail, M. (2012) 'The coming of age of Scottish social services?' in G. Mooney and G. Scott (eds) *Social justice and social welfare in contemporary Scotland.* Bristol: Policy Press.

Easen, P., Atkins, M. and Dyson, A. (2000) 'Inter-professional collaboration and conceptualisations of practice', *Children and Society*, 14, 5, 355–67.

Egan, G. (2002) *The skilled helper: A problem-management and opportunity-development approach to helping* (7th ed). Belmont, CA: Thomson Brooks/Cole.

Elsley, S. (2010) *Media coverage of child deaths in the UK: The impact of baby P: A Case for Influence? CLiCP Briefing.* Edinburgh: The University of Edinburgh/NSPCC.

Emde, R.N., Wolfe, D.P. and Oppenheim, D. (eds) (2003) *Revealing the inner worlds of young children: The MacArthur story stem battery and parent-child narratives.* Milton Keynes: Open University Press.

Erikson, E.H. (1950) *Childhood and society*. New York: Norton.

Erskine, R.G, Moursand, J.P.& Trautmann, R. L. (1999) Beyond empathy A therapy of contact-in-relationship. Philadelphia: Brunner/Mazel.

Ferguson, H. (2003) 'Outline of a critical best practice perspective on social work and social care', *British Journal of Social Work*, 33, 8, 1005–24.

Ferguson, H. (2008) 'The theory and practice of critical best practice in social work' in K. Jones, B. Cooper and H. Ferguson (eds) *Best practice in social work: Critical perspectives*. Basingstoke: Palgrave Macmillan.

Ferguson, H. (2011) *Child protection practice*. London: Palgrave MacMillan.

Finlay, L. and Ballinger, C. (2008) 'The challenge of working in teams' in S. Fraser and S. Matthews (eds) *The critical practitioner in social work and health care*. London: Sage/ Milton Keynes: The Open University.

Fisher, D.V. (1991) *An introduction to constructivism for social workers*. New York: Praeger.

Flouri, E. and Buchanan, A. (2002) 'What predicts good relationships in parents in adolescence and partners in adult life', *Journal of Family Psychology*, 16, 2, 186–98.

Fook, J. (2002) *Social work: Critical theory and practice*. London: Sage.

Fook, J. (2012) *Social work: A critical approach to practice*. London: Sage.

Forrester, D., Copello, A., Waissbein, C. and Pokhrel, S. (2008) 'Evaluation of an intensive family preservation service for families affected by parental substance misuse', *Child Abuse Review*, 17, 6, 410–26.

Forrester, D., Holland, S., Williams, A. and Copello, A. (2012) *An evaluation of the option 2 intensive family preservation service*. Final research report for alcohol research UK. Cardiff University and University of Bedfordshire. http://alcoholresearchuk.org/downloads/finalReports/FinalReport_0095.pdf

Foucault, M. (1972) *The archaeology of knowledge*, AM Sheridan-Smith, Trans. London: Tavistock.

Foucault, M. (1975) *Discipline and punish*, AM Sheridan-Smith, Trans. Harmondsworth: Penguin.

Frost, N., Robinson, M. and Anning, A. (2005) 'Social workers in multidisciplinary teams: Issues and dilemmas for professional practice', *Child and Family Social Work*, 10, 3, 187–96.

Fursland, E. (2010) *Social networking and contact: How social workers can help adoptive families*. London: BAAF.

Fursland, E. (2013) *Facing up to facebook: A survival guide for adoptive families*. London: BAAF.

Garrett, P. (2005) 'Social work's "electronic turn": Notes on the deployment of information and communication technologies in social work with children and families', *Critical Social Policy*, 24, 4, 529–53.

Gelatt, H.B. (1989) 'Positive uncertainty a new decision making framework for counseling', *Journal of Counseling Psychology*, 36, 2, 252–6.

Giddens, A. (1990) *The consequences of modernity*. Cambridge: Polity Press.

Gilbert, T. and Powell, J. (2010) 'Power and social work in the United Kingdom: A Foucauldian excursion', *Journal of Social Work*, 10, 1, 3–22.

Gilligan, R. (1998) 'The importance of schools and teachers in child welfare', *Child and Family Social Work*, 3, 1, 13–25.

Glaister, A. (2008) 'Introducing critical practice' in S. Fraser and S. Matthews (eds) *The critical practitioner in social work and health care*. London: Sage/ Milton Keynes: The Open University.

Gordon, J. and Cooper, B. (2010) 'Talking knowledge – Practising knowledge', *Practice*, 22, 4, 245–7.

Gray, M., Plath, D. and Webb, S.A. (2009) *Evidence-based social work: A critical stance*. Abingdon: Routledge.

Hackett, S., Phillips, J., Masson, H. and Balfe, M. (2011) *Recidivism, desistance and life course trajectories of young sexual abusers: An in depth follow up study, ten years on*. Durham: Durham University http://www.dur.ac.uk/resources/sass/research/briefings/ResearchBriefing7-Recidivismdistanceandlifecoursetrajectoriesofyoungsexualabusersanin-depthfollow-upsstudy10yearson.pdf (accessed 12 August 2012).

Hannon, C., Bazalgette, L. and Wood, C. (2010) *In Loco Parentis: 'To deliver the best for children the state must be a confident parent'*. London: Demos.

Harbin, F. (2006) 'The roller coaster of change: The process of parental change from a child's perspective' in F. Harbin and M. Murphy (eds) *Secret lives: Growing with substance use – Working with children and young people affected by familial substance use*. Lyme Regis: Russell House.

HM Government (2013) *Working together to safeguard children: A guide to inter-agency working to safeguard and promote the welfare of children*. London: HM Government.

Hochschild, A.R. (1979) 'Emotion work, feeling rules and social structure', *American Journal of Sociology*, 85, 3, 551–75.

Hogg, V. and Wheeler, J. (2004) 'Miracles R Them: Solution-focused practice in a social services duty team', *Practice: Social Work in Action*, 16, 4, 299–314.

Hollis, F. (1964) *Casework: A psychosocial therapy*. New York: Random House.

Howe, D (1993) *On being a client: Understanding the process of counselling and psychotherapy*. London: Sage.

Howe, D. (1996) 'Surface and depth in social work practice' in N. Parton (ed.) *Social theory, social change and social work*, pp. 77–97. London: Routledge.

Howe, D. (2009) *A brief introduction to social work theory*. Basingstoke: Palgrave Macmillan.

Ingleby, D (1985) 'Professionals as socialisers: The "psy complex,"' in A. Scull and S. Spitzer (eds) *Research in law, deviance and social control*, pp. 79–109. New York: JAI Press.

International Federation of Social Workers (2012) *Definition of social work*. Berne: IFSW http://ifsw.org/policies/definition-of-social-work/ (accessed 28 September 2012).

Jackson, S. (1998) 'Education and children in care', *Adoption and Fostering*, 12, 4, 6–11.

Jobe, A. and Gorin, S. (2013) '"If kids don't feel safe they don't do anything": Young people's views on seeking and receiving help from Children's Social Care Services in England', *Child and Family Social Work*, 18, 429–38.

Jones, D. (2003) *Communicating with vulnerable children*. London: Gaskell.

Jones, K., Cooper, B. and Ferguson, H. (2008) *Best practice in social work: Critical perspectives*. Basingstoke: Palgrave Macmillan.

Jones, K. and Watson, S. (2013) *Best practice with older people: Social work stories*. Basingstoke: Palgrave MacMillan.

Keating, M. (2010) 'Policy convergence and divergence in Scotland under devolution', *Regional Studies*, 39, 4, 453–63.

Kelly, G. (1991) *The psychology of personal constructs* (Originally Published 1955, New York: Norton). London: Routledge.

Kemshall, H. (2007) 'Risk assessment and management: An overview' in J. Lishman (ed.) *Handbook for practice learning in social work and social care: Knowledge and theory*. London: Jessica Kingsley.

Kilbrandon, L. (1964) *Report of the committee on children and young persons, Scotland*, Cmnd 2306. Edinburgh: Scottish Office, HMSO.

Laming, L. (2003) *The Victoria Climbié inquiry: Report of the inquiry by Lord Laming, Cm 5730*. London: Stationery Office.

Laming, L. (2009) *The protection of children in England: A progress report*. London: The Stationery Office.

Larsson, S. and Sjoblom, Y. (2010) 'Perspectives on narrative methods in social work research', *International Journal of Social Welfare*, 19, 272–80.

Lave, J. and Wenger, E. (1991) *Situated learning*. Cambridge: Cambridge University Press.

LeCroy, C.W. (2002) *The call to social work: Life stories*. London: Sage.

Lester, S. (1999) 'From map-reader to map-maker: Approaches to moving beyond knowledge and competence' in D. O'Reilly, L. Cunningham and S. Lester (eds) *Developing the capable practitioner: Professional capability through higher education*, pp. 45–53. London: Kogan Page.

Littlechild, B. (2008) 'Child protection social work: Risks of fears and fears of risks – impossible tasks from impossible goals?' *Social Policy and Administration*, 42, 6, 662–75.

Lowe, N., Murch, M., Borkowski, M., Weaver, A., Beckford, V. and Thomas, C. (1999) *Supporting adoption: Reframing the approach*. London: BAAF.

Macdonald, A. (2011) *Solution-focused therapy: Theory, research & practice*. London: Sage.

McGraw, S. (undated) *Parent assessment manual*. http://www.pillcreekpublishing.com/pams3–0.html (accessed 20 December 2012).

McLeod, A. (2010) 'A friend and an equal': Do young people in care seek the impossible from their social workers?' *British Journal of Social Work*, 40, 772–88.

Marsh, P. and Fisher, M. (2008) 'The development of problem-solving knowledge for social care practice', *British Journal of Social Work*, 38, 5, 971–87.

Miller, W. and Rollnick, S. (2002) *Motivational interviewing: Preparing people for change*. New York: Guildford Press.

Morgan, R. (2005) 'Finding what children say they want: Messages from children', *Representing Children*, 17, 3, 180–8.

Morrow, G.H. (2003) 'Capacity to consent to sexual relationships in adults with learning disabilities', *Journal of Family Planning and Reproductive Health Care*, 29, 3, 148–9.

Munro, E. (1996) 'Avoidable and unavoidable mistakes in child protection', *British Journal of Social Work*, 26, 6, 793–808.

Munro, E. (2002) *Effective child protection*. London: Sage.

Munro, E. (2011) *The Munro review of child protection. Final report: A child centred system*. London: Department for Education.

Narey, M. (2014) *Making the education of social workers consistently effective*. London, Department of Education https://www.gov.uk/government/uploads/system/uploads/attachment_data/file/287756/Making_the_Education_of_social_workers_con-sistently_Effective.pdfhttps://www.gov.uk/government/uploads/system/uploads/attachment_data/file/287756/Making_the_Education_of_social_workers_consist-ently_Effective.pdf (accessed 7 March 2014).

Neil, E. (2002) 'Contact after adoption: The role of agencies in making and supporting plans', *Adoption & Fostering*, 26, 1, 25–38.

Neil, E. (2003) 'Adoption and contact: A research review' in A. Bainham, E. Lindley, M. Richards and L. Trinder (eds) *Children and their families: Contact, rights and welfare*. Oxford: Hart Publishing.

Neil, E. (2004) 'The "Contact after Adoption" study: Indirect contact and adoptive parents' communication about adoption' in E. Neil and D. Howe (eds) *Contact in adoption and permanent foster care: Research, theory and practice.* London: BAAF.

Neil, E. (2010) 'The benefits and challenges of direct post-adoption contact: Perspectives from adoptive parents and birth relatives', *Aloma*, 27, 89–115.

Neil, E., Beek, M. and Schofield, G. (2003) 'Thinking about and managing contact in permanent placements: The differences and similarities between adoptive parents and foster carers', *Clinical Child Psychology and Psychiatry*, 8, 3, 401–18.

Office of the Children's Commissioner (2011) *Don't make assumptions: Children's and young people's views of the child protection system and messages for change.* Norwich: University of East Anglia.

Ofsted (2011) *The voice of the child: Learning lessons from serious case reviews.* Manchester: Ofsted. http://www.ofsted.gov.uk/resources/voice-of-child-learning-lessons-serious-case-reviews (accessed 20 October 2013).

Okitikpi, T. (2011) *Social control and the use of power in social work with children and families.* Lyme Regis: Russell House.

O'Connell, B. (2005) *Solution-focused therapy.* Sage: London.

O'Sullivan, T. (2011) *Decision making in social work* (2nd ed). Basingstoke: Palgrave Macmillan.

Paley, J. and Eva, G. (2005) 'Narrative vigilance: The analysis of stories in health care', *Nursing Philosophy*, 6, 83–97.

Paris, M.E. and Epting, F.R. (2004) 'Social and personal construction: Two sides of the same coin' in J.D. Raskin and S.K. Bridges (eds) *Studies in meaning 2: Bridging the personal and social in constructivist psychology.* New Paltz: Pace University Press.

Parker, R. (1999) *Adoption now: Messages from research.* London: The Stationery Office,

Parton, N. (1998) 'Risk, advanced liberalism and child welfare: The need to rediscover uncertainty and ambiguity', *British Journal of Social Work*, 28, 1, 5–28.

Parton, N. (2000) 'Some thoughts on the relationship between theory and practice in and for social work', *British Journal of Social Work*, 30, 4, 449–63.

Parton, N. (2011) 'Child protection and safeguarding in England: Changing and competing conceptions of risk and their implications for social work', *British Journal of Social Work*, 41, 854–75.

Parton, N. (2012) 'The Munro review of child protection: An appraisal', *Children and Society*, 26, 150–62.

Parton, N. and Marshall, W. (1998) 'Postmodernism and discourse approaches to social work' in R. Adams, L. Dominelli and M. Payne (eds) *Social work: Themes, issues and critical debates*, pp. 240–50. London: Macmillan.

Parton, N and O'Byrne, P. (2000) *Constructive social work.* London: Palgrave Macmillan.

Pawson, R., Boaz, A., Grayson, L., Long, A. and Barnes, C. (2003) *Types and quality of knowledge in social care.* London: Social Care Institute for Excellence.

Perlman, H. (1979) *Relationship: The heart of helping people.* Chicago: Chicago Press.

Petrie, P. (2011) 'Children's associative spaces and social pedagogy' in P. Foley and S. Leverett (eds) *Children and young peoples spaces: Developing practice.* Basingstoke: Palgrave Macmillan/Milton Keynes: The Open University.

Phillips, J., MacGiiollaRi, D. and Callaghan, S. (2012) 'Encouraging research in social work: Narrative as the thread integrating education and research in social work', *Social Work Education*, 31, 6, 785–93.

Pithouse, A., Broadhurst, K., Hall, C., Peckover, S., Wastell, D. and White, S. (2012) 'Trust, risk and the (mis)management of contingency and discretion through new information technologies in children's services', *Journal of Social Work*, 12, 2, 158–78.

Polkinghorne, D.E. (1992) 'Postmodern epistemology of practice' in S. Kvale (ed.) *Psychology and postmodernism*, pp. 146–165. London: Sage.

Pollio, D.E. (2006) 'The art of evidence-based practice', *Research on Social Work Practice*, 16, 2, 224–31.

Power, M. (2004) *The risk management of everything: Rethinking the politics of uncertainty*. London: Demos.

Prochaska, J.O. and DiClemente, C.C. (1984) *The transtheoretical approach: Towards a systematic eclectic framework* . Homewood, IL, USA: Dow Jones Irwin.

Prynn, B. (2008) 'Reflections on past social work practice: The central role of relationship' in S. Fraser and S. Matthews (eds) *The critical practitioner in social work and health care*. London: Sage/Milton Keynes: The Open University.

Quinton, D., Rushton, A., Dance, C. and Mayes, D. (1997) 'Contact between children placed away from home and their birth parents: Research issues and evidence', *Clinical Child Psychology and Psychiatry*, 2, 3, 393–413.

Quinton, D. and Selwyn, J. (1998) 'Contact with birth parents after adoption: A response to Ryburn', *Child & Family Law Quarterly*, 10, 4, 349–61.

Quinton, D., Selwyn, J., Rushton, A. and Dance, C. (1999) 'Contact between children placed away from home and their birth parents: Ryburn's "reanalysis" analysed', *Clinical Child Psychology and Psychiatry*, 4, 4, 519–31.

Riessman, C. (1993) *Narrative analysis*. California: Sage.

Riessman, C.K. and Quinney, L. (2005) 'Narrative in social work: A critical review', *Qualitative Social Work*, 4, 3, 391–412.

Rixon, A. (2012) 'Child care social work: Perspectives on the professional' in M. Robb and R. Thomson (eds) *Critical practice with children and young people*. Bristol: Policy Press.

Rojek, C., Peacock, C. and Collins, S. (1988) *Social work and received Ideas*. London: Routledge.

Roscoe, K.D. and Madoc-Jones, I. (2009) 'Critical social work practice: A narrative approach', *International Journal of Narrative Practice*, 1, 9–18.

Rose, N. (1985) *The psychological complex: Psychology, politics and society in England 1869–1939*, London: Routledge & Kegan Paul.

Rose, N. (1996) 'The death of the social? Re-figuring the territory of government', *Economy and Society* 25, 3, 327–56.

Rose, W. (2011) 'Effective multi-agency work in children's services' in J. Seden, S. Matthews, M. McCormick and A. Morgan (eds) *Professional development in social work*. Abingdon: Routledge.

Ruch, G. (2005) 'Relationship-based practice and reflective practice: Holistic approaches to contemporary child care social work', *Child and Family Social Work*, 10, 2, 111–123.

Ruch, G. (2012) 'Where Have All the Feelings Gone? Developing reflective and relationship-based management in child-care social work', *British Journal of Social Work*, 42, 7, 1315–32.

Ruch, G., Turney, D. and Ward, A. (2010) *Relationship based social work: Getting to the heart of practice*. London: Jessica Kingsley.

Ruch, G. (2010) 'The contemporary context of relationship-based practice' in Ruch, G., Turney, D. and Ward, A. (2010) *Relationship based social work: Getting to the heart of practice*. London: Jessica Kingsley.

Ryburn, M. (1996) 'A study of post-adoption contact in compulsory adoptions', *British Journal of Social Work*, 26, 5, 627–46.

Ryburn, M. (1998) 'In whose best interests? Post adoption contact with the birth family', *Child and Family Law Quarterly*, 10, 1, 53–70.

Ryburn, M. (1999) 'Contact between children placed away from home and their birth parents: A reanalysis of the evidence in relation to permanent placements', *Clinical Child Psychology and Psychiatry*, 4, 4, 505–18.

Satyamurti, C. (1979) 'Care and control in local authority social work' in N. Parry, M. Rustin and C. Satyamurti (eds) *Social work, welfare and the state*, pp. 89–103. London: Edward Arnold.

Scottish Executive (2002) *It's everybody's job to make sure I'm alright*, Edinburgh, Scottish Executive http://www.scotland.gov.uk/Resource/Doc/47007/0023992.pdf (accessed 21 March 2014).

Scottish Executive (2006) *Changing lives: Report of the 21st century review of social work*. Edinburgh: Scottish Executive.

Scottish Government (2008) *Taking forward the government economic strategy: A discussion paper on tackling poverty, inequality and deprivation in Scotland*. Edinburgh, Scottish Government. http://www.scotland.gov.uk/Resource/Doc/210936/0055757.pdf (accessed 21 March 2014).

Scottish Government (2010) *National guidance for child protection in Scotland*. Edinburgh: Scottish Government.

Scottish Government (2012) *A guide to getting it right for every child*. Edinburgh: Scottish Government.

Scottish Social Services Council (2008) *The framework for continuous learning in social services*. Dundee: SSSC.

Scottish Social Services Council (SSSC) (2009) *The codes of practice for Scottish social services workers and their employers*. Dundee: SSSC.

Searle, J. (1995) *The construction of social reality*. London: Allen Lane/Penguin.

Seden, J. (2008) 'Organisations and organisational change' in S. Fraser and S. Matthews (eds) *The critical practitioner in social work and health care*. London: Sage.

Seebohm Report (1968) *Report of the committee on local authority and allied personal social services*. London: HMSO.

Seed, P. (1973) *The expansion of social work in Britain*. London: Routledge & Kegan Paul.

Senior, B. with Loades, E. (2008) 'Best practice as skilled organisational work' in K. Jones, B. Cooper and H. Ferguson (eds) *Best practice in social work: Critical perspectives*. Basingstoke: Palgrave Macmillan.

Sheldon, B. and Chilvers, R. (2000) *Evidence-based social care: A study of prospects and problems*. Russell House: Lyme Regis.

Sikes, P. and Gale, K. (2006) *Narrative approaches to education research*. University of Plymouth, http://www.edu.plymouth.ac.uk/resined/narrative/narrativehome.htm (accessed 21 August 2013).

Smeeton, J. (2012) 'Child protection social work in practice' in M. Davies (ed.) *Social work with children and familie*. Basingstoke: Palgrave Macmillan.

Smith, R. (2008) *Social work and power*. Basingstoke: Palgrave MacMillan

Smith, R. (2010) 'Social work, risk, power', *Sociological Research Online*, 15, 1, 4, http://www.socresonline.org.uk/15/1/4.html (accessed 28 August 2013).

Social Care Institute for Excellence (2010) *Enabling risk, ensuring safety: Self directed support and personal budgets*. London: SCIE.

Social Work Inspection Agency (2006) *Extraordinary lives: Creating a positive future for looked after children and young people in Scotland*. Edinburgh: SWIA.

Social Work Reform Board (2010a) *Building a safe and confident future: One year on. Overarching professional standards for social workers in England*. London: Crown Copyright.

Social Work Reform Board (2010b) *Building a safe and confident future: One year on.* London: Crown Copyright.

Social Work Task Force (2009) *Building a safe, confident future. The final report of the social work task force.* London: Department of Health/ Department of Schools, Children and Families.

Squire, C., Andrew, M. and Tamboukou, M. (2008) What is narrative research? in M. Andrews, C. Squire and M. Tamboukou (eds) *Doing narrative research.* London: Sage.

Staudt, M.M., Dulmus, C. and Bennett, G.A. (2003) 'Facilitating writing by practitioners who have published', *Social Work,* 48, 1, 75–83.

Stein, M. (2009) *Quality matters in children's services: Messages from research.* London: Jessica Kingsley.

Thompson, S. and Thompson, N. (2008) *The critically reflective practitioner.* Basingstoke: Palgrave Macmillan.

Titterton, M. (2011) 'Positive risk taking with people at risk of harm' in H. Kemshall and B. Wilkinson (eds) *Good practice in assessing risk.* London: Jessica Kingsley Publishers.

Titterton, M. and Hunter, S. (2011) 'Risk, professional judgement and the law: Antimony and antagonism in an age of uncertainty' in R. Davis and J. Gordon (eds) *Social work and the law in Scotland* (2nd ed). London: Palgrave/Milton Keynes: The Open University.

Trevithick (2003) 'Effective relationship-based practice: A theoretical exploration', *Journal of Social Work Practice,* 17, 2, 163–76.

Trevithick, P. (2005) *Social work skills: A practice handbook* (2nd ed). Milton Keynes: Open University Press.

Triseliotis, J., Shireman, J. and Hundleby, M. (1997) *Adoption: Theory, policy and practice.* London: Cassell.

Turner, C. (2003) *Are you listening?' What disabled children and young people in Wales think about the services they use.* Cardiff: Welsh Assembly.

Turney, D. (1999) 'Speaking up and speaking out: A dialogic approach to anti-Oppressive practice' in A. Jokinen, K. Juhila and T. Posco (eds) *Constructing social work practices,* pp. 257–73. Aldershot: Ashgate.

Turney, D. (2010) 'Sustaining relationships: Working with strong feelings' in G. Ruch, D.Turney and A. Ward (eds) *Relationship based social work: Getting to the heart of practice.* London: Jessica Kingsley.

Turney, D., Platt, D., Selwyn, J. and Farmer, E. (2011) *Social work assessment of children in need: What do we know? Messages from research.* London: Department of Education.

UNICEF (1989) *The united nations convention on the rights of the child,* UNICEF http://www.unicef.org/crc/ (accessed 21 March 2014).

Vandiver, D.M. (2006) 'A prospective analysis of Juvenile male sex offenders: Characteristics and recidivism rates as adults', *Journal of Interpersonal Violence,* 21, 5, 673–88.

Ward, A. (2010) 'The learning relationships: Learning and development for relationship-based practice' in G. Ruch, D. Turney and A. Ward (eds) *Relationship based social work: Getting to the heart of practice.* London, Jessica Kingsley.

Wastell, D., White, S., Broadhurst, K., Peckover, S. and Pithouse, A. (2010) 'Children's services in the iron cage of performance management: Street-level bureaucracy and the spectre of Švejkism', *International Journal of Social Welfare,* 19, 310–20.

Webb, S.A. (2006) *Social work in a risk society.* Basingstoke: Palgrave Macmillan.

Welsh Assembly Government (2007) *One Wales: A progressive agenda for the government of Wales.* Cardiff: Welsh Assembly Government, http://webarchive.nationalarchives.

gov.uk/20081023141438/http://new.wales.gov.uk/strategy/strategies/onewales/one-walese.pdf?lang=en (accessed 28 August 2013).

Welsh Assembly Government (2010) *The report of the social care and social work workforce task group*, Cardiff: WAG, http://wales.gov.uk/docs/dhss/publications/110524workforceen.pdf (accessed 4 November 2013).

Welsh Assembly Government (2011) *Sustainable social services for Wales: A framework for action.* Cardiff: Welsh Assembly Government, http://wales.gov.uk/docs/dhss/publications/110216frameworken.pdf (accessed 28 August 2013).

Welsh Assembly Government (2012) *Research,* http://wales.gov.uk/about/aboutresearch/?lang=en (accessed 4 November 2013).

Wenger, E. (1998) *Communities of practice: Learning, meaning and identity.* Cambridge: Cambridge University Press.

Whittington, C. (2007) *Assessment in social work: A guide for learning and teaching.* London: Social Care Institute for Excellence.

Wiles, F. (2013) 'Not easily put into a box': Constructing professional identity', *Social Work Education,* 32, 7, 854–866.

Winter, K. (2009) 'Relationships matter: The problems and prospects for social workers' relationships with young children in care', *Child and Family Social Work,* 14, 450–60.

Witkin, S. (2011) *Social construction and social work practice: Interpretations and innovations.* New York: Columbia University Press.

Worling, J.R. (2004) 'The estimate of risk of adolescent sexual offense recidivism (ERASOR): Preliminary psychometric data', *Sexual Abuse: Journal of Research and Treatment,* 16, 3, 235–54.

Wright, P., Turner, C., Clay, D. and Mills, H. (2006) *The participation of children and young people in developing social care.* Social Care Institute for Excellence: London.

Index

Q 15